University of Plymouth Library

Subject to status this item may be renewed
via your Voyager account

http://voyager.plymouth.ac.uk

Exeter tel: (01392) 475049
Exmouth tel: (01395) 255331
Plymouth tel: (01752) 232323

Migration, Minorities and Citizenship

General Editors: **Zig Layton-Henry**, Professor of Politics, University of Warwick; and **Danièle Joly**, Professor, Director, Centre for Research in Ethnic Relations, University of Warwick

Titles include:

Muhammad Anwar, Patrick Roach and Ranjit Sondhi (*editors*)
FROM LEGISLATION TO INTEGRATION?
Race Relations in Britain

Sophie Body-Gendrot and Marco Martiniello (*editors*)
MINORITIES IN EUROPEAN CITIES
The Dynamics of Social Integration and Social Exclusion at the
Neighbourhood Level

Naomi Carmon (*editor*)
IMMIGRATION AND INTEGRATION IN POST-INDUSTRIAL SOCIETIES
Theoretical Analysis and Policy-Related Research

Malcolm Cross and Robert Moore (*editors*)
GLOBALIZATION AND THE NEW CITY
Migrants, Minorities and Urban Transformations in Comparative Perspective

Adrian Favell
PHILOSOPHIES OF INTEGRATION
Immigration and the Idea of Citizenship in France and Britain

Agata Górny and Paolo Ruspini (*editors*)
MIGRATION IN THE NEW EUROPE
East-West Revisited

Simon Holdaway and Anne-Marie Barron
RESIGNERS? THE EXPERIENCE OF BLACK AND ASIAN POLICE OFFICERS

Danièle Joly (*editor*)
GLOBAL CHANGES IN ASYLUM REGIMES
Closing Doors

HAVEN OR HELL?
Asylum Policies and Refugees in Europe

SCAPEGOATS AND SOCIAL ACTORS
The Exclusion and Integration of Minorities in Western and Eastern Europe

Christian Joppke and Ewa Morawska
TOWARD ASSIMILATION AND CITIZENSHIP
Immigrants in Liberal Nation-States

Atsushi Kondo (*editor*)
CITIZENSHIP IN A GLOBAL WORLD
Comparing Citizenship Rights for Aliens

Zig Layton-Henry and Czarina Wilpert (*editors*)
CHALLENGING RACISM IN BRITAIN AND GERMANY

Jørgen S. Nielsen
TOWARDS A EUROPEAN ISLAM

Jan Rath (*editor*)
IMMIGRANT BUSINESSES
The Economic, Political and Social Environment

Peter Ratcliffe (*editor*)
THE POLITICS OF SOCIAL SCIENCE RESEARCH
'Race', Ethnicity and Social Change

John Rex
ETHNIC MINORITIES IN THE MODERN NATION STATE
Working Papers in the Theory of Multiculturalism and Political Integration

Carl-Ulrik Schierup (*editor*)
SCRAMBLE FOR THE BALKANS
Nationalism, Globalism and the Political Economy of Reconstruction

Steven Vertovec and Ceri Peach (*editors*)
ISLAM IN EUROPE
The Politics of Religion and Community

Östen Wahlbeck
KURDISH DIASPORAS
A Comparative Study of Kurdish Refugee Communities

John Wrench, Andrea Rea and Nouria Ouali (*editors*)
MIGRANTS, ETHNIC MINORITIES AND THE LABOUR MARKET
Integration and Exclusion in Europe

Migration, Minorities and Citizenship
Series Standing Order ISBN 0–333–71047–9
(*outside North America only*)

You can receive future titles in this series as they are published by placing a standing order.
Please contact your bookseller or, in case of difficulty, write to us at the address below with
your name and address, the title of the series and the ISBN quoted above.

Customer Services Department, Macmillan Distribution Ltd, Houndmills, Basingstoke,
Hampshire RG21 6XS, England

Migration in the New Europe

East-West Revisited

Edited by

Agata Górny
Social Scientist
Warsaw University

Paolo Ruspini
Political Scientist
Centre for Research in Ethnic Relations
University of Warwick

First published 2004 by
PALGRAVE MACMILLAN
Houndmills, Basingstoke, Hampshire RG21 6XS and
175 Fifth Avenue, New York, N. Y. 10010
Companies and representatives throughout the world

PALGRAVE MACMILLAN is the global academic imprint of the Palgrave Macmillan division of St. Martin's Press, LLC and of Palgrave Macmillan Ltd. Macmillan® is a registered trademark in the United States, United Kingdom and other countries. Palgrave is a registered trademark in the European Union and other countries.

ISBN 1–4039–3550–5 hardback

This book is printed on paper suitable for recycling and made from fully managed and sustained forest sources.

A catalogue record for this book is available from the British Library.

Library of Congress Cataloging-in-Publication Data

Migration in the new Europe: East-West revisited / edited by Agata Górny, Paolo Ruspini.
    p. cm.– (Migration, minorities, and citizenship)
  Includes bibliographical references and index.
  ISBN 1–4039–3550–5
    1. Europe–Emigration and immigration. 2. Europe–Emigration and immigration–Government policy. 3. Europe–Economic integration–Europe, Eastern. I. Górny, Agata, 1974–II. Ruspini., Paolo, 1966–III. Series.

JV7590.M5254 2004
325.4–dc22

2004056072

10   9   8   7   6   5   4   3   2
13 12 11 10 09 08 07 06 05

Printed and bound in Great Britain by
Antony Rowe Ltd, Chippenham and Eastbourne

To my sister Małgosia
Agata Górny

To Franco, Giuliana and Luca who never stop encouraging me
Paolo Ruspini

Contents

List of Tables, Figures and Maps

Foreword

The story of this book began with the hosting of Paolo Ruspini, a Marie Curie post-doctoral fellow, and Agata Górny, a visiting fellow, at the Centre for Research in Ethnic Relations. This is where we mooted the idea of a conference to bring together scholars from the East and the West of Europe, which was splendidly organized by my two colleagues in March 2002. This book developed from it, which could not be more timely due to the urgency of the topic.

The European Economic Community, originating through the treaty of Rome, has developed and enlarged in leaps and bounds from its six founding member states of Belgium, France, Germany, Italy, Luxembourg and the Netherlands. What would become the European Union has expanded through four waves of accession: Denmark, Ireland and the United Kingdom in 1973, Greece in 1981, Spain and Portugal in 1986, and Austria, Finland and Sweden in 1995. Further strides were taken with the introduction of mechanisms to bring down internal borders and the creation of a European currency, the Euro, compounding the implications of expansion and integration. A European constitution is now in the making, which seems to carry the nostalgia expressed by Paul Valéry in the wake of the Great War whilst pondering over the crossroads facing Europe's destiny.

A momentous historical development opened greater opportunities for European integration in the 1990s. The fall of the Berlin wall and the collapse of communist regimes have meant the definite end of the cold war political division of Europe into East and West. The new millennium has now witnessed the integration of ten additional member states to the European Union, eight of which belong to Central/Eastern Europe: the Czech Republic, Estonia, Hungary, Latvia, Lithuania, Poland, Slovakia and Slovenia. There is a potential for the new Europe of 25 to respond to the 'American challenge', as elucidated by Jean-Jacques Servan-Scheiber, but there is also the spectre of a neo-liberal economic project due to accelerated globalization.

The face of Europe is being transformed not only through geopolitical enlargement. Substantial minorities of immigrant origin are already settled in the Western part while Eastern European countries are themselves experiencing the whirlwind of international migration.

The European Union has prioritized two issues pertaining to migration and settlement: discrimination and asylum. The new accession countries will take on the *acquis communautaire* in those areas. On the one hand, they need to introduce anti-discrimination measures and practices in accordance with Article 13 of the Treaty of Amsterdam enabling the Council to 'take appropriate action to combat discrimination based on sex, racial or ethnic origin, religion or belief, disability, age or sexual orientation'; the two European Union directives on discrimination will also have to be incorporated into national laws. Meanwhile, the new member states are eager to adopt the Schengen Convention and the EU restrictive approach to asylum. They thus risk embracing the prevalent hostility to asylum-seekers and refugees without an established body of laws and institutions to cushion the impact of this negative paradigm.

Migration will continue to figure prominently on the agenda of the EU and the new accession countries. This was brought home by the now well-known UN report (*Replacement Migration. Is it a Solution to Declining and Ageing Populations?*, New York, 2000) documenting the dramatic demographic curve in industrialized countries and their critical need for immigrant labour. However, the long experience of migration and settlement in the west of Europe might fruitfully yield lessons for the fledgling migration and settlement in the new accession countries by providing them with the wisdom of good and bad practices.

This book makes a valuable contribution to this debate.

Danièle Joly

Preface

Migration is currently a topical issue in discussions concerning the future of the European Union (EU). Although efforts to derive the principles for a common European approach to migration date back to the early 1990s, the need for a common EU immigration policy has been fully recognized by all the member states only since the October 1999 Tampere meeting of the European Council. Migration has gained particular importance in light of the European Union's eastward enlargement. This, to be the Union's widest-ever enlargement, moves the Schengen border further east and symbolizes the end of the East-West division of Europe. It also brings a variety of economic and political consequences, including the need to gradually remove barriers to human mobility between accession countries and the rest of the EU. In fact, negotiations concerning restrictions on such mobility have been quite heated and several policy issues relating to countries beyond the new Eastern border still remain high on the EU political agenda. In consequence, there exists a widely-recognized need to reinforce dialogue and exchange of expertise concerning migration between academics and policy makers from East (accession, candidate and neighbouring countries) and West (member countries). It is our intention that this volume contribute to this important element of European integration.

Work on this book began in Coventry, United Kingdom in the spring of 2001 with a meeting of the coeditors, Agata Górny and Paolo Ruspini, at the Centre for Research in Ethnic Relations of the University of Warwick (CRER). It was then that the idea to develop cooperation between their research institutes, the CRER and the Centre of Migration Research of Warsaw University (CRM) was born.

The first fruit of the cooperation was a conference titled 'In Search for a New Europe: Contrasting Migratory Experiences', held at the University of Warwick in March 2002. The conference was devoted to discussing and investigating the interrelationships between migratory flows and policies in the contemporary and forthcoming European migration space. In this crucial period during which the European Union is being reshaped by the enlargement process, the conference brought together top scholars and migration practitioners from Central and Eastern Europe, Western Europe and the United States. They sought to evaluate selected elements of immigration policies already in place in the 'old' immigration countries and to identify best practices for the countries of Central and Eastern Europe, which have only recently begun attracting migrants and immigrants. The most promising outcomes of the conference discussions are included in this volume. The collection of papers presented here covers a variety of themes debated in this context for the first time. The papers were selected through a comparative mode of analysis focusing on international migration similarities; however, existing differences in the volume and patterns of migratory flows due to European countries' varying stages of migratory experience were also taken into account. This approach was chosen to satisfy the urgent need to implement a model for a common EU immigration policy that would encompass member and accession countries while balancing the prerogatives of the nation states' sovereignty and the increasing transfer of power to the developing supranational entity.

Acknowledgements

This book would have been inconceivable without the support of many people. In particular, we are grateful for the financial support that we received to develop this fascinating project. We want to express our thankfulness to the German Marshall Fund of the United States and the British Council for their financial assistance in organizing the conference 'In search for a New Europe: Contrasting Migratory Experiences' and preparing this book for publication. We also want to thank the Barrow Cadbury Trust for its valuable financial contribution in the course of the editing process.

As editors of the book, we are much indebted to all our contributors for their willingness to discuss their ideas throughout the editing process. We are grateful to our series editors, Zig Layton-Henry and Danièle Joly, for their inspiring advice. We would also like to thank Piotr Koryś from the Centre of Migration Research, Institute for Social Studies, Warsaw University for his insightful help in improving the material presented in this book. Our gratitude goes out likewise to Darren Luck, Beata Kaliciuk and Dariusz Dejnarowicz for helping with the final manuscript as well as to Sam Hundal and all the support staff from the Centre for Research in Ethnic Relations for their assistance in managing the project. Finally, Maria Teresa Garetti and Ardita Demneri, librarians of the Fondazione ISMU in Milan, provided us with valuable assistance in acquiring absolutely any reference book that we could think of.

List of Abbreviations

CEE	—	Central and Eastern Europe
CEC	—	Commission of the European Communities
CEU	—	Council of the European Union
CIS	—	Commonwealth of Independent States
EC	—	European Commission
ECRE	—	European Council on Refugees and Exiles
EEA	—	European Economic Area
EU	—	European Union
GNP	—	Gross National Product
GDP	—	Gross Domestic Product
ILO	—	International Labour Office
IOM	—	International Organization for Migration
OECD	—	Organization for Economic Co-operation and Development
NATO	—	North Atlantic Treaty Organization
PHARE	—	Poland and Hungary Action for Reconstructing the Economy
UN	—	United Nations
UNHCR	—	United Nations High Commissioner for Refugees
USSR	—	Union of Socialist Soviet Republics

Notes on the Contributors

Christophe Bertossi is a Research Fellow at the French Institute of International Relations in Paris, and lectures in political sociology at the Institut d'Etudes Politiques de Toulouse. His research interests focus on citizenship, nationality and immigration within the European context.

Dusan Drbohlav is Associate Professor of social geography at Charles University, Prague. He was a Senior Fulbright Fellow at the California State University in 1999–2000. He specializes in international migration (mainly the Czech Republic and Central and Eastern Europe) and migrants' integration.

Agata Górny is Assistant Professor at the Faculty of Economic Sciences and a Research Fellow at the Centre of Migration Research, Warsaw University. Her research focuses on patterns of migration and adaptation of ex-USSR migrants coming to Poland, and particularly on the application of qualitative methods in migration research.

Krystyna Iglicka is Associate Professor at the L.K. Academy of Management, Warsaw. She has been a Visiting Professor at several European and American Universities and was a Senior Fulbright Fellow at the University of Pennsylvania in 1999–2000. She is the author of over 30 publications on international migration, migration policy and particularly on East-West migration.

Vladimir Iontsev is Head of the Department of Population at the Faculty of Economics, Moscow State 'Lomonosov' University, where he coordinates demographic teaching and training courses. The author of over 90 publications, his particular sphere of interest is theory of international migration of population, including its impact on demographic development and international migration management.

Irina Ivakhniouk is a Senior Researcher at the Faculty of Economics of the Moscow State 'Lomonosov' University. The author of over 30 publications, she is a specialist in international migration, its trends, consequences and regulation, and is particularly interested in labour migration and irregular migration.

Eva Janská is a Research Fellow at the Faculty of Science, Charles University, Prague, in the department of social geography and regional development. Her research interests include: international migration, migration policy and integration/adaptation of foreigners.

Paweł Kaczmarczyk is Assistant Professor at the Faculty of Economic Sciences and a Research Fellow at the Centre of Migration Research, Warsaw University. His main field of interest is causes and consequences of labour migration, with special emphasis on migration in CEE countries and Polish migration to Germany.

Lynnette Catherine Kelly is a Research Fellow at the Centre for Research in Ethnic Relations, University of Warwick. She lectures on refugee policy and ethnic relations. Her main research interests are the settlement and integration of refugees and asylum seekers, employment of refugees and ethnic minorities, and methodologies of researching refugee populations.

Ewa Kępińska is a Research Fellow at the Centre of Migration Research, Warsaw University. Her main interest is the role of gender in international migration and differences between determinants of male and female international labour migration, and their origins. She is a SOPEMI/OECD national correspondent.

Marek Okólski is Professor at the Warsaw University and at the School of Advanced Social Psychology, Warsaw, where he teaches demography and migration. He heads the Centre of Migration Research, Warsaw University, is a member of the Academic Advisory Board of the International Organization for Migration and a SOPEMI/OECD national correspondent

John Rex is Professor Emeritus at the University of Warwick. His long and distinguished career has included posts at the University of Leeds, Birmingham, Durham, Warwick, Aston, Toronto, Capetown and New York. He has been a member of UNESCO International Experts Committee on Racism and Race Prejudice and was President of the Research Committee on Racial and Ethnic Minorities in the International Sociological Association.

Paolo Ruspini is a political scientist researching for the Centre for Research in Ethnic Relations, University of Warwick where he was Marie Curie Research Fellow; the ISMU Foundation, Initiatives and Studies on Multi-ethnicity, Milan; and the Catholic University of Milan. His main research interests include migration, European integration and political psychology.

Giuseppe Sciortino is Assistant Professor at the Università di Trento, Italy. His main areas of expertise are immigration policy, ethnic relations and sociological theory. He has published a comparative and historical study of immigration control policies in Western Europe as well as several articles in both Italian and international journals.

Dariusz Stola is a Fellow at the Institute for Political Studies, Polish Academy of Sciences, Centre of Migration Research, Warsaw University and Professor of History at the Collegium Civitas. His research focuses on Poland's twentieth century history, in particular, on international migrations, Polish-Jewish relations, and the communist regime.

Edward Tiryakian is Professor of Sociology at Duke University, where he has served as Director of International Studies. He has conducted research and published on various aspects of national identity and nationalism in Western and Eastern Europe. He served as Fulbright project director for the New Century Scholars 2003 programme devoted to 'Sectarianism, Ethnicity, and Culture within and across National Borders'.

1
Introduction

Agata Górny, Paolo Ruspini

International mobility and everyday contact with immigrants' rich variety of cultures is the reality for millions of European citizens. Foreign visitors, workers and residents have become a permanent element of the European Union's societies. As well, it is widely understood that Europe needs and will continue to need immigrants due to the alarmingly low fertility rates of most European countries. However, the accession to the European Union by Central and Eastern European countries was preceded by anxiety about the future of East-West European migration. The most pessimistic scenarios foretell the destabilization of the European migration system and a flood of Central and Eastern Europeans into the West upon the opening of the Union's borders and labour markets. Such predictions are unquestionably exaggerated; however, the EU's eastward enlargement will most likely accelerate ongoing movements, in particular East-West mobility.

The enlargement of the European Union entails the eastward expansion of its migration space,[1] as demarcated by the Schengen borders. The common European migration space is, *ipso facto*, a result of European integration and globalization processes. This is so because integration implies closer links among European countries, thereby stimulating migration, whereas globalization, with its concurrent technological developments and related changes in economic and socio-demographic performance, is diminishing geographical distances between countries. Remarkable for its freedom of international human mobility and dismantlement of barriers to economic cooperation, the European migration space emerged despite the existence of regional differences, attributable to divergent historical experiences and dissimilar economic development. Nonetheless, the inclusion of Central and Eastern

1

European countries in this space is usually perceived as particularly challenging given the real and perceived differences between the East and West of Europe. This perception has shaped discussions about the future of Europe and consequently of the European migration space.

The future of the European migration space is directly related to the process of European policy integration; EU migration policy has been under formation since the Tampere meeting of the European Council in October 1999. Integration requires the interaction and attentive co-ordination of different levels of governance. The balance between three levels — regional, national and European — represents the basis of the European polity and the realization of the careful and progressive design of its Founder Fathers. The obligation to satisfy European (that is EU) prerogatives is most apparent in the case of the accession countries,[2] which had to fulfil all the necessary *acquis* to be admitted to the Union. The European level of governance influences, however, the national policies of all member countries. This has led to the problem of determining and ensuring a degree of state sovereignty that would enable national governments to satisfactorily address country-specific aspects of both immigration and emigration. Finding such a balance between the European and nation-state levels is to be accomplished through discussions and negotiations involving actors from all present and prospective member states.

The upcoming, widest ever enlargement of the European Union is viewed as a challenge to the formation of a common EU immigration policy. This perception is due to two considerations. Firstly, as with any endeavour, the more stakeholders, the more difficult it is to reach a consensus; the EU is now faced with the task of creating a policy framework applicable and befitting for the 25 member countries of the enlarged Union. Secondly, the Union needs to enact particular policy measures for accession countries, at least in the short-term perspective. It can be argued, however, that the 2004 enlargement of the Union has sped up work on forming EU migration policy, since effort has had to be made to anticipate difficulties in incorporating the accession countries into the European migration system[3] and provide them with appropriate policy recommendations to smooth the way for their implementation of the *acquis* in migration matters. Thus, the two political processes — enlargement and formation of a common European migration policy — are simultaneous and interrelated and any careful analysis must acknowledge their close relationship.

This book aims to demonstrate the scope of differences and similarities between East and West in terms of migration and related policy developments. We argue that differences between accession and member countries, while sizeable and unquestionable, are overstated in the light of the pre-existing differences among 'old' member countries. Following Claire Wallace's (2001, p. 3) reasoning, we seek to argue that 'we too easily transpose onto Central and Eastern Europe a reversed mirror image based on a misleading simplification, implying a contrast between a relatively homogeneous Western Europe and a fragmented and segmented Eastern Europe'. The division between core and periphery in Europe is one that cuts across state borders and across the East-West divide. Furthermore, Giuliano Amato and Judy Batt (1999a, p. 7) point out that the focus on the East-West division 'should not allow us to forget the salience of the long-standing North-South divide in Western Europe, which will not disappear with the enlargement'.

While stressing the importance of present-day or foreseen similarities in migratory phenomena between European countries, it is worth recalling an analysis of Stephen Castles and Mark J. Miller (1993).[4] In comparing how highly-developed western countries had experienced large-scale immigration since 1945, they found the following common characteristics: (i) a dynamic process of migration, which transformed the temporary entry of workers and refugees into permanent settlers who form distinct ethnic groups; (ii) the economic and social marginalization of the immigrants; (iii) community formation among immigrants; (iv) increasing interaction between immigrant groups and the local population; and (v) the imperative for the state to react to immigration and ethnic diversity (Castles, 1995, p. 293). These immigration stages can be detected, albeit in slightly different forms, in all the country cases discussed in this book. As concluded by Krystyna Iglicka (Chapter 7 in this volume), the globalization of migration will likewise involve Central and East European countries in ways that will soon exemplify the above model.

This book's mapping of differences and similarities between East and West Europe in migration and migration-related policy, in the light of existing already European diversity, allows us to argue that the key task in forming a common EU immigration policy is to find an appropriate level of harmonization. Enlargement does indeed complicate this task but does not redefine the general framework of the problem. In order to deal with this aspect, this book relies on a two-level — national and European — mode of analysis. We have opted for such a twin approach because the prerogatives of immigration policy are usually formulated at these two levels, although the importance of the regional level is increasing in the overall policy-making process.

Due to the diversity of European migration, common European migration guidelines should, generally speaking, leave enough leeway for states to deal with migratory phenomena particular to themselves. At the same time, we see no satisfactory alternative to a common approach in the field of European migration policy. European integration is proceeding slowly but steadily and the management of migratory flows towards and within the European Union requires appropriate coordination. For accession countries, the European level of governance has certainly already been playing an important role as they adjust their policy framework to EU standards. Having had only recent experience with migration, these countries need much consultancy, but simultaneously require some freedoms to develop their own respective policies. On the one hand, their immigration laws, for example, are under-developed compared to those of 'old' member countries and so they would certainly benefit from adopting some solutions already in force in the Union. On the other hand, since accession countries are at earlier stages of development in their migratory processes than other European countries, they require some solutions than cannot be fully copied from contemporary western practice. Thus, *ad hoc* solutions need to be developed for this region and countries therein. In our view, this represents the greatest challenge that the enlargement confronts the formation of the common EU immigration policy with.

* * *

Even though this book is about migration and respective European policy formation, its theme is grounded in broader problems of European identity, European integration and intra-European divides, in particular the dichotomy of East vs. West Europe. This book views differences between East and West of Europe as only a part of the variety and richness of European diversity. Europe was for a long time a plural, not a singular, reality: Greece and Rome, East and West, Orthodox and Catholics, Catholics and Protestants. The idea of Europe (and so of the European Union) as a cultural and geographical space has been conceived in opposition to specific inspiring and/or threatening 'out-groups' over various historical periods (Triandafyllidou, 2002, p. 10). It has been argued that

Europe, as an identity and concept, was formed by encounter and resistance to other religions — specifically, the Muslim religion. It was largely in response to the Muslim threat that Europe drew together.[5]

Historically, two stages in the development of the notion of Europe can be traced (Delanty, 1995). The first covers the period leading up to the late fifteenth century. At that time, the term 'Europe' was used mainly as a geographic expression demarcating the Christian world. Since the fall of Constantinople to the Turks in 1453 and the Europeans powers' post-1492 colonial expansion, the European identity as a system of 'civilization values' has been developing. The Eastern region of Europe fell conceptually out of the notion of 'Europe' after the fall of Constantinople, when the Greek Christian East Empire disappeared and 'Europe' was confined to the Latin West. Simultaneously, the idea of Europe started to distinguish itself from strictly Christendom and become 'the cultural frame of reference for new processes of identity formation' (Delanty, 1995, p. 30).

The term 'Eastern Europe' did not enter popular discourse until the Enlightenment era and was used to denote the part of Europe that differed from 'civilized' Western Europe. The term encompassed the region from the Baltic Sea to the Ottoman Empire and from the western border of Poland to Siberia (Wolff, 1994).[6] The origins of a tangible East-West division can be traced, however, back to the late medieval era, when nascent forms of capitalism were forming in Europe (Wallerstein, 1976).

The centres of European (and world) capitalism evolved and shifted, starting from Italian cities, moving to Amsterdam in the sixteenth century and to the British Empire in the seventeenth. Nevertheless, the core of economic development remained in the western portion of the continent and other countries gradually became peripheries of this core (Wallerstein, 1976). The centre-periphery division was not stable and in Europe the core expanded as Scandinavian countries caught up and became a part of the developed industrial European centre in the nineteenth century (Berend, 1996). It can be argued, however, that Central and Eastern Europe failed to do so and, instead by the sixteenth century had become a chief supplier of food and other primary goods to the developing capitalistic economies in the West of Europe. Certainly, there was diversity within this region. For example, industrialization in the Czech Republic, being under 'western influence', was much faster than in Poland.

Thus, even though a core and periphery were distinguishable in Europe that overlapped the East-West division in the mid-twentieth century, both halves were internally diverse. The peripheral countries differed not only in terms of economic development, but also in the intensity of their contacts with the Western core. In fact, there were strong cultural, economic and political links between the Eastern and Western parts of Europe. In this realm, East-Central Europe — Poland, the Czech Republic and Hungary — is sometimes distinguished as the most westernized, and indeed as oscillating between East and West of Europe (see, for example, Szűcs, 1994).

The mid-twentieth century East-West division was entrenched by the Yalta agreement. The pact forced almost a half-century of political separation between the East and West of Europe. The idea of Western Europe as the true Europe, a Cold War construct, served as a legitimization for a costly readiness for a potentially cataclysmic war (Delanty, 1995). Europe's eastern frontier constricted back to the Elbe, leaving Eastern Europe a semi-periphery of the USSR. At the time, the notion and term of 'Eastern Europe' almost always designated the Soviet Union and all countries of the Socialist bloc (Sosnowska, 2004).

The East-West division, stemming from the seventeenth century, appeared to be very stable and was even a justification of the Yalta division of Europe. The differences and supposed division was even used to suggest the existence of different civilizations in Europe: an advanced western one versus a backward eastern civilization (Wolf, 1994). The foundation of the European Economic Community in the 1950s challenged but did not change the above perspective. In the Founder Fathers' vision, Europe encompassed a sphere of common values, such as democracy and human rights, bounded within a clearly defined geographic, historical and civilization space. Until the late 1980s, the European Union comprised countries sharing not only a geographical space (the western half of the European continent) but also a set of cultural and political values. Such relative homogeneity gave rise to various 'fault lines' in Europe, particularly the elaboration of a concept of 'Western civilization', from which Eastern Europe was excluded (Davies, 1996).[7] The West and the East were very clearly defined in this conceptualization. Consequently, Europe's historic mission at the demise of communism was to stretch out her hand to her eastern siblings and to absorb the one-time democracies of Eastern Europe (Soutou, 2000).[8]

The discussion concerning the position of Eastern Europe in European history and civilization would be impossible if not for the collapse of the communist system (Wolf, 1994). Thus, this book uses the term 'East of Europe' to designate post-communist countries. We use this term interchangeably with the term 'Central and Eastern Europe' which is, along with the term 'East-Central Europe', used to emphasize the existence of historical links between this part of Europe and both the East and West portions of the continent. Central and Eastern Europe, as a term and notion, became particularly popular in the 1980s and demonstrates the ongoing process of redefinition and blurring of the frontiers of East and West Europe.

This redefinition and reconceptualization has been invigorated by the eastward enlargement of the European Union and the historic opportunity to re-integrate most of the European continent. On the one hand, East and West are geographical and historical constructions, entrenched by the Cold War to dichotomize areas of Europe in terms of political and socio-economic developments. On the other hand, however, East and West represent also psycho-sociological ('mindset') categories. In particular, decades of communism and isolation have strongly shaped the attitudes and behavioural reflexes of the peoples of Central and Eastern Europe. Their differing attitudes and behaviours have nourished Western Europeans' long-lasting perceptions about the East as 'backward' and less 'civilized' than the West and not fully 'part of Europe'.[9] Even though material differences between East and West, stemming from their unequal speed of economic development, are going to require decades to be reduced, the EU enlargement should be an occasion to tackle the existing psycho-sociological and political aspects of the East-West dichotomization.

The historically-determined differences will not disappear upon new member states' entrance to the Union. Thus, in this book, we hope to demonstrate both the specificity of Central and Eastern Europe (accession area) and the diversity that Western Europe already features. At the same time, in turning our attention more specifically to the field of migration, we intend to present similarities and potential areas of convergence for Europe's East and West and for the future Union as a whole. In particular, we want to trace similarities in the interaction between the supranational (European) and national levels of governance in immigration policy formation in European countries. The material demonstrated in this book is by no means exhaustive and does not cover the enormous complexity of the European migratory reality. The presented case studies provide, however, valuable insights and evidence for further discussion about the future of the European migration space.

* * *

In tracing differences and similarities in European migration and related policy developments, two aspects should be taken into consideration: migratory trends and the integration of migrant and ethnic minorities in European countries. These two aspects can be directly translated into two respective sub-components or sub-goals of immigration policy: efficient management of migratory flows and successful integration of the migrant and ethnic minorities present in a given country.

Management of migratory flows in the enlarged Europe is an issue that is attracting most attention at the moment. Inclusion of the CEE countries in the European migration space is bringing about a lot of speculation concerning the future of European migration. Experts are divided concerning possible scenarios for migratory trends in the accession area and the consequences that the inclusion of CEE in the European migration space will bring. This issue is dealt with in the first section of this book, 'Present and Future East-West Migratory Trends in the Enlarged European Union'.

This section opens with a contribution of Marek Okólski, 'Migration Patterns in Central and Eastern Europe on the Eve of the European Union Enlargement', which provides a broad and complex overview of migration in CEE. As Okólski shows, the migration space of the accession countries itself has its own peculiarities. CEE as a whole has even become a separate migration space recently, with its own logic, structure and dynamic; most flows of Central and Eastern European migrants are contained within the region itself. This space covers CEE as the whole post-Communist area relative to the rest of the European continent. Consequently, the author states that the widely stressed, nowadays, importance of emigration from CEE to the West is an exaggeration. In Okólski's view, forecasts concerning post-enlargement migratory trends are most problematic in the case of East-East and East-Central movements, as the shift of the Schengen border will divide areas where international barriers are currently small and rather conducive to international migration.

The problem of East-Central movements is dealt with in the subsequent chapter 'Current Ukrainian and Russian Migration to the Czech Republic: Mutual Similarities and Differences', by Dusan Drbohlav and Eva Janská. Their contribution is devoted to immigration to the Czech Republic, as part of a broader phenomenon of immigration *to* (as opposed to migration from and through) CEE countries, a quite new element of the overall migratory picture of this region. The largest segment of immigration to the accession countries consists of citizens of ex-USSR countries. Based on theoretical concepts of 'transnationalization theory', the authors argue that there has been a gradual transformation from circular migration into more permanent forms of migration and settlement in the Czech Republic. It seems, therefore, that emigration from ex-USSR countries (particularly from Russia and Ukraine) is likely to influence the future shape of the European migration space. This reshaping is due to the fact that these latter forms of migration are now typically more stable than the shuttle, irregular and short-term movements that were predominate in migration from the former Soviet Union to Central Europe (Poland, Czech Republic and Hungary) at the beginning of the 1990s.

The last chapter of Section I — 'Future Westward Outflow from Accession Countries: the Case of Poland' — deals with the prospects of emigration from CEE to the old EU members. Paweł Kaczmarczyk argues that there will be neither a migratory 'big-bang' nor 'invasions' of Western labour markets. He discusses the prospects of limited out-migration from accession countries, basing his theses on a wide selection of different models used to estimate future flows from accession to older EU member states. His focus is on Poland, but as part of a wider Central European framework. Demonstrating that differences in wages and per capita national incomes are pre-conditions for mobility but not sufficient causes for it, Kaczmarczyk's conclusions echo Wallace's belief that 'being poor is not enough to become a migrant'. In other words, he argues, East-West European economic differences are not sufficient to initiate a large wave of East-West post-enlargement migration. Another important refutation to pessimistic outflow scenarios — for the author the most important point of his paper — is the reminder that labour migration is most of all a function of demand. In his words, 'There is no economic migration without demand for foreign labour in the destination country'.

Section I demonstrates main aspects of migratory movements in the accession area. In doing so, the section rebuts those simpler forecasts concerning the future of the enlarged European migration space that overemphasize wage differentials between the East and West of Europe. On the one hand, these differences are insufficient to induce a mass East-West migration. On the other hand, other factors, such as social, economic and cultural links already existing in the region and enforced by particular structural factors, have created a framework for migration in CEE. This framework will neither disappear nor be made irrelevant overnight upon the EU's absorption of some CEE countries and so should be taken into consideration in making any forecast about the future of the enlarged European migration space.

Generally speaking, Section I stresses the peculiarities of the accession area. In contrast, the second section of the book, 'The Struggle for Recognition: New and Old Minorities in Europe', demonstrates some important similarities between Eastern and Western experiences. Its broad theme — integration of migrant and ethnic minorities in European countries — is an important policy issue at the top of the European agenda at the moment. This problem, even though a subject of immigration policies, overlaps the broader issue of European identity and, what is at stake at the moment, European citizenship and the rights of representatives of migrant and ethnic minorities to it. Beyond the Euro-rhetoric, there is a widespread need to act in order to create an inclusive idea of an enlarged Europe — a Europe that is open and tolerant of cultural diversities and whose concept of citizenship features characteristics similar to multicultural, pluralistic models.

The section opens with a general chapter, 'Multiculturalism and Political Integration in Modern Nation States', by John Rex. In it, the author expounds on the philosophical and social science view of multiculturalism and compares different integration models adopted by some European countries. The author covers also the 'devolution'[10] issue, using several examples ranging from EU member and accession countries to the former Soviet Union and Yugoslavia. He shows that, for post-communist countries (especially Yugoslavia), 'It was easy to suggest new multicultural constitutions but harder to put them into practice'. He deals with the settlement of immigrant minorities, who, for now, cannot make the same demands as certain sub-nationalities do. In advocating the role of negotiations and compromise to overcome the conflicts of ideas and interests between different groups, he promotes a viable multicultural policy that is neither devised nor imposed from above. At the same time, however, he stresses that, in Europe, issues of integration and devolution of immigrant and ethnic minorities are inseparable from the discourse (sympathetic or hostile) about multiculturalism.

Rex's detailed overview of different European integration models is followed by the contribution titled 'Politics and Policies of French Citizenship, Ethnic Minorities and the European Agenda' by Christophe Bertossi. His chapter deals with the issue of ethnic minorities viewed from the particular, but overwhelmingly important in the present European political context, perspective of citizenship policy. Interestingly enough, the author argues that the notion of integration is not relevant anymore in the French policy-making process. Because of the overloaded legacy of French Republicanism, the issue of recognition is no less important than policies of distribution and welfare. Bertossi ascribes this to the way anti-discrimination policies are becoming a 'common denominator' in Europe. Quoting the French case, he points out how these pluralistic policies could assist in developing a common citizenship framework in Europe that would subsume national models of citizenship. Bertossi stresses the pan-European nature of the issue in his attempt to relate how two levels of governance — the national and supranational (European) one — interplay to explain the importation of the European agenda into French citizenship politics and policies. In particular, he demonstrates how the ongoing European legislation process has been shaping national policies.

Notwithstanding existing differences, Rex and Bertossi demonstrate the importance of modern and contemporary multi-cultural policies and anti-discrimination measures in the light of the growing and diversifying minority groups in all the countries of Europe. As far as the accession area is concerned, the region is similar to the rest of Europe in securing anti-discrimination measures, but the introduction of multicultural policies in CEE has not happened yet. However, Krystyna Iglicka, in her chapter 'The Revival of Ethnic Consciousness: the Case of Poland', argues that ethnic and cultural diversity is a crucial issue in CEE, as the collapse of the communist system brought about a subsequent revival of 'ethnic consciousness' in Poland. This is not specific to Poland, as similar phenomena have also been observed in other Central and Eastern European countries since the break-up of the communist bloc. Thus, although the term 'multiculturalism' may sound out-of-place for 'ethnically homogenous' Poland and other Central and Eastern European countries, Iglicka proves that the problem of ethnic minorities in the region deserves careful attention. She sees more and more similarities between East and West as to their societies' cultural diversity and a common need for accommodating different cultures and ethnic groups in their societal structures.

In general, the formulation of national integration policies remains up to the respective governments; furthermore, experience shows that there can be no universal integration model that would work in all countries and contexts. However, the issue of integration of migrants and ethnic minorities has many common denominators throughout Europe. The unifying ideas of multiculturalism and anti-discrimination measures are implicit in the democratic values underlying the idea of European civilization such as tolerance, securing human rights and human dignity. In terms of protecting immigrants' and refugees' human rights, CEE has already joined the group of Western European countries.

Further similarities between the East and West of Europe and among all European countries are outlined in the third section of the book, 'Migration Policies at Different Stages of Development: between National and European'. The country-studies of Poland, Italy and Great Britain included in this section demonstrate the way in which national migration policies affect migrants and how the adoption of EU legal requirements and binding international conventions have shaped the development of their respective immigration policies. However, the studies' foremost conclusion is that the unpredictable nature of migration makes it difficult to create structured recommendations for the harmonization of immigration policies in the European Union.

The first chapter of this section is 'Migration Policies and Politics in Poland' by Ewa Kępińska and Dariusz Stola. It demonstrates how the immigration policy of the major country of Central and Eastern Europe — Poland — has been highly influenced by the need to fulfil the requirements of the *acquis*. The authors do not hesitate to call that policy formation a reactive response to EU demands. Consequently, consistent with European trends, the increasing restrictions on migration to and through Poland are the major feature of state policy. Poland's reactiveness can be also observed in the way contemporary migratory phenomena are accommodated there. Kępińska and Stola argue, however, that though the requirement to meet *acquis* was an unprogressive contributor to Polish migration policy itself, accession to the European Union has importantly contributed to the advancement of immigration policies in Poland. In their view, however, the reactiveness of the process is a factor of concern. Thus, they argue that further advantage should be taken from the current environment by formulating coherent postulates for Polish immigration policy, taking into account particularities of CEE migratory phenomena as soon as possible. Although the chapter focuses on Poland, it illustrates how immigration policy is developed on the eve of a country's accession to the European Union. Evidently, the salient points of this chapter are applicable to other countries of Central Europe.

The circumstances requiring Poland to adapt itself to new contingencies and the EU legislative and political framework are not typical only of the accession area. In fact, they can be compared to the experiences of member countries, such as like Italy and France, in the way unexpected migratory developments affect the development of migratory policies. Both those countries, although at different stages of their migratory process, had to develop/change their policies to be in accordance with the European Union agenda. Italy's experience is analysed by Giuseppe Sciortino in the chapter 'When Domestic Labour is not Native Labour: the Interaction of Immigration Policy and the Welfare Regime in Italy'. He provides a striking example of the danger of implementing simplified policy solutions to some migratory phenomena. The author attempts to develop a new direction of research in order to question the widespread conviction that migrants affect the welfare regimes solely as consumers of benefits. Interestingly enough, as Sciortino shows, foreign labour is vital to the Italian welfare regime. He stresses that the connection between foreign labour and welfare activities is mainly a function of the kind of labour demand that welfare regimes actually produce and of the niches migrants occupy on a domestic labour market. The chapter characterizes the Italian welfare system as one of several Western European welfare regimes wherein the family plays a central role as a caregiver. Sciortino draws comparisons between the Italian welfare and other European welfare regimes, arguing that culture, welfare model and immigration policy are important causes of differences among European countries. This piece of research is useful in a broader, comparative European perspective because it emphasizes how the design of Italy's immigration policy was constrained by international conventions and the European level of governance.

The following chapter 'Bosnian Refugees in Britain: a Question of Community' by Lynnette Kelly presents another example of the ambiguous influence of international conventions and the supranational level of governance on the process of dealing with immigrants. Her chapter is devoted to the problem of refugees in the United Kingdom — an important issue not only in the UK but also in the European Union as a whole. Kelly focuses on the so-called 'Bosnia Project' for Bosnian refugees given temporary status in Britain due to the Balkan conflicts between 1992 and 1995. The chapter's focus on Bosnian community formation shows how such formation was mainly the result of aid and emergency responses addressed to them. That's why their formal communities are said to be 'contingent', and the real communities only 'imagined'. In the author's view, a true, inclusive Bosnian community cannot be said to exist and the *raison d'etre* of Bosnian community associations has always been the acquisition of benefits that British society gives to the community associations. She criticizes the social policies that imposed an external construct on the Bosnians and argues that these contingent communities are in reality a reaction to prevailing policies rather than an example of refugees' initiatives or even inclinations.

In general, the contributions included in Section III, despite their presentation of selected problems of interaction between national and supranational (European) level of governance, do not challenge the idea of a common immigration policy for the European Union. They illustrate, however, the need for careful examination of European-level recommendations and some widely-held beliefs before implementing them at the national level. All together, Sections I–III present not only dissimilarities between East and West of Europe, the breadth and diversity of European migratory issues and country-specific scenarios, but also some common denominators that can be used to underline the future development of a European policy.

It can be also argued that, even though the diversity of Europe is unquestionable, the countries of the European Union share common interests and values supported by a unifying notion of a common European civilization.[11] These 'common' aspects are discussed in the fourth and final section of the book, 'The Enlargement of the European Union and the Creation of a Common Policy on Immigration'. It includes American and Russian scholarly perspectives on the new, expanding EU migration space and an analysis of the main lines of debate taking place during the difficult process of setting up a common EU immigration policy.

The United States is the most powerful political actor in the international arena and does keep its eye on the ongoing process of European integration. Since the September 11 attacks, the US administration has been exercising its military and political power to exert influence on the foreign policy choices of the present and future members of the European Union. The choices and related political orientations selected by European actors, as individual players and/or as a whole polity, are strongly related to the nature of the European identity formation/transformation. This is true not only for the economic and political sphere but also in societal and cultural dimensions. This topic is broadly demonstrated in Edward Tyriakian's contribution, '"Old Europe/New Europe": Ambiguities of Identity'. Writing about the European identity, the author uses

European integration and the evolution of its political apparatus to tackle three of its historical and contemporary challenges: expansion, immigration and the 'new' American challenge posed by the present US administration. This 'view from outside' offers an important insight that may bear on the processes analysed in the book: since Europe has historically drawn together because of external pressure, the new American assertiveness might even strengthen Europe's determination to become more autonomous in the international arena (Calleo, 2003).

Russia is another influential political actor that closely follows European integration and developments in the migration field. Some elements of Russia's stance are presented in the chapter 'Russia and the Enlargement of the European Union', by Vladimir Iontsev and Irina Ivakhniouk. The authors cover a wide selection of key issues relating to Russia's role as the peripheral zone of exodus of migrants heading to the West, but explain as well how Russia also represents the core of a new migration space in the territory of the former Soviet Union. Presenting current migratory trends, the authors explain why the European Union should look at its eastern neighbours with unprejudiced consideration. They discuss also the problem of regulating migration between Russia and accession Central and East European countries. The authors advocate moving migration management policy from solutions designed to deal with forced migration to ones designed to adequately cover labour migration, above all to its irregular component. It is in fact due to its lack of control on entry and strict control on exit that the huge Russian geographical space has become a 'settling tank' for irregular, would-be westward migrants. The authors also describe the related matter of the Kaliningrad enclave as one of the critical issues in relations between the European Union and Russia. This chapter demonstrates how the enlargement of the European Union, not only in the field of migration, represents a crucial redefinition of East-West relations in Europe.

The final chapter of Section IV and of the book overall is Agata Górny and Paolo Ruspini's contribution, titled 'Forging a Common Immigration Policy for the Enlarging European Union: for Diversity of Harmonization', devoted to the prospects for a common EU immigration policy. Their analyses are based on European experts' opinions on prospects for a European migration policy voiced at the conference 'In Search for a New Europe: Contrasting Migratory Experiences', held on 22–24 March 2002. Górny and Ruspini argue that harmonization of EU immigration policy should be secured to the extent that European countries share not only common problems but also common interests. Namely, the authors propose three fields for effective European-level management: asylum versus migration, labour markets and enlargement. Efforts in all three fields, they argue, must be dealt with an eye on the formation of a common EU immigration policy. The recommendations included in this chapter show how the optimal degree of harmonization varies in different fields of policy formation. Thus, the contribution attempts to sum up the richness of the overall material presented in the book and provides analyses of the interrelation between European and national levels of governance in the process of European Union policy formation.

* * *

The outcomes of contemporary discussions and negotiations on the shape of the European Union and a common EU immigration policy are still to come. Notions of 'commonalities' and 'differences' have changed throughout the course of European history. Factors supposedly 'unifying' Europe in some historical periods have become 'dividing lines' in other times and contexts. Nevertheless, European integration is proceeding slowly but uninterruptedly. European countries' strong awareness of their individual national interests and the exceptional dynamics of migration, which are difficult to encapsulate in a highly structured policy framework and strict legislative solutions, are likely to keep challenging European efforts to harmonize policies. All this makes the issue of European migration in the context of European integration a fascinating object of research.

Although East-West differences, not only in the realm of migration, are clearly visible in the contributions presented in this volume, the selection of problems presented here shows that there are many existing and anticipated similarities among the interests, views, and circumstances of present and prospective members of the European Union. In the course of the 'East-West reintegration' now underway, these similarities will bear growing importance over current differences. Thus, not only students of migration should find here inspiration for forming views unbiased by the 'erected walls' of misjudgement and free of ignorance of the long-past and most recent histories of Europe.

Notes

1   The term 'migration space', as used in this book, is based primarily on the term 'social space' that comprises the 'everyday life and concentrated social "interlacing coherence networks" and social institutions that structure a human life' (Pries, 1999, p. 3). It designates the space on which mutual migratory links between various countries have developed. In particular, 'migration space' refers also to the geographical space that is characterised by a lack of barriers for human mobility, for example, the Schengen area. Usually, both aspects of the 'migration space' — geographical and social — are interrelated as freedom of movements stimulates formation of migratory links.

2. With reference to the 1993 Copenhagen European Council's framework and the following April 2003 signature of the EU Accession Treaty, in this book, when writing of 'accession/acceding' countries we refer to the eight CEE countries, that is the Czech Republic, Estonia, Hungary, Latvia, Lithuania, Poland, Slovakia, Slovenia, which have joined the EU on 1 May 2004 together with the two Mediterranean islands of Cyprus and Malta. We mean for 'candidates' the other three countries, that is Bulgaria, Romania, Turkey, which still need to satisfy the convergence criteria to join the Union.

3   The term 'migration system', as used in this book, is similar to the concept of 'migration space'. The term 'migration system' designates, however, not only extensive migratory flows and links but also development of social functions (by means of particular migration patterns and policy developments) that secure the equilibrium of a given migratory reality (compare, for example, Zlotnik, 1992).

4   From Iglicka (Chapter 7 in this volume).

5   From Mongols and Tartars from the east and from Arabs and Turks in the south. One may argue that Europe is a product, perhaps ironically, of its history with Muslims, Muslim empires and Islamic culture. Muslims have contributed to the formation of Europe not only as Europe's 'other' but directly, as philosophers, scientists and scholars (Kumar, 2004).

6   Although the status of Greece — as the 'cradle of Western civilisation' — was hard to pin down (Wolff, 1994).

7   From Kumar (2004). For elaboration on the concept of Western civilization, see Huntington (1997, pp. 157–63).

8   In anthropological perspective, the West and the East are only seemingly separate but are really bound by a consanguineous continuity nexus: Phoenix is brother of Europe; Aeneas, the defeated of Troy, builds Rome (Ferrara, 1998).

9   A product of the so-called 'Wall in our Heads', termed by Czech President Vaclav Havel to name the mutual ignorance and prejudices built up during the decades of the Cold War division of Europe (Amato and Batt, 1999b).

10 Concession of power from central national governments to regionally-based, sub-national groups with the possibility of power sharing at the centre.

11 For François Guizot in his *History of Civilization in Europe* (1828), the European civilization distinguished itself from all past civilizations precisely by its principle of diversity, which, paradoxically, also provided its unity.

References

Amato, G., J. Batt (eds), 'The Long-Term Implications of EU Enlargement: Culture and National Identity', Report of the Reflection Group on 'Long-term Implications of EU Enlargement: the Nature of the New Border', *RSC Policy Paper*, No. 99/1 (San Domenico di Fiesole (FI): European University Institute, 1999a).

Amato, G., J. Batt (eds), *The Long-Term Implications of EU Enlargement: The Nature of the New Border* (San Domenico di Fiesole (FI): European University Institute, 1999b).

Berend, I., *Central and Eastern Europe 1944–1993: Detour from the Periphery to the Periphery* (Cambridge, MA: Cambridge University Press, 1996).

Calleo, D. P., 'Europe's Future and America's War on Terrorism', afterword in D. P. Calleo, *Rethinking Europe's Future* [First edition, 2001], (Princeton and Oxford: Princeton University Press — The Century Foundation, 2003).

Castles S., M. J. Miller, *The Age of Migration: International Population Movements in the Modern World* (London: Macmillan, 1993).

Castles, S., 'How nation-states respond to immigration and ethnic diversity', *New Community*, Vol. 21, No. 3 (1995), pp. 293–308.

Davies, N., *Europe: A History* (Oxford and New York: Oxford University Press, 1996).

Delanty, G., *Inventing Europe. Idea, Identity, Reality* (London: MacMillan, 1995).

Ferrara, P., 'L'unità molteplice dei popoli', *Politica Internazionale*, Vol. 28, No. 6 (1998), pp. 169–73.

EC, *Equality, Diversity and Enlargement. Report on measures to combat discrimination in acceding and candidate countries* (Brussels: European Communities, 2003).

Guizot, F., *The History of Civilization in Europe*, translated by W. Hazlitt, edited by L. Siedentop [First edition, 1828], (London: Penguin Books, 1997).

Huntington, S. P., *The Clash of Civilizations and the Remaking of World Order* (New York: Touchstone, 1997).

Kritz, M. M., H. Zlotnik, 'Global Interactions: Migration Systems, Processes and Policies', in M. M. Kritz, L. L. Lim, H. Zlotnik (eds), *International Migration Systems* (Oxford: Clarendon Press, 1992), pp. 1–16.

Kumar, K., 'The Idea of Europe: Cultural Legacies, Transnational Imaginings and the Nation-State', in M. Berezin, M. Schain (eds), *Europe without Borders: Remapping Territory, Citizenship and Identity in a Trans-national Age* (Baltimore, MD: Johns Hopkins University Press, 2004), forthcoming.

Nolte, H. H., '"Spóźnione" narody w Europie Środkowej i Wschodniej', *Przegląd Zachodni*, No. 1 (1995), pp. 31–6.

Pries, L., 'New Migration in Transnational Spaces', in L. Pries (ed.), *Migration and Transnational Social Spaces* (Aldershot, Brookfield, Singapore, Sydney: Ashgate, 1999), pp. 1–35.

Sosnowska, A., *Socjologia zacofania. Spory historyków o Europę Wschodnią (1947–1994)*, (Warszawa: Wydawnictwo Trio, 2004), forthcoming.

Soutou, G. H., 'Il sonno della geopolitica genera mostri', *Limes*, No. 3 (2000), pp. 37–8.

Szűcs, J., *Trzy Europy* [First edition, Budapest, 1983], (Lublin: Instytut Europy Środkowo-Wschodniej, 1994).

Triandafyllidou, A., *Negotiating Nationhood in a Changing Europe: Views from the Press*, (Ceredigion, Wales and Washington, DC: Edwin Mellen Press, 2002).

Wallace, H., 'Introduction: Rethinking European Integration', in H. Wallace (ed.), *Interlocking Dimensions of European Integration* (Basingstoke: Palgrave, 2001), pp. 1–22.

Wallerstein, I., *The Modern World System. Capitalist Agriculture and the Origins of the European World-Economy in the Sixteen Century* (New York: Academic Press, 1976).

Wolf, L., *Inventing Eastern Europe. The Map of Civilisation on the Mind of Enlightement* (Stanford, CL: Stanford University Press, 1994).

Part I

Present and Future East-West Migratory Trends in the Enlarged European Union

2

Migration Patterns in Central and Eastern Europe on the Eve of the European Union Expansion: an Overview[1]

Marek Okólski

2.1. CEE in View of the Coming EU Expansion

The recognition of Central and Eastern Europe as a separate and distinct migration space in the global migration system first arose in the 1990s.[2] Particular interest in CEE resulted from many factors, such as a widely-expected, protracted and massive flow of persons from that part of Europe to the West, the perceived strong impact of CEE migration upon regional political changes (especially the pace of the post-communist transition) and the emergence or radical intensification of certain new or then-marginal East-West human flows, like illegal transit migration, movements of *mala fide* refugees, circular movements of false tourists or petty traders, and so on.

Surprisingly, despite extensive research and public debate for more than ten years now, there exists no universal definition of CEE,[3] especially in terms of its geographical coverage. Although most analyses include all former communist countries of Europe, some literature regards the CEE as only the countries that transformed themselves before the collapse of the Soviet Union (that is the Baltic States, Hungary, Slovakia, the Czech Republic and Poland) or before the disintegration of Yugoslavia (therefore, additionally ex-Soviet republics as well as Romania and Bulgaria). In some research and policy-oriented reports, however, the set of CEE member-states is tailored to the needs of specific aims or focuses of those reports and often encompasses only a narrow selection of post-communist European countries. This seems to be the case of most recent discussions on migration effects of the accession of CEE countries to the European Union.

Despite the ambiguity of substantive evidence, the imminent eastward expansion of the EU is sometimes seen as an additional challenge to the fragile stability of the European migration system. Namely, the enlargement is viewed as a vehicle of increasing (uncontrolled or undesirable) inflow of immigrants into the present EU. This view stems above all from that eight formerly communist countries of Europe that are likely to become new EU members on 1 May 2004.[4] These eight states substantially lag behind Community standards in terms of standard of living, while representing great demographic potential (if not surplus).

Table 2.1 Population, GDP (per capita) and monthly wage in the CEE countries that are likely to enter the EU in 2004 (data for 1999)

Country	Population in millions	Gross domestic product per capita in PPP[a] (as % of EU-15 average)	Gross monthly wage (USD equivalent) (as % of EU-15)
Czech Republic	10.4	59.0	13.2
Estonia	1.4	36.3	11.5
Hungary	10.0	50.5	12.4
Latvia	2.4	27.4	5.4
Lithuania	3.5	29.2	9.6
Poland	38.6	36.8	17.7
Slovakia	5.4	48.6	9.7
Slovenia	2.0	70.8	41.1
All eight countries	73.7	39.0	13.8

[a] In purchasing power parity
Source: United Nations (2001), European Commission (2001)

As evident from Table 2.1, at the turn of the millennium workers in accession countries earned much less (between one-sixth and one-tenth)[5] than workers in the EU; likewise, GDP per capita in those countries was generally significantly lower than in the EU. According to mainstream migration theory, such a situation is conducive to labour supply transfers from CEE to EU countries.

Those differences relative to the EU, however, were much smaller than the differences between EU and major non-European countries of migrant workers' origin. Furthermore, they were not substantially higher than those observed between the most well-off and the least affluent EU member states, or even between rich and poor regions in certain EU countries (for example Germany or Italy), in which, despite the differentials, only moderate flows of people continue to exist.

An income gap *per se*, as follows from various empirical investigations, does not present a sufficient stimulus for migration. The gap, however, might be conceived as merely *conditio sine qua non* for mobilization of labour's migratory potential in low-wage countries. It is rather the pull of continuous excess labour demand (and low unemployment) in countries offering higher wages, combined with active worker recruitment by employers (or their agents), that contributes most to actual flows of people from poorer to richer areas. Such a situation was typical of western Europe in the 1960s and early 1970s; however, recently it can be observed only in a very truncated and highly selective form, which hardly fosters large flows of migrant labour.

In terms of demographic potential, the 1999 total population of the eight accession countries was just below 74 million, or around 10 per cent of Europe's population and 20 per cent of EU-15 population. Excluding the three most populous countries (the Czech Republic, Hungary and Poland), the remaining five countries were jointly populated by some 15 million. This represents both a tiny fraction of the EU-15 population and is significantly fewer than their total number of (legal) foreign inhabitants. With regard to the Czech Republic and Hungary, it should be kept in mind that, in the 1990s, both countries became net immigration areas. Therefore, only one country, Poland, with its population of above 38 million and continuous net emigration, can be considered a potential pool of large-scale inflow into the EU. Besides, all prospective new EU member states (including Poland) are among the world's leaders in fertility decline, feature stagnant or decreasing population size and are (or soon will be) experiencing a decline in the 'mobile segment' of working-age population (below the age of 45).

The above leads me to conclude that predictions of migration from the eight accession countries to EU-15 ones based solely on CEE population size and income gaps were too ill-founded to represent reliable forecasts of likely migration. Besides inaccurately forecasting out-migration from the eight accession countries, such analyses also fail to take the whole CEE region into account. Furthermore, the analyses, perhaps illegitimately, group the eight accession countries together as co-members of a single region.[6] Additionally, any discussion of the migratory potential of the entire CEE region based on economic and demographic data from the eight imminent member countries will suffer from unrepresentativeness, as those countries significantly differ from other countries in Central and Eastern Europe. Indeed, the eight countries:

- are a distinctly better-off fraction of an area comprising the 19 post-communist countries of Europe (CEE in the wider sense),
- account for only 22 per cent of the total CEE population,
- do not include a number of CEE countries of vital importance for intra-CEE and pan-European migration, most notably Ukraine,
- do not constitute a homogeneous entity with respect to migration.[7]

For this reason, in the analysis to follow I will adopt a different perspective, one that focuses on intrinsic migratory trends and structural characteristics in the CEE, here understood as the whole post-communist area relative to the rest of the continent. Following this approach, however, I will not delve into the issues and problems specific to intra-CIS (and Ukrainian) migration unless they are relevant to broader issues in CEE and pan-European migration.[8]

2.2. Migration in CEE *vis-à-vis* a General Pattern of European Migration

Present migration throughout Europe is, at least to some extent, historically determined. Modern history offers clues for many similarities and contrasts between countries and regions. For instance, modernization brought about mobility transition in practically all parts of Europe and so population surpluses throughout Europe could emigrate overseas during times of rapid population growth and demographic transition. On the other hand, many differences in current population movements in Europe are due to differing times of initiation and courses of modernization. Regional interdependencies that led to stable local (usually bipartite) patterns of migratory flows, such as between Sweden and Finland, Britain and Ireland, France and Italy or Germany and Poland, are also rooted in European history. Furthermore, migration trends found in former colonial powers, such as Britain, France, Spain, Portugal and the Netherlands, are affected by past political and economic links to their colonies and dependencies and considerably differ from trends observed in European countries with either no colonial history or only brief colonial episodes. In turn, migration on the territory of the former multinational or multiethnic empires (Austro-Hungarian, Ottoman and Tsarist) also displays distinct characteristics. By the same token, it is no wonder that current migration in CEE is influenced by a more recent history of political isolation and forcibly repressed spatial mobility.

Distinct migration trends in CEE are attributable less to political developments of the second half of the twentieth century than to historical factors, of which the following four seem to be prominent:
- relative economic and institutional backwardness (compare to the West),
- a relative abundance of labour,
- relative instability of state boundaries,
- relative instability of a (comparatively diverse) ethnic mix in the population.

Nonetheless, some facts concerning migration pertaining to the entire continent's history or characterizing an increasing number of its populations can be selectively presented. Those facts include massive (and permanent) transfers of people from rural to urban areas and strong outflow to non-European destinations, particularly between the early ninetieth and early twentieth centuries, and a more recent phenomenon — a transformation from net emigration to net immigration involving smaller outflows and greater inflows, especially from non-European countries.

Even if only the three above-mentioned generalizations are considered, the specificity of CEE is quite clear if not striking. Here, rural-to-urban migration was both greatly delayed and generally low, at least (with the distinct exception of the Czech Republic) until the post-World War II period. The outflow overseas started much later than the respective outflow from western or northern Europe and did not reach the pace of the latter. Certain CEE countries, notably those belonging (before 1918) to the Austro-Hungarian and Ottoman empires, contributed just moderately to migratory flows to non-European territories. In contrast to most western European countries, in the early decades of modernization a large part of the superfluous rural population emigrated to or sought seasonal employment in other European countries (mainly Germany).[9] Finally, the notion of a shift from net emigration to net immigration (pertaining to almost all non-CEE, European countries in recent decades) is inapplicable to a majority of CEE countries because the latter were closed to international movements of people for nearly half of the twentieth century. When freedom of movement was restored around 1990, some countries instantly experienced strong outflow (and weak inflow), some others went through moderate inflow (and weak outflow), and still other countries saw moderate outflows and inflows.

2.3. Current *vis-à-vis* pre-1990 Migration in CEE[10]

A statistical overview of major recent migratory flows in CEE can be found in Table 2.2. In that table, countries[11] have been classified according to the relative intensity of movements of each type of international mobility.

One of the important traits of migration in CEE nowadays is its two-tier legal status. Due to institutional underdevelopment of CEE countries, only a relatively little of the inflow can be channelled into the regular sphere of activities and so migrants often resort to irregularity. Similarly, the outflow to non-CEE countries encounters various administrative barriers, such as limited access to labour markets, which prompts many migrants to opt for clandestine residence and employment. Below I begin with the regular (documented) movements.

Around the year 2000, the intensity and volume of regular migration flows in CEE were surprisingly low. First of all, while a few countries in the region became net immigration areas, in no country did immigration reach a high level. For instance, in 1999 the Czech Republic and Hungary, considered as rare cases of a migrant attracting countries in CEE, recorded only 9900 and 15,000 immigrants, of whom the largest national groups were Slovaks in the Czech Republic (33 per cent) and ethnic Hungarians, mainly from Romania, in Hungary (51 per cent). Although emigration was generally higher than immigration in CEE, the outflow from the principal sending countries (Poland and Romania followed by Lithuania)[12] barely exceeded 20,000. In Lithuania (like other Baltic States), a large majority of emigrants headed to other former Soviet republics.

In turn, the flows of temporary labour were rather low. The Czech Republic followed by Hungary and Poland were the only countries regularly receiving foreign labour in excess of 10,000 persons per annum. In 1999, the Czechs authorized as many as 16,600 migrant workers and issued 19,500 business licenses to foreigners, whereas the total number of work permits issued in Hungary was 34,100 and in Poland 20,600. In all three countries, migrants from former communist countries strongly predominated (80–90 per cent). The same holds for other CEE countries.

Only one country sent large number of migrant workers. Around 300,000 persons from Poland were employed abroad of whom 230,000 as seasonal workers in Germany. A mention might be made here about Ukraine, which (as a member-state of the CIS) is left aside in the present discussion. That country is not only another important labour sending area (around 150,000 persons worked abroad in 2000) but also a major foreign labour supplier for such countries as the Czech Republic (37,200), Hungary (3700) and Poland (3200). The outflow of temporary labour from other countries was drastically smaller and indeed insignificant (usually below 10,000 per annum per country).

Other flows, such as repatriation- or asylum-related ones, were by no means sizeable either. Romania experienced moderate outflow of ethnic Hungarians but at the same time received return migration. Some outflow of Russian-speaking persons was observed in the Baltic States (notably in Latvia). As far as flows of asylum seekers were concerned, almost all CEE countries received a few thousand applications per year[13] whereas very few refugees from those countries (except representatives of Roma population)[14] were recorded elsewhere in the world.

Finally, movements of false tourists, the main source of un-documented migration, were rather intensive. The inflow, however, was much larger than the outflow. Three sub-groups of incoming irregular foreigners may be distinguished: transit migrants, migrant workers and petty traders.

With the exception of Estonia and Latvia, all CEE countries experienced significant irregular transit migration at around the turn of the century. Destination countries were almost exclusively in the West. Besides using tourism as a cover, irregular migrants often resorted to smugglers' networks. The Czech Republic and Hungary received more irregular transit migrants than other countries. Major regions of non-CEE migrant origin included the Middle East and southern and central Asia. At around 2000, the citizens of the ten CEE countries listed in Table 2.2 hardly participated in those movements although in the early 1990s Bulgarians and, especially, Romanians belonged to largest national groups.

The Czech Republic, Hungary and Poland hosted large numbers of irregular migrant workers and self-employed foreigners, a great majority of whom arrived officially as tourists. A predominant proportion of those migrants originated from the neighbouring ex-communist countries: from Slovakia and Ukraine in the Czech Republic, from Romania and Ukraine in Hungary and from Belarus and Ukraine in Poland.[15] A distinct characteristic of that flux was its circulatory, repetitive character. In the course of time, however, many shuttle migrants became undocumented long-term (or permanent) residents

Table 2.2 Levels and natures of Central and Eastern European countries'[a] international migration[b] immediately before the onset of the transition and ten years afterward

Type of migration[c]	1985–1989[d]				1996–2000			
	High	Medium	Low	Negligible	High	Medium	Low	Negligible
Outflow								
1 Emigration	E, LA, LI, P, R		B, C	H	B, LI, P	LA, R	C, E	H, SA, SE
2 Temporary employment abroad[e]	P	C, H, R	R, LI	B, C, E, H, LA	P	R	H, LI, SE	B, C, E, LA, SA
3 Ethnicity-based outflow	B, P, R		C, LA, LI	E, H		R, LA	E, LI	B, C, H, P, SA, SE
4 Outflow of refugees and/or asylum seekers	P		B	E, LA, LI	B, LI, P, R	B, R	C, LI, SA	E, H, LA, P, SE
5 Outflow of false tourists[f]	P		H	B, C, E, LA, LI, R		C	E, H, LA, SA, SE	
Inflow								
1 Immigration		H		B, C, E, LA, LI, P, R		C, H, R, P, SE	B, E, LA, LI,	SA
2 Employment of foreigners[e]		C	H	B, E, LA, LI, P, R	C	H	P, LI, SA	B, E, LA, RSE
3 Ethnicity-based inflow	E, LA, LI	H		B, C, P, R		R	E, H, LA, LI, P	B, C, SA, SE
4 Inflow of refugees and/or asylum seekers				All	H	C, P, SA, SE	B, R	E, LA, LI
5 Inflow of false tourists and/or illegal migrants[f]								
a for transit to the West				All	P	C, H	B, LI, P, R, SA, SE	E, LA
b for work				All		C, H	SA	B, E, LA, LI, R, SE
c for petty trade		H	C	B, E, LA, LI, P, R	P	C, H, SA		B, E, LA, LI, R, SE

[a] 10 countries (**B**ulgaria, the **C**zech Republic, **E**stonia, **H**ungary, **LA**tvia, **LI**thuania, **P**oland, **R**omania, **S**lov**A**kia, **S**lov**E**nia); [b] Intensity of migration measured in absolute terms; for defining criteria of each category see Appendix; [c] Types from 1 to 5 comprise flows (in the case of type no. two — stocks) recognised as regular (legal) ones in the respective host countries; [d] In 1985–89: C denotes the former Czechoslovakia; data for Slovenia not available; migration in the Baltic States includes inter-republic flows within the former USSR; [e] Average annual stock; [f] Guesstimates based on police or research reports rather than estimates based on statistical sources

Source: National OECD/SOPEMI reports; Eurostat statistics.

Nevertheless, the strongest flow of false tourists into CEE countries was by far that of petty traders, who stayed very briefly in a host country. Such traders as a rule lived close to their destination countries, usually in the immediate borderlands. The movements were repetitive, even more than the movements of irregular labour. A metamorphosis from entering the country for street-corner or bazaar trading to moving for other purposes, mainly gainful employment, was quite common.

Apart from receiving or hosting irregular or illegal migrants, the region itself sent out a strong outflow of false tourists. All countries contributed to that phenomenon, but Bulgarians, Lithuanians, Poles and Romanians visibly outnumbered citizens of other CEE countries. Interestingly, while Lithuanians mainly headed for Poland, most migrating Poles went to Germany. Whereas the destinations of false tourists from Bulgaria and Romania were geographically highly dispersed, most of them went to other countries of the region. Irregular migrants from CEE engaged in gainful employment, petty trade and other activities, such as begging, street or road prostitution and petty crime.

What has been observed in the late 1990s (around 2000) differed significantly from the phenomena characteristic of the late 1980s and even early 1990s. The major changes can be summarized as follows:
- in terms of outflow: the number of net emigration countries and, particularly, countries encountering high emigration decreased; the volume of ethnicity-based outflow declined and fewer countries recorded such outflow; considerably fewer of their citizens attempted to emigrate as asylum-seekers, and, lastly, many more countries became involved in movements of irregular migrants (notably false tourists);
- in terms of inflow: generally, flows (except ethnicity-based movements in the Baltic States) became much larger and less regular and inter-country diversification emerged; in most countries, the number of asylum seekers rose from nil to a few thousand a year.

It is also noteworthy that the early 1990s witnessed one important but transient migratory phenomenon in CEE that had not occurred in the late 1980s and would reoccur in the late 1990s: intensified illegal transit movements from Africa and Asia (and certain CEE countries) to the West. This process was associated with international criminal networks of smugglers and traffickers. Oftentimes, illegal border crossings were executed in large groups and assisted by professional smugglers. All CEE countries sharing a border with an EU member (as well as Lithuania) were seriously affected.

2.4. The Impact of Political and Economic Transition upon Migration Patterns

Since 1989, CEE countries have been introducing democratic and market oriented reforms. The most important, and one of the first, effect of the transition on international migration was the rejection of what had been a uniform restrictive policy on population movements. Citizens of CEE countries acquired the unlimited right to freely leave their country and return; similarly, the regulations on foreigners' entry became more liberal.

Those changes had a tremendous impact on the so-called 'suspended movements' of people who, under the communist rule, had been denied international mobility. Between 1989 and 1991, tens of millions of inhabitants of that part of Europe found themselves on the move. International journeys resulted mainly from a curiosity; it was like tasting a previously-forbidden fruit. Constrained financially and by inexperience, travellers usually visited neighbouring countries and did not venture on long-distance trips. For instance, since 1989 Poland started to receive a great number of visitors from the USSR. Between 1988 and 1991, the number of arrivals from that country increased by around 5.8 million (to reach 7.5 million), that is more than quadrupled.[16] Sparse and understaffed checkpoints became dramatically overburdened with the control of traffic, condemning visitors to very long (often overnight) border queues.

Another significant effect of the collapse of the former political and economic system was the disruption of societal tissue and, particularly, certain artificial and forcibly-created social entities, such as multiethnic societies. In effect, national or ethnic identities, once concealed under the communist regimes and subsumed into the state identity, revived and national or ethnic groups occasionally clashed with each other. That in turn led to the fragmentation of three former federal states: Czechoslovakia, the Soviet Union and Yugoslavia and consequent massive ethnicity-based population movements among newly emerged states and/or a flight of refugees to other countries.

A third consequence of the transition was the economic differentiation of CEE as a result of deregulation and liberalization itself as well as diversified strategies of post-communist development. The growing income gap itself may not have been pivotal; perhaps more important was the rapid deterioration of living conditions in certain countries and their inhabitants' impoverishment. In effect, two sizeable flows of migrants have been generated: one of people seeking means of subsistence abroad and another of people wanting to exploit opportunities stemming from the 'gap'. An additional mobility factor within individual CEE countries was a change in and probably deepening of social stratification. A typical case presented members of 'losing groups' who, in order to maintain their status, adopted highly proactive strategies and, by and large, became inclined to seeking extra income in foreign countries.

Last but not the least, the transition had two important effects on the inflow of people from outside of CEE. First, liberalization of migration policy and the respect for human rights attracted many migrants from other parts of the world who could not get into the West. Those migrants came from a large variety of African and Asian countries, but primarily from the Horn of Africa, the Middle East, China and Vietnam. Second, the transition also created relatively favourable political and institutional environments for the economic activity of non-national agents, particularly for foreign investment. The flow of foreign capital and expansion of global corporations were followed by migration of highly-qualified personnel (top managers). Other stimuli for labour inflow were market imbalances originating from an acute skill deficit. Demand generated by certain emerging sectors (banking and public finance, real estate, insurance services, and so on) and by the mass popularity of foreign languages and its reorientation — from mainly Russian to mainly English — attracted immigrants, mainly citizens of western countries, especially the EU.

The inflow of the highly skilled frequently comprised former CEE émigrés or their descendants. Poland, which had lost over a million inhabitants to emigration in the 1980s (many more than any other CEE country), witnessed a strong wave of return migration. It featured a great diversity in return migrants' motives, skills and professions.

2.5. Intra-CEE Movements: towards a New Migration Space

Prior to 1990, CEE (comprising all communist countries of Europe) was a relatively uniform economic area with respect to capital ownership, unemployment rate,[17] labour mobility, even production sector structure, and so on. Income levels varied among countries, but owing to huge price-subsidies of many consumer goods, differences in living standards were not striking. Table 2.3 indicates that, in terms of wage rates, four countries, namely Slovenia, Russia, Bulgaria and Ukraine, were (in 1990) in a highly privileged situation with average hourly wages 2–4 times higher than the next five top-paying countries.[18]

Table 2.3 Wage ratio between Russia and selected CEE countries (USD equivalent according to official exchange rates); Russia = 100

Country	1990	1993/94	1997
Bulgaria	93.0	125.4	47.1
Czech Republic	35.4	261.8	215.7
Hungary	41.1	181.8	196.1
Poland	21.0	265.4	217.6
Romania	26.7	127.3	70.6
Russia	*100.0*	*100.0*	*100.0*
Slovakia	34.6	220.0	172.5
Slovenia	173.7	832.7	558.8
Ukraine	82.7	105.4	52.9

Source: International Labour Office

In the 1990s, Slovenia retained its top position, but the divide relative to Bulgaria, Romania, Russia and Ukraine increased whereas it dwindled relative to the Czech Republic, Hungary, Poland and Slovakia. Barring Slovenia, a very small economy, a new, distinct bipolar division of CEE economies has been observable since 1997. Namely, the Czech Republic, Hungary, Poland and Slovakia recorded average wages and salaries 2–4 times higher than the remaining four countries. Thus, the post-1990 transition seems to have brought about a dramatic shift in the attractiveness of labour markets within CEE.

It might be suggested that in the course of the transition, CEE economies were being deeply polarized according to the strength, extent and consistency of the transition. In effect, the countries that radically reformed their economies became a strong magnet for labour. The three largest, the Czech Republic, Hungary and Poland, became a destination for many employment seekers from the CEE countries that were furthest behind in economic reforms.

It should be noted that the Czech Republic and Hungary received many more documented migrant workers than Poland, especially relative to the size of their labour markets. On the other hand, from the very moment of its economic liberalization, Poland became a major host for migrants earning money in the informal economy by engaging in petty trade and doing various odd jobs.

Varied courses and paces of the transition have led to many other differences among CEE countries related to levels of such phenomena as: internal security, deregulation, market imbalances with regard to consumer goods, currency convertibility, black market and other economic pathologies, and so on. Countries where market equilibrium has quickly been installed and liberal policies widely adopted started to host circular travellers from many other CEE countries, who were able to earn a living purchasing and reselling small quantities of merchandize and currencies. Again, the three above-mentioned countries became the most-preferred destinations, especially since they offered a relatively high degree of security for migrants' activities. Poland, with its relatively large internal market and sizeable informal economy, probably offered more opportunities to such migrants than the two other countries, and ultimately hosted the greatest number of those migrants.

In contrast to Western predictions from 1989 or 1990, there was no mass exodus from Central and Eastern Europe to Western Europe after the liberalization of CEE states' (e)migration policies. An overwhelming proportion of international mobility was contained within the region itself. Apparently, in the 1990s the former communist countries of Europe received more migrants from other regions overall than they sent beyond the region's boundaries. Why the predictions did not come true? There can be no simple answer because the reasons were complex and differentiated. Some of the obvious factors, besides anticipatory controls on entry introduced by the member countries of the Schengen agreement, included:

- the very existence of CEE's magnets of the Czech Republic, Hungary and Poland (and a few other but much smaller countries),
- cost-benefit calculus of individual migrants, which often suggested that potentially higher economic benefits associated with travelling to the West *vis-à-vis* Central and Eastern Europe were insufficient to offset the related greater costs, inconveniences and risks,
- the existence or fast development of migration networks in Central and Eastern Europe and migrants' familiarity with a common post-communist reality.

As a result, a new international migration space emerged in that part of the world, with its own sending and receiving countries, specific categories of migrants and specific flow dynamics and directions. Its prominence has been fuelled, especially in the early 1990s, by intense intra-CEE movements of refugees and displaced persons from territories experiencing ethnic conflicts or civil wars who sought temporary protection abroad.

2.6. The Inflow from non-European Countries: does it Really Matter?

In the early 1990s, developments in migratory phenomena in CEE might have suggested a similar course to that experienced earlier by other countries of Europe. Even rare individual cases of migrant arrival from remote areas of the globe, not to mention group inflows of foreigners, made policy makers in many CEE countries concerned and the public opinion curious if not excited.

After dozen or so years of intensifying population movements in CEE, however, a striking difference appeared relative to a trend observed in western countries. The geographical diversity of migrant-sending countries turned out to be very low and a great majority of migrants originated from neighbouring countries. In fact, practically no foreigners were coming from such renowned sending countries of the world as Cambodia, Iran, Iraq, Morocco, Tunisia, Pakistan, the Philippines, Senegal, Sri Lanka, Turkey, and so on.

In 2000, two countries — the Czech Republic and Hungary — hosted nearly the same number of immigrants ('long-term' or 'permanent'), around 130 thousand each, which was many more than recorded in any other CEE country. However, in Hungary as many as 71 per cent of those immigrants were citizens of CEE countries (15 per cent from ex-USSR), 11 per cent EU citizens and 4 per cent citizens of other OECD countries. Analogically in the Czech Republic — 76 per cent came from CEE (44 per cent from ex-USSR), 5 per cent from the EU and 3 per cent from other OECD countries.

Strikingly then, in both countries a similar small proportion of foreigners (16 per cent in the Czech Republic and 14 per cent in Hungary) originated from neither CEE nor the OECD. Of those immigrants, a large majority came from just three countries: China, Vietnam and Mongolia (15 per cent of the total in the Czech republic and 8 per cent in Hungary). Only five non-CEE, non-OECD countries (Algeria, India, Libya, Nigeria and Pakistan) were represented by more than 100 immigrants in the Czech Republic, each of which sent fewer than 225 immigrants. Typically, those tiny national groups comprised mostly former asylum seekers than proper economic migrants.

Though it might be argued that towards the end of the 1990s Vietnam or China ranked amongst the top-five foreign nationalities residing in the Czech Republic and Hungary (and Poland), these nationalities' top positions seemed peculiar and exceptional rather than normal or regular. For migrants from China and Vietnam, their movement was towards a familiar post-communist milieu. Moreover, an important pull factor in the flow of citizens of those two countries was the existence of well-integrated ethnic minorities established decades earlier (in the 1960s and 1970s) by former Chinese and Vietnamese students and relatively strong cultural and economic links between the respective countries.

All in all, shortly before their accession to in the EU, the main migrant receiving countries of CEE proved insufficiently attractive to people (in particular, migrant workers) from non-European renowned sending countries. This might be related to the relatively short time since the transition began. If so, at the beginning of the twenty first century, the immigration process was still yet to gain momentum. For this to occur, however, there would have to be proof of central Europe's CEE's magnet countries' enduring political stability and CEE wage rates would have to approximate those offered in labour-receiving western countries.[19]

2.7. Migration between CEE and in the EU: Myths and Reality

One of hardest issues in the negotiation process related to the upcoming EU expansion (set for May 1, 2004) was free labour mobility for citizens of the new member states. CEE was generally perceived as a region of a tremendous migratory potential that, once released, might destabilize the EU labour market. Both the European Commission and governments of EU member-countries expressed endless objections to the idea of immediate such freedom. In effect, that freedom has become subject to severe but temporary restrictions.

Whether the anxiety expressed in the EU was justified is only to be seen. Nevertheless, analyses devoted to the future migratory consequences of the accession of the eight CEE countries came up with conflicting and confusing results. That ambiguity and anxiety, however, will not be without precedent.

In 1989 and 1990, discussions concerning European migration at various international forums focused on the risk of uncontrolled, mass East-West migrations. When discussing the lifting of internal administrative barriers to migration in post-communist countries,

Table 2.4 Population and immigrant-population of selected EU countries (the eight countries with highest absolute number of nationals from CEE) by citizenship, with particular reference to nationals of selected CEE countries, 1 January 1998; in thousands

	Germany	Greece	Austria	Italy	Sweden	France	Finland	United Kingdom
Total population	82,057.4	10,486.6	7,795.8	57,461.0	8,847.6	56,651.9	5,147.3	58,185.0
Total non-national population of which:	7,365.8	161.1	517.7	884.5	522.0	3,596.6	79.9	2,121.0
CEE population[a] number	729.8	41.3	65.3	106.4	32.6	63.0	31.8	67.0
share in total population (%)	*0.9*	*0.4*	*0.8*	*0.2*	*0.4*	*0.1*	*0.6*	*0.1*
share in non-national population (%)	*9.9*	*25.6*	*12.6*	*12.0*	*6.2*	*1.7*	*39.8*	*3.2*
Albania	11.3	5.0	0.9	55.6	0.1	–	0.0	5.0
Bulgaria	34.5	6.1	3.6	3.6	1.3	1.0	0.3	1.0
ex-Czechoslovakia	55.8	1.0	11.3	3.2	1.4	2.4	0.1	7.0
Hungary	52.0	0.6	10.6	2.4	2.9	2.7	0.4	3.0
Poland	283.3	5.0	18.3	16.6	15.8	47.1	0.7	25.0
Romania	95.2	5.6	18.5	17.9	3.2	5.1	0.4	3.0
ex-USSR	254.0	15.9	2.1	7.4	4.0	4.7	30.2	23.0

[a] Former Yugoslavia excluded
Source: Eurostat

many experts predicted an almost instant inflow of many millions from CEE into in the EU. This, however, never came true.

Despite their relatively great demographic potential and at times intensive outflow of their inhabitants to western Europe, currently people from CEE countries are insignificant in the population statistics of the EU member-countries. This can clearly be seen in Table 2.4. In virtually no EU country did the share of the Central and East Europeans (taken as a whole) in the total population exceed 1 per cent. It surpassed 0.5 per cent in only three countries: Austria, Finland and Germany whereas in some other countries (France or the United Kingdom) it oscillated around 0.1 per cent.

Moreover, the population that originated from CEE in some EU countries constituted a tiny fraction of even just the non-national population, in certain cases (for example France) even less than 2 per cent. In other countries, however, immigrants from that part of Europe have recently become a visible and statistically significant segment of the immigrant population. Those countries where the proportion of Central and Eastern Europeans reached or exceeded 10 per cent include Germany (10 per cent) and Austria (13 per cent), both of whom have had strong political and economic ties with certain CEE countries. However, it was some countries that quite recently joined the ranks of net immigration areas, such as Finland (40 per cent), Greece (26 per cent) and Italy (12 per cent), that featured a high proportion of CEE citizens represented in their overall populations of foreigners.

Interestingly, the contribution of individual CEE countries in the stocks of non-national populations in those EU countries with significant proportions of Central and Eastern Europeans relative to total immigrants varied greatly. In Finland, a substantial majority of non-nationals from CEE came from the ex-USSR, mainly from Russia and Estonia; in Italy, Albanians were by far the main CEE nationality, followed by Poles and Romanians. In Greece, the contribution of immigrants from the former Soviet Union was the largest of all ex-communist countries similar to the aggregate number of people from the following three Balkan countries: Albania, Bulgaria and Romania. In Germany, Poles shared the lead with people from the ex-USSR but the proportion of Romanians was also considerable. Finally, there were significant numbers of people from the Czech Republic, Slovakia, Poland and Hungary in Austria.

There was an estimated 814,000 citizens of CEE countries living (legally) in the EU in 1996 and almost 850,000 within the European Economic Area (EEA). That was comparatively few given the over

17 million foreign residents in the EU and more than 19 million in the EEA. In relative numbers, Central and East Europeans accounted for 4.7 per cent of total immigrant population in the EU and 4.4 per cent in the EEA (Salt, Clarke and Schmidt, 2000).

The stock of Central and East Europeans in western Europe was highly concentrated. Nearly 64 per cent of them lived in Germany alone, and more than 90 per cent in just six countries (Germany, France Austria, the United Kingdom, Italy and Sweden).

Obviously, certain CEE countries had many more nationals in the EU than other countries, with Poland being a clear leader. In the Eurostat ranking of the 15 top non-national citizenship groups in western Europe (EEA) as of 1 January 1998, there was hardly mention of Central and Eastern Europeans, except for Poland ranking tenth, behind four non-EEA countries (Turkey, ex-Yugoslavia, Morocco and Algeria) and five EEA countries (Italy, Portugal, Ireland, Spain and Greece) but ahead of the USA, the United Kingdom, Germany, France, Tunisia and all other countries (Eurostat, 2000). In contrast, there were very few Hungarians in almost all western countries. Likewise, various EU countries' statistics of top ten immigrant nationalities rarely reveal the presence of CEE states. Poland ranked tenth in Finland, ninth in France and seventh in Sweden. The former Soviet Union occupied a very high second place in Finland but that was the stark exception. No other CEE countries appeared in its statistics at all.

Although the numbers residing in the EU are low, recently the inflow of migrants from CEE into the EU seems rather strong relative to their proportion of the overall immigrant population. In six of the eight host EU countries with available data for 1997, the percentage of new arrivals from CEE exceeded 10 per cent, of which in three (Austria, Germany and Italy) it was close to one-quarter and in two (Finland and Greece) it was over 40 per cent (Table 2.5). The magnitude of the inflow in each receiving country was in the thousands (or in tens of thousands for Germany and Italy) for at least one (usually more than one) CEE country. Immigration to France presented an opposite case, with only hundreds of individuals arriving (annually) from any individual CEE country.

In the light of official data, the numerical impact on the West of the intra-European, East-West migrant flows seems rather moderate at present. This is because, despite increasing numbers of immigrating nationals of CEE countries, more and more *émigrés* started to return to their countries of origin, in sharp contrast to the late 1980s and

Table 2.5 Immigration of non-nationals to selected EU countries (eight countries selected according to the criteria cited in Table 2.4) by citizenship, with particular reference to nationals of selected CEE countries[a], 1997

	Germany	Greece	Austria	Italy	Sweden	France	Finland	United Kingdom
Total no. of non-national immigrants	615,298	22,078	56,859	143,151	33,302	15,020	8,098	188,000
Immigrants from CEE countries number	173,397	9,736	14,030	35,287	2,384	2,003	3,378	4,000
share of all non-national immigrants (%)	*28.2*	*44.1*	*24.7*	*24.6*	*7.2*	*13.3*	*41.7*	*2.1*
Citizenship of origin								
Albania	2,175	589	247	20,508	24	53	7	..
Bulgaria	6,433	2,076	645	1,070	92	114	27	..
ex-Czechoslovakia	14,599	192	2,983	1,273	75	85	17	2,000
Hungary	11,140	122	1,939	380	164	85	46	..
Poland	71,322	586	5,521	3,262	601	525	23	..
Romania	14,144	1,162	1,569	6,701	224	421	36	..
ex-USSR	79,645	6,109	1,210	2,248	1,279	868	3,280	2,000

[a] Former Yugoslavia excluded
Source: Eurostat

early 1990s. It follows from Table 2.6 that in most EU countries the net migration in 1997 compared to 1991 remained positive but rather small (below 5000 annually). Two clear exceptions point to different trends: in Germany, high net immigration was even replaced with a moderate net emigration, and in Italy an almost zero balance evolved into moderate net immigration.[20] In addition, like Germany, in 1997 Austria recorded a small net emigration between itself and CEE. On aggregate, the migration balance between the EU (the eight major countries with available statistics)[21] and CEE changed from strongly positive in 1991 to slightly negative in 1997 for the EU, and from strongly negative to slightly positive for the CEE.

Table 2.6 Net migration between selected countries of the European Union and CEE countries[a] as a whole in 1991 and 1997; in thousands

Country	1991	1993	1997[b]
Austria	no data	no data	−1.1 (−0.6)
Belgium	0.9	1.4	2.1 (1.7)
Denmark	1.7	1.3	2.7 (1.9)
Finland	7.1	6.2	3.1 (0.1)
Germany	467.8	181.3	−79.4 (−124.2)
Italy	4.7	no data	43.2 (41.0)
Sweden	5.9	25.8	6.3 (5.2)
United Kingdom	1.0	5.0	2.0 (0.0)

[a] ex-USSR included
[b] Figures in brackets: ex-USSR excluded
Source: Eurostat

Obviously, the official immigration statistics compiled by Eurostat are not fully adequate to evaluate the true magnitude or structural complexity of population movements or to assess the trends with regard to the duration or stability of immigrants' stays in host countries. This seems of special relevance in the case of the inflow from CEE, since in the recent past very diverse forms of movements (going far beyond the form of regular immigration) from that area to western Europe were observed.

Since 1990, those forms have mainly been related to labour migration. The bulk of migration for work has, in turn, been associated with certain marginal segments of the EU economy, such as the activities of sub-contracting foreign firms or highly labour-intensive but variable (as a rule, seasonal) demand for labour. In the 1990s, most of the related movements were to Germany, where they were subject to effective administrative control (OECD, 2001).

Given strong excess demand for non-highly skilled (and cheap) labour in practically all EU countries coinciding with substantial excess labour supply in many countries of CEE, the previously weak and repressed migratory flows have given way to a peculiar circulation of labour, which might be called incomplete migration. Incomplete migration is the movements of false tourists who, during their legal stay in the EU (nominally as tourists), seek short-term, informal employment in the secondary segment (usually, foreigners' segment) of the labour market. This seems a major trait of the present East-West migration pattern (Okólski, 2001).

Both major types of present-day migration from CEE to the EU, that is migration for regular seasonal/sub-contracted work and incomplete migration, reveal several common characteristics. Above all, they are relatively stable over time and their size is low compared to the total human inflow to the EU and the total foreign participation in the EU labour market. As well, those movements are of a highly temporary nature. Migrants rarely stay longer than three months in the destination countries. Moreover, taking into account migrants' relatively low earnings and the relatively high cost of living in the EU, the profitability of those movements strongly depends on their ability to economize and live apart from their family and social milieu. This, by itself, tends to prompt the migrants to choose short rather than long sojourns in destination countries. Finally, the flows that belong to those two types of migration are, so to speak, demand-driven and, due to the specificity of the demand for labour, hardly involve metamorphoses to other types of movements and occupational or any other mobility in EU countries. This may additionally suggest that current migration from CEE accession countries to the EU may be relatively easily controlled by the latter.

Statistics prove that the feared exodus from what used to be the communist bloc did not materialize; indeed, migrants from CEE represent a small fraction of the EU's population of legally-resident and irregular foreigners. Furthermore, no large-scale labour migration is foreseeable and the flows that do exist from CEE tend to be both temporary (more often short-term than medium-term) and relatively easily manageable.

2.8. A Word of Final Conclusion

After several years of complex developments in human territorial mobility, the situation in CEE seems to be simplifying. The importance of Western Europe as the main destination for CEE migrants has diminished. Also, the related pre-1990 predominant forms of the outflow, namely family emigration overseas (and to certain EU countries) fuelled by migrant networks, out-movements of 'privileged' ethnic minorities (ethnic Germans and Jews) and emigration of politically-motivated asylum seekers, have become marginal. On the other hand, temporary movements of workers into in the EU have substantially intensified.

By all accounts, strong, economically-motivated mobility seems to be the principal feature of current migration in, from and through CEE. This is equally true as far as intra-CEE flows are concerned, as well as flows outside of CEE or non-European flows into CEE.

Regarding migration to non-CEE countries, the EU has become, unsurprisingly, the main magnet for CEE labour (and thus for all migrants from that region), and will probably strengthen its role in CEE population movements in the years to come. On the other hand, CEE has failed to attract statistically significant numbers of migrants from outside itself.

As a matter of fact, CEE has recently been recognized as a separate migration space, with its own logic, structures and dynamics. Indeed, most CEE migrant flows are contained within the region itself. This appears to be the paramount characteristic of current migration in CEE.

All those characteristics notwithstanding, the population movements in CEE on the eve of so-called eastern enlargement of the EU are by no means structurally stable or at least orderly. Migration flows frequently change their forms, intensity and direction, and hardly any clear durable trends or regularities can be discerned. This makes the respective generalizations and predictions very difficult, if not risky.

Notes

1   In drafting of this chapter, I have extensively used statistical data contained in (unpublished) national OECD/SOPEMI reports, especially those prepared by: D. Bobeva, B. Froehlich, D. Gheorghiu, J. Juhas, E. Kępińska, M. Lubyova, J. Maresova, M. Okólski, A. Sipaviciene, L. Zsoter.

2   Major early works include: Council of Europe (1991); Simon (1992); Ardittis (1993); Castles and Miller (1993); Rudolph and Morokvasic (1993); Fassmann and Münz (1994); Stalker (1994); Frejka (1996).

3   In fact, various names were (sometimes interchangeably) used, such as Central Europe, Eastern Europe, Central and Eastern Europe or Central Eastern Europe.

4   For full list of those countries, see Table 2.1.

5   With two distinct exceptions: Slovenia, where the wage level was almost at a half of the EU average, and Latvia where it was at one-twentieth of the EU average.

6   According to a routine UN definition of major areas and regions, Europe is composed of four parts and the eight accession countries belong to three of those parts: Eastern, Northern and Southern Europe. In each of those parts, the accession countries constitute a minority in terms of number of countries and population size.

7   This point will be elaborated in further parts of this chapter.

8   The reason for making this exception (and in a way for being inconsistent in the analysis to follow) is a specificity and exclusiveness of international migration in the CIS countries relative to other countries of CEE. Above all, it is the fact that a predominant part of what now qualifies as 'international' would be non-existent or 'internal' provided no break-up of the Soviet Union occurred. For instance, in 1997 925.8 thousand persons emigrated from all CIS countries of whom only 220.6 thousand to non-CIS area (in 2000: 595.3 thousand and 156.5 thousand, respectively) (IOM, 1999; 2002). Those figures do not account for sizeable flows of asylum seekers/refugees and persons repatriated within the CIS nor for the flows of undocumented migrants. A totality of those intra-CIS international migration constitutes a topic in itself, the one to be discussed separately.

9   A plausible estimate for inter-war Poland's territory suggests that, between the late ninetieth century and 1914, around 4.1 million persons emigrated or migrated for temporary work, of whom 87 per cent were emigrants. As much as 52 per cent of migrants went overseas (of whom nearly a half from the former Russian empire) and 35 per cent emigrated to European countries (mainly within the Russian and Austro-Hungarian empires or to Germany). A predominant majority (around 90 per cent) of the reminder migrated to Germany for seasonal employment (Gliwic, 1934).

10   For a more exhaustive description of migration in CEE, see Okólski (1998; 2000).

11   Only ten countries were considered. For missing countries (Albania, Croatia, Yugoslavia, Bosnia and Herzegovina, FYR Macedonia) reliable data were largely unavailable. Omission of the CIS countries was explained in an earlier part of this chapter.

12   Bulgaria probably belonged to the group of CEE countries with the largest emigration. However, only indirect and very vague estimates of Bulgarian emigration are available.

13   It should be noted here that for a majority of migrants who entered a refugee recognition process in CEE, the requesting of refugee status there was part of their more far-reaching migration strategy, which was to ultimately get to one of western countries. Indeed, even those (very rare cases) to whom asylum in CEE was granted gradually 'disappeared', only to be found as illegal migrants in the West.

14   A considerable inflow of asylum seekers representing that ethnic group was observed in Ireland and the United Kingdom, among others.

15   Ukraine is, after Russia, by far the most populous post-communist country of Europe, and borders Hungary and Poland (and is linked with the Czech

Republic through Slovakia). It is no wonder that the inflow from that country mattered so much.

16   In the same period, the number of arrivals from Romania increased 20 times (and approached 400 thousand) a year.

17   Universally, no open unemployment; rather over-employment on a macro-economic scale that resulted from labour hoarding by enterprises.

18   The same pertains to Croatia and other ex-Yugoslav republics as well as Belarus and probably the Baltic states.

19   In 2000, the average wage in the Czech Republic stood at 14.2 per cent and in Hungary at 12.2 per cent of the EU average (EC, 2001).

20   In Germany a major factor was a change of a migration balance with former Yugoslavia from +169,200 to –106,900, and in Italy an increase in the positive balance with Albania — from almost zero to 20,300.

21   France, the Netherlands and Spain are the most significant countries for which there are no available statistics. Nevertheless, it could be assumed from other sources that the importance of those countries for the migration between the EU and Central and Eastern Europe is by no means pivotal.

References

Ardittis, S. (ed.), *The Politics of East-West Migration* (New York: St. Martin's Press, 1994).

Castles, S., M. J. Miller, *The Age of Migration: International Population Movements in the Modern World* (Houndmills: Macmillan, 1993).

Council of Europe, *People on the Move. New Migration Flows in Europe* (Strasbourg: Council of Europe Press, 1992).

EC, *The Impact of Eastern Enlargement on Employment and Labour Markets in the EU Member States; Final Report of European Integration Consortium* (Brussels: EC, Directorate-General for Employment and Social Affairs, 2001).

Eurostat, *European Social Statistics. Migration: 2000 Edition* (Luxembourg: EC, 2000).

Fassmann, H., R. Münz (eds), *European Migration in the Late Twentieth Century* (Aldershot: Ashgate, 1994).

Frejka, T. (ed.), *International Migration in Central and Eastern Europe and the Commonwealth of Independent States* (New York, Geneva: United Nations, 1996).

Gliwic, H., *Materiał ludzki w gospodarce światowej* (Warsaw: Trzaska, Evert & Michalski, 1934).

IOM, *Migration in the CIS 1997–98. 1999 Edition* (Geneva: IOM, 1999).

IOM, *Migration Trends in Eastern Europe and Central Asia. 2001–2002 Review* (Geneva: IOM, 2002).

OECD, *Trends in International Migration. SOPEMI 2001* (Paris: OECD, 2001).

Okólski M., 'Incomplete migration: a new form of mobility in Central and Eastern Europe. The case of Polish and Ukrainian migrants', in C. Wallace, D. Stola (eds), *Patterns of Migration in Central Europe* (Houndmills: Palgrave, 2001), pp. 105–28.

Okólski M., 'Recent trends and major issues in international migration: Central and East European perspectives', *International Social Science Journal*, Vol. 52, No. 165 (2000), pp. 329–42.

Okólski M., 'Regional dimension of international migration in Central and Eastern Europe', *Genus*, Vol. 54, No. 1–2 (1998), pp. 11–36.
Rudolph H., M. Morokvasic (eds), *Bridging States and Markets. International Migration in the Early 1990s* (Berlin: Sigma, 1994).
Salt J., J. Clarke, S. Schmidt, *Patterns and Trends in International Migration in Western Europe* (Luxembourg: EC, 2000).
Simon G. (ed.), 'L'Europe de l'Est, la Communaute et les migrations', *Dossier of Revue Europeenne des Migrations Internationales* (Poitiers: University of Poitiers, 1992).
Stalker P., *The Work of Strangers: A survey of international labour migration* (Geneva: ILO, 1994).
UN, *World Population Prospects. The 2000 Revision* (New York: UN, 2001).

Appendix

The criteria used for categorising particular migratory flows considered in Table 2.2.
1. Emigration/immigration (flow; average annual number of persons):
    *   high: 20,000 or more,
    *   medium: 5000–20,000,
    *   low: 1000–5000,
    *   negligible: fewer than 1000.
2. Temporary employment (stock; average annual number of workers):
    *   high: 75,000 or more,
    *   medium: 25,000–75,000,
    *   low: 10,000–25,000,
    *   negligible: fewer than 10,000.
3. Ethnicity-based migration (flow; average annual number of persons):
    *   high: 20,000 or more,
    *   medium: 5000–20,000,
    *   low: 1000–5000,
    *   negligible: fewer than 1000.
4. Migration of refugees and/or asylum seekers (flow; average annual number of applications):
    *   high: 5000 or more,
    *   medium: 1000–5000,
    *   low: 500–1000,
    *   negligible: fewer than 500.
5. Movements of false tourists and/or illegal migrants (flow; approximate annual number of persons):
    *   high: 150,000 or more,
    *   medium: 50,000–150,000,
    *   low: 5000–50,000,
    *   negligible: fewer than 5000.

3

Current Ukrainian and Russian Migration to the Czech Republic: Mutual Similarities and Differences[1]

Dusan Drbohlav, Eva Janská

3.1. Basic Overview

The combination of such factors as political stability, geographical location (bordering on the classical Western World, which has had no history of a communist era), and the strict migration policies of western developed democracies has led to the creation of a migratory 'buffer zone' between the West and the East (see also Wallace and Stola, 2001b; Wallace, Chmuliar and Sidorenko, 1995). This buffer zone comprises the Czech Republic, Poland, Slovakia and Hungary — countries which, despite many problems, are progressing through the politico-economic transition successfully relative to many other ex-communist countries and have been able to maintain reasonable living standards (for example Garson, Lemaitre and Redor, 1996). Their labour markets have also been able to absorb a foreign labour force — both legal and illegal/irregular.

The Czech Republic has specific characteristics with respect to labour migration from the 'East' and its attractiveness to international migrants. For example, in contrast with Poland, Hungary and partly Slovakia (see Wallace and Stola, 2001a; Stola, 2001), it is not characterized by short-term migration and so-called 'petty traders',[2] but rather by circulating labour, long-term migration movements and even by migrants who stay and work permanently (for example Wallace and Stola, 2001b). As far as labour immigration in CEE countries[3] is concerned, one important fact should be emphasized: among the buffer states, in spite of some similarities, the Czech Republic represents an important exception in terms of the quantity of the foreign labour force on its territory. Its contingent, at least of documented foreign workers with work permits, has been and is much more numerous than in any other buffer zone country (see Wallace and Stola, 2001b).

Among the post-communist countries, the Ukrainian[4] migrant community, together with Slovaks, is by far the largest in the Czech Republic. Apart from Slovaks, who have special permit conditions,[5] Ukrainian immigrants hold the largest number of residence permits (long-term residence permit or visa over 90 days and permanent residence permit[6] — see Table 3.A1 in Appendix). Out of 211,000 foreigners who had been granted residence permits in the Czech Republic as of 31 December 2001, 25 per cent originated from the Ukraine. Similarly, while the total employment of foreigners in the Czech Republic (comprising those with working permits, trade licenses and Slovaks registered at job centres) was approximately 168,000 on the same date, Ukrainians themselves made up 23 per cent (see Table 3.A2 in Appendix). In geographical terms, measured via long-term visas issued for a period exceeding 90 days (as of the very end of 2000), the largest absolute representation of Ukrainians was in Prague (15,990), followed by Central Bohemia (6434) and Southern Moravia (5228) (Drbohlav, 2003). Although for many well known reasons it is very difficult to estimate the number of illegal/irregular or clandestine migrants, it is highly probable that Ukrainians represent the largest group (Drbohlav, 1997; Drbohlav, 2003). Based on consultations with officers at the Ministry of Labour and Social Affairs and the Research Institute of Labour and Social Affairs (2001, 2002), it is possible to assume that the number of illegal/irregular labour immigrants might roughly be equal to the number of legal economic migrants.[7] These estimates are, to some extent, also supported by relevant studies (namely, for example Drbohlav, 1997; Lupták and Drbohlav, 1999; Drbohlav, 2003).

In terms of quantitative parameters, currently the Russian immigrant community makes up only 1/15 of all legal foreign residents in the Czech Republic. Russians significantly differ from Ukrainians (and many other ethnic groups who migrate to the Czech Republic from other CEE states) as they hold a much higher share of permanent residence permits[8] (33 per cent in 2001) than do Ukrainians (only 19 per cent). Thus, their intention to stay in the country of destination, or at least make their residence official, appears to be more stable than in the case of other CEE immigrants. As well, there is some evidence that their position in the Czech labour market is different than that of many other CEE immigrants — they are more likely to be involved in white-collar types of work. Regarding the spatial distribution patterns of (economic) immigrants, Russians tend to concentrate in Prague much more than Ukrainians do (60 vs. 39 per cent — holders of visas for a period exceeding 90 days in 2000). Also, the Russian influence in the spa town of Karlovy Vary is enormous.

Such discrepancies between those two communities from the former Soviet Union in the Czech Republic attracted us and inspired us to make a more systematic and deeper analysis. What both immigrant communities share is that their presence has been pretty unpopular among the Czech majority population (Institute for Opinion Polls, 2000). This reaction is the result of two main reasons: 1) Czech society's general, negative attitude towards all things 'Soviet' as a result of their famous 1968 occupation, and 2) the tendency to connect 'Soviets' to specific forms of mafia criminality, which, from time to time, have been significantly manifested in Czech territory.

3.2. Main Goals and Theoretical Concepts

The primary goal of this contribution is to answer, in practical terms, important questions connected to fundamental socio-demographic and geographical parameters of respondents, their mechanisms of entry into the Czech Republic and the conditionality of the migration itself. A secondary aim is to analyse important similarities and differences between Ukrainians and Russians and how both groups relate to their mother countries and to the domestic majority population. In doing so, we shall determine the type of social communication, the living conditions (including character of work performed) and the pragmatic integration of both groups into Czech society by the particular determinants of various dimensions of integration: economic, social, legal, cultural and political (see more in Drbohlav et al., 1999a and 1999b; Drbohlav, 1997).

In trying to fulfil the first goal, the two following issues have also been addressed:

1) To consider to what extent Ukrainian/Russian migration to the Czech Republic fits the concept of migratory transnationalism. Portes, Guarnizo and Landolt (1999, pp. 217–18), characterize transnationalism in the following way:

The events in question pertain to the creation of a transnational community linking immigrant groups in the advanced countries with their respective sending nations and hometowns ... This field is composed of a growing number of persons who live dual lives:

speaking two languages, having homes in two countries, and making a living through continuous regular contact across national borders. Activities within the transnational field comprise a whole gamut of economic, political and social initiatives ranging from informal import-export business, to the rise of a class of bi-national professionals, to the campaigns of home country politicians among their expatriates.

In addition, some other well-known migratory theories are simply tested, in particular the network theory and the dual labour market theory.

2) To confirm the hypothesis of the gradual transformation of circular migration into permanent immigration and settlement among Ukrainians. The question is whether this trend does exist, and, if so, whether it follows Martin's and Taylor's (1995) 'S' curve pattern (based, for example, on former migratory realities in Western Europe, Singapore, and the Gulf States — see Figure 3.1[9]). The authors argue that:

First guest workers are typically young men, and dependence or settlement refers to the fact that some of them invariably develop ties to the host country and settle there ... The settlement process often accelerates over time ... in many cases, settlement patterns have an S-pattern. Initially, few migrants settle, then unification and perhaps (the threat of) a recruitment stop prompt a sharp increase in settlement. After two or three decades, the percentage of workers who settle stabilizes at 30 to 50 percent of peak migrant worker levels, and the total foreign population can be 10 to 300 percent larger than guest worker employment. (Martin and Taylor, 1995, p. IV in abstract).

In fact, both concepts need not be in contradiction. According to Portes, Guarnizo and Landolt, (1999, p. 233), a transnational migration system can also be created by migrants who 'settle abroad but sustain significant ties with their places of origin'. As long as contacts between countries of origin and destination are intensive and 'productive' (immigrants maintain contacts either via direct and permanent circulation — moving 'back and forth' — or via other communication channels) the 'S' curve formation may only be one of several ways by which transnationalism is reached.

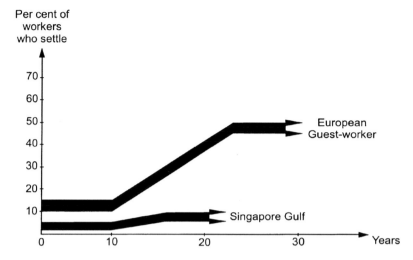

Figure 3.1 Guest-worker settlement
Source: Martin and Taylor (1995, p. 19)

3.3. Research Methods

Questionnaire surveys (semi-structured, in-depth interviews) were the main research tool used in the research on both communities. In the case of Ukrainians, the survey was carried out in the capital city of Prague in October and November 1999; regarding Russians, in addition to Prague, the city of Karlovy Vary was included as a very important Russian enclave, likewise in October and November 1999.

Selection of respondents could not be carried out through random or quota sampling, as it was not possible to obtain a basic group with its structural characteristics intact. Official statistical data do not provide us with detailed information about immigrants' fundamental socio-demographic characteristics, including localities of residence or work. In addition, we assume that a significant proportion of immigrants (mainly Ukrainians) reside and/or work in the Czech Republic illegally/irregularly. Therefore, we selected localities with a marked concentration of the population under study and applied a version of the so-called 'snowball' method (see, in this context, for example, Fawcett and Arnold, 1987 or Massey, 1987). In the case of Ukrainians, we used an intermediary of Ukrainian origin who distributed 130 questionnaires, of which we got back 100. In the case of Russians, national associations and groups[10] helped us to contact respondents. Out of 100 distributed questionnaires, 70 were returned (43 in Prague and 27 in Karlovy Vary). In order to better interpret the results, 20 interviews were also carried out for each community.

By using methods and approaches similar to those used in 1995 and 1996 research on the Ukrainian immigrant community (Drbohlav, 1997 — see footnote 1), we were able to try to evaluate the development of migratory reality over time. Nevertheless, one has to point out that, from a purely statistical point of view, a comparison itself is impossible (non-longitudinal approach; unrepresentative samples). Hence, in this regard the below comparison over time is rather hypothetical in its character.

Our main results are discussed below, while more detailed information with supporting figures is available from other sources (see Drbohlav et al., 1999a and 1999b; Drbohlav, 1997).

3.4. Results of the Surveys

3.4.1. *Ukrainians*

The results of the research demonstrate that the migration of a Ukrainian labour force to the Czech Republic is neither a chance nor a short-term phenomenon. It has clearly been indicated that Ukrainian migration to the Czech Republic has marked characteristics of 'transnationalization' (see more, for example, Portes, 1999; Pries, 1999) as well as of the 'S' curve formation.

It is evident that Ukrainians' migration to the Czech Republic is stimulated particularly by the catastrophic state of the Ukrainian economy and the resultant low standard of living. Present and past research (Drbohlav, 1997) has confirmed that, for the present time, young (and mostly married) men predominate amongst Ukrainian workers, whose family and children remain in the Ukraine. Generally, Ukrainians' relatively high level of education (which, in the Czech Republic as in other countries of the world, is very often under- or unexploited) does not correspond with their jobs (work) in the host country. Typically, they are employed mostly in unskilled occupations, predominantly in construction (it is clearly consistent with the dual labour market theory). Persistent features typical of Ukrainians in the Czech Republic include a high level of working activity, the difficult nature of the work engaged in, and frequent abuse and exploitation by employers and various intermediaries (namely low wages, unsatisfactory or even terrible working conditions/environment, withholding of documents, and so on). It is possible to observe a certain stabilization of Ukrainians' position in

Czech society and on the Czech labour market. This stabilization especially concerns their mechanisms of arrival (it used to be bilaterally agreed official networks and annual quotas for Ukrainian migrant workers; now it is the unofficial recruitment organization and practices having, in fact, the same 'effect') and their behaviour patterns in Czech society. When characterizing 'more permanent' features of Ukrainians in the Czech Republic, one has to identify their generally poor knowledge of foreign languages (including the Czech language), poor cultural life and minimal attempts to lead an 'organized' social life. It has also been demonstrated that illegal/irregular residence is more typical of younger immigrants while the intention to return to Ukraine tends to be declared predominantly by married migrants.

A comparison of the surveys from the mid-1990s vs. at the very end of the decade alludes to some possible shifts in the behaviour of the Ukrainian immigrant community over time. Some of these changes are, logically, linked with the ongoing transformation process in the Czech Republic as well as with more general economic, social, and migratory changes at the global level. For instance, research has indicated a shift in Ukrainians' employment from the sphere of industrial production to the construction and service sectors, particularly in small, privately-owned Czech companies. Ukrainians' temporary lack of organization in the Czech Republic, their limited cultural life and proclaimed desire to return to their home country suggest a 'permanent mobility' (circulation) that fits within the conceptual framework of transnationalization. This trend does not support the idea that soon the Ukrainians will be willing and able to create a strong 'segregated community' in the host country. On the other hand, other ascertained facts evince the so-called 'S' curve (but not necessarily contradicting transnationalism) that confirms a strong settlement process — it seems that more Ukrainians are preferring to stay in Czech territory, that there is more intensive communication within the Ukrainian community in the destination country, and that there are more and more relatives and friends who have joined respondents and operate/stay in the new country (clearly validating the network theory). Moreover, illegal/irregular immigration continues (at a given moment, 31 per cent of the respondents confessed that either their stay or work or both were not legalized at all)[11] and 'underground activities' have been initiated through, for example, more numerous opportunities for the 'legalization' of residence/work through the offer of counterfeit documents or bogus marriages.[12]

Regarding Ukrainians, it is clear that the two processes of transnationalism and 'S' curve formation are in an immature, initial stage in the Czech Republic. At this stage in the migration process, even settlement that will eventually demonstrate an S-curve pattern may take the form of transnationalization. Thus, Ukrainians present migration patterns can fit within both frameworks. Only time will tell us which pattern of migration will prevail: 'constant circulation' (with firm transnational ties in countries of origin and destination) or the permanent and significant transformation of circulation into permanent settlement in the destination country — either with continuation of strong contacts (within the transnationalist paradigm) or self-dissociation from the mother country.

Systematic endeavours to improve certain aspects of the integration of this immigrant community into Czech society are very difficult at present, given the migrants' notable mobility, which itself actually precludes integration in the true sense of the word. The probably high level of Ukrainians' internal mobility within the Czech Republic and their often-illegal/irregular status similarly exacerbate this matter. It is clear that for any kind of normal 'communication process' to begin between Ukrainians and the majority, the state must logically and legitimately bring most Ukrainian migrants under its control, a matter which, in spite of increased restrictions (introduction of visas, annual immigration quotas), has so far been relatively unsuccessful.

3.4.2. Russians

Another aim of the study was to identify main features of typical Russian migration to the Czech Republic.[13] The group of immigrants contacted was of younger or middle age, composed of both men and women and often of whole families (two thirds of respondent-immigrants were between 21–40 years old, married and with at least one child), and was characterized by a relatively high level of education. This group is also typified by its relatively high level of economic activity, particularly in the realm of business and employment (the dual labour market theory is not borne out at all). A distinguishing characteristic is that Russian respondents do not have significant problems providing material security for their families, since their impetus to migrate is generally not economic but rather problems associated with political instability in Russia and fear for their own safety (connected primarily with the growth in crime). Though at a macro level the reality corresponds to a neo-classical economic approach (see for example Massey et al., 1998), at an individual level, factors such as wage levels and work opportunities in the host country do not dominate. Rather, the motivation behind migration is based on a whole complex of 'push' factors in connection with finding satisfaction in one's (or one's family's) life.

The factor: having friends and relatives penetrates the entire process of migration and adaptation of the given immigrants (44 per cent of the respondents had relatives in the Czech Republic) and, thus, the network theory has been validated.

The studied sample of immigrants demonstrates a minimum level of participation in organizations of all types, within both the majority society and their own ethnic communities. For the moment, the relatively short period elapsed since the first transition-period migration of Russians to the Czech Republic is evidently hampering the initiation of an otherwise natural trend of institutionalization (be it part of a pattern of the transnationalism or not).

A process of separation/segregation has been demonstrated among the Karlovy Vary cohort, in the spheres of economic activity (there is indication of an 'ethnic economy' — employment of workers from their 'own' ethnic group) and of social contacts, as well as partly in terms of the spatial concentration of housing. It seems that this 'separatist behaviour' is not necessarily a reaction to the attitude of the majority population but, rather, was initiated by the immigrants themselves. This fact is strengthened by the character of the city, which was historically and continues to be a 'Russian island', and by the Russian clientele of its spas, which constantly stimulates and bolsters the settled ethnic population. The survey research proves integration into the majority population is not taking place as much as it could. The integration process may be taking place in the case of isolated or numerically limited groups of immigrants (again, for the moment, probably the case of Prague), or for segments of the population with fewer property or business opportunities, who would be forced to learn the Czech language in order to get a job in a non-homogenously Russian working environment. There is no doubt that knowledge of the language is one of the most crucial factors for successful adaptation.

Within the realm of social integration, a comparison offers itself in the realm of employment, in which a mere 11 per cent of respondents are unemployed[14] (compared to approximately 9 per cent for Czech society as a whole). A number of Russian entrepreneurs positively evaluate their current situation and prospects, but they mostly employ only their own compatriots. It also follows from the research that more than one third of respondents are now used to their way of life in the Czech Republic. From a legal perspective, the majority of Russians in the Czech Republic hold long-term residence permits but demonstrate no great interest in obtaining other forms of residence (for example permanent residence permit and, subsequently, naturalization by obtaining Czech citizenship).

For the present time, Russians' interest in learning Czech is rather only marginal. They prefer to attend Russian cultural performances (mostly theatre) and other Russian cultural activities (concerts, exhibitions, and so on). Despite the majority of respondents indicating their satisfactory relationships with Czechs, they rather prefer to socialize with their own compatriots.

3.4.3. Similarities

In summary, one can identify several features common to the both ethnic immigrant groups.
- Holding mostly 'long-term' types of residence permits/visas.
- Poor knowledge of the Czech language.
- Minimal participation in the cultural and social life of the majority society, minimal 'institutionalization'.
- Interaction is largely within one's their own ethnic communities, little integration into the majority society.

3.4.4. Differences

Where are the differences?

Ukrainians
- A long-term trend of circular migration has been confirmed, ensuing from the abominable socio-economic situation in Ukraine (very low living standards).
- Married men coming without their families continue to predominate amongst Ukrainian labour migrants in the Czech Republic.
- Ukrainian migrants' relatively high level of education does not correspond with the nature of their jobs (unskilled, manual, low-paying jobs).
- Illegal/irregular residence and work is omnipresent (along with related underground activities — for instance counterfeit documents) and typical mostly of young (as compared to middle age) immigrants.
- There is a huge 'microconcentration' of Ukrainians in workers' hostels, located mostly in Prague suburbs.

Russians
- The main reasons Russian citizens migrate to the Czech Republic are political instability and high crime rates in their mother country.
- Relatively close-knit immigrant community typically engaged in business activities.
- The majority of respondents fall within the 21–45 age category, are married and live in the Czech Republic with their entire nuclear families.
- There is a concentration of Russians in a limited numbers of cities (Karlovy Vary and Prague), whilst the 'internal Russian island' in the centre of Karlovy Vary represents the only larger spatial concentration of Russians in the whole Czech Republic at this time.

3.5. Final Remarks

The relationship between two broad migratory conceptual frameworks (see Chapter 3.2 above) and the situation of Ukrainian and Russian immigrant communities in the Czech Republic (see Chapter 3.4 above) is rather complicated. It is clear that both of the processes of transnationalism and of 'S' curve formation (which are not mutually exclusive) are in an immature, initial stage in the Czech Republic. In this initial stage, the migratory process may be consistent with both conceptual frameworks. Only time will show us which pattern of migration will prevail: 'constant circulation' (with firm 'transnational' ties in the countries of origin and of destination) or the permanent and significant transformation of circulatory movement into permanent settlement in the destination country — with migrants either maintaining strong bonds with (within transnationalism) or to some extent cutting themselves off from the mother country. While it makes sense to ask this question about future developments in Ukrainian migration to the Czech Republic (so far they have fit the frameworks), the Russians in Czechia do not match either framework from the very beginning — for example they do not circulate at all and their contacts with the mother country are very limited, they immigrate with their families, they immediately enter the middle-class echelons of the labour market but separate themselves as much as possible from the majority population. This 'strong separatism' clearly is going to hinder them from reaching a positively routed final stage of the 'S' curve (to be satisfied and fully stabilized in a destination country). Obviously, further juxtaposing both given concepts with heterogeneous migratory reality is worth working on. In any case, what the research makes clear and illustrates is that the former Soviet Union is composed of many different nations. Their populations may significantly differ in motives and, correspondingly, the migration patterns and strategies they favour or resort to.

Studies like this one cannot be ambitious. Our research has been heavily limited by methodical barriers (see Chapter 3.3 above) and it must be taken only as a sort of introduction to its field of inquiry. It is essential to further research migration and immigration/integration processes typical of individual ethnic and citizenship groups in the Czech Republic and to refine and cultivate the data and information that have been found out so far.

Notes

1   This contribution is based on results of two research projects: MV ('Ukrainian community in the Czech Republic' and 'Russian community in the Czech Republic'). Nevertheless, a reader is referred to another project: RSS/HESP ('Immigrants in the Czech Republic — with special regard to Ukrainian workers and western companies operating in Prague'), which is 'older' but was designed in a very similar way as the two recent research activities. The topic of this paper also fits the current MSM grant ('Geographical structure and development of interaction between natural environment and society').

2   'In Poland they [petty traders] come mostly from Ukraine, Russia and Belarus, ... in Slovakia they are from Ukraine and Romania, ... in Hungary they are from Federal Republic of Yugoslavia, ... Romania and Bulgaria' (Wallace and Stola, 2001a, p. 30).

3   The CEEc are the former socialist/communist countries of the region, including those of the former Soviet Union.

4   Unless otherwise specified, all references to Ukrainians, Russians, Slovaks, and so on, pertain to citizenship rather than ethnicity/nationality.

5   Regarding working activities in the Czech Republic, Slovaks have a special, freer regime as compared to any other ethnic immigrant communities. For example, they do not have to ask for a work permit; they only have to be registered at a job centre.

6   To a large extent, holders of long-term residence permits and visas over 90 days represent a classical economic migration. While former permits was used before 2000, the latter came with a new legislation in 2000. On the other hand, the permanent residence permit represents, at least in the Czech case, migration movements that are mostly tied to a family migration process.

7   Those who hold work permits, trade licenses and Slovaks registered at job centres.

8   That is the proportion of immigrants who hold a permanent residence permit of those with a permit to stay (permanent residence permits plus visa for more than 90 days).

9   See also the 'four stages model' in Castles and Miller (1993, p. 25).

10 Organizations that assisted us included the Russian Union in the Czech Republic, the Civic Association of Russian Speaking and Sympathizing Inhabitants of the Czech Republic, and the General Consulate of the Russian Federation in Karlovy Vary.

11 21 per cent has entered the country without necessary legal support and 10 per cent continued to stay whereas their permits have already expired.

12 During their stay, 26 per cent have been offered false documents and 19 per cent a marriage with a citizen of the Czech Republic.

13 However, it does not mean that other Russian immigrants do not follow patterns typical of the above-analysed Ukrainian labour circular migrants.

14 Besides unemployed respondents, we know that 39 per cent were employed, 36 per cent owned their own business, 9 per cent were students and 3 per cent were housewives.

References

Castles, S., M. J. Miller, *The Age of Migration; International Population Movements in the Modern World* (New York: The Guilford Press, 1993).

Czech Statistical Office, *Cizinci v České republice* (Prague: Scientia, s.r.o, 2001).

Drbohlav, D., 'Immigration and the Czech Republic (with a Special Focus on the Foreign Labor Force)', *International Migration Review*, Vol. 37, No. 1 (2003), pp. 194–224.

Drbohlav, D., 'Imigranti v České republice (s důrazem na ukrajinské pracovníky a 'západní firmy' operující v Praze)', Research report for RSS/HEPS — the Research Support Scheme, the Higher Education Support Programme of the Open Society Institute, No. 622/1995 (Prague, 1997).

Drbohlav, D., M. Lupták, E. Janská, J. Bohuslavová, 'Ruská komunita v České republice', Research report of the Grant of the Ministry of the Interior of the Czech republic — MV ČR čj. U-2115/99 (Prague: Faculty of Science, Charles University in Prague, 1999a).

Drbohlav, D., M. Lupták, E. Janská, P. Šelepová, 'Ukrajinská komunita v České republice', Research report of the Grant of the Ministry of the Interior of the Czech republic — MV ČR čj. U-2116/99 (Prague: Faculty of Science, Charles University in Prague, 1999b).

Fawcett, J. T., F. Arnold, 'The Role Of Surveys in the Study of International Migration: An Appraisal', *International Migration Review*, Vol. 21, No. 4 (1987), pp. 1523–40.

Garson, J. P., G. Lamaitre, D. Redor, 'Regional Integration and the Outlook for Temporary and Permanent Migration in Central and Eastern Europe', in G. Biffl (ed.), *Migration, Free Trade and Regional Integration in Central and Eastern Europe* (Vienna: OECD, WIFO, Österreichische Staatsdruckerei, 1996), pp. 299–334.

Horáková, M., 'Mezinárodní pracovní migrace v ČR', *Bulletin*, No. 2 (Prague: the Research Institute for Labour and Social Affairs, 1999).

Horáková, M., 'Mezinárodní pracovní migrace v ČR', *Bulletin*, No. 4 (Prague: the Research Institute for Labour and Social Affairs, 2000).

Horáková, M., I. Macounová, 'Mezinárodní pracovní migrace v ČR', *Bulletin*, No. 8 (Prague: the Research Institute for Labour and Social Affairs, 2002).

Institute for Opinion Polls, *O vztahu k u nás žijícím národnostem* (Prague: Institute for Opinion Polls, 2000).

Lupták, M., D. Drbohlav, 'Labour Migration and Democratic Institutions in the Czech Republic (on the Example of the Ukrainian Workers)', Research report within the programme: Democratic Institutions Fellowship (NATO), (1999), www.nato.int.

Martin, P., J. E. Taylor, *Guest Worker Programs and Policies* (Washington: the Urban Institute, 1995).

Massey, D. S., 'The Ethnosurvey in Theory and Practice', *International Migration Review*, Vol. 21, No. 4 (1987), pp. 1498–522.

Massey, D. S., J. Arango, G. Hugo, A. Kouaouci, A. Pellegrino, J. E. Taylor, *Worlds in Motion; Understanding International Migration at the End of the Millennium* (New York: Oxford University Press Inc, 1998).

Portes, A., 'Conclusion: Towards a New World — The Origins and Effects of Transnational Activities', *Ethnic and Racial Studies*, Vol. 22, No. 2 (1999), pp. 463–77.

Portes, A., L. I. Guarnizo, P. Landolt, 'The Study of Transnationalism: Pitfalls and Promise of an Emergent Research Field', *Ethnic and Racial Studies*, Vol. 22, No. 2 (1999), pp. 217–37.

Pries, L. (ed.), *Migration and Transnational Social Spaces* (Aldershot: Ashgate, 1999).

Stola, D., 'Two Kinds of Quasi-Migration in the Middle Zone: Central Europe as a Space for Transit Migration and Mobility for Profit', in C. Wallace, D. Stola (eds), *Patterns of Migration in Central Europe* (New York: Palgrave Macmillan, 2001), pp. 84–104.

Wallace, C., D. Stola (eds), *Patterns of Migration in Central Europe* (New York: Palgrave Macmillan, 2001b).

Wallace, C., D. Stola, 'Introduction: Patterns of Migration in Central Europe', in C. Wallace, D. Stola (eds), *Patterns of Migration in Central Europe* (New York: Palgrave Macmillan, 2001a), pp. 3–44.

Wallace, C., O. Chmouliar, E. Sidorenko, 'The Eastern Frontier of Western Europe: Mobility in the Buffer Zone', *New Community*, Vol. 22, No. 2 (1996), pp. 259–86.

Appendix

Table 3.A1 Foreigners with residence permits by citizenship in the Czech Republic in 1994 and 2001(as of December 31)[a]

Country	1994	%	2001	%
Slovakia	16,778	16.0	53,294	25.3
Ukraine	14,230	13.6	51,825	24.6
Vietnam	9,633	9.2	23,924	11.3
Poland	20,021	19.2	16,489	7.8
Russia	3,611	3.5	12,423	5.9
Germany	4,195	4.0	4,937	2.3
Bulgaria	3,772	3.6	4,101	1.9
China	2,907	2.8	3,309	1.6
Yugoslavia	4,026	3.8	3,269	1.6
USA	3,490	3.3	3,160	1.5
Others	21,680	21.0	34,063	16.2
Total	104,343	100.0	210,794	100.0

[a] Residence permition = permanent residence permition + 90 and more days visa (long-term residence)
Source: Horáková-Macounová (1999; 2002)

Table 3.A2 Foreigners employed by citizenship in the Czech Republic (as of December 31)[a]

Country	1995	1997	1999	2000	2001
Slovakia	62,272	77,294	59,803	70,237	70,606
Ukraine	27,557	33,862	36,197	37,155	39,063
Vietnam	8,092	24,863	19,000	19,382	20,466
Russia	973	2,018	2,701	2,858	2,777
Poland	12,400	14,574	7,913	8,712	7,712
'Other' former	1,180	6,181	4,609	4,740	4,448
Soviet Union	34,504	34,705	21,070	21,657	21,884
Others					
Total	148,855	194,296	151,852	164,987	167,652

[a] Employment = valid trade licenses + work permits + Slovak citizens registered by job centres
Source: Horáková-Macounová (2000; 2002)

Table 3.A3 Foreigners with permanent residence permits by citizenship in the Czech Republic (as of December 31); selected years

Group of migrants	1994	1995	1997	1999	2000	2001
Ukrainians	1,563	2,120	4,632	7,790	8,774	9,909
Russians	1,734	1,670	2,475	3,486	3,806	4,097
Total	32,468	38,557	56,281	66,754	66,891	69,816

Source: Horáková-Macounová (1999, pp. 46–47; 2002, pp. 43–44)

Table 3.A4 Foreigners with long-term residence permits (until 1999) and visas for more than 90 days (since 2000) by citizenship in the Czech Republic (as of December 31)

Group of migrants	1994	1995	1997	1999	2000	2001
Ukrainians	12,667	26,038	38,770	58,083	41,438	41,916
Russians	1,877	2,717	6,463	13,420	9,158	8,326
Total	71,230	120,060	153,516	162,108	134,060	140,978

Source: Horáková-Macounová (2002, pp. 43–44), Cizinci (2001, pp. 19–20)

4

Future Westward Outflow
from Accession Countries:
the Case of Poland

Paweł Kaczmarczyk

4.1. Introduction

For some time there has been a discussion on the potential consequences of Central and Eastern European countries' accession to the EU, and especially on the introduction of one of the fundamental European Community values — unfettered freedom of movement for individuals. There are concerns within the present EU members that abolition of existing barriers to labour mobility may have a number of undesirable effects on labour markets and income distribution in the EU.

As part of the planning and preparation for the accession of selected Central and Eastern European accession countries into the EU, in recent years there have been attempts to estimate the migratory potential[1] from this area. Such attempts fall into two categories: model-based studies and survey-based estimates. The first category employs advanced modelling techniques and uses aggregate data. Researchers involved in the second method poll a population about their migratory intentions and plans (declarations). Both methods produce specific numbers, which then serve as a basis for sometimes dramatic discussion on different levels.

In my opinion, the widely held, rather pessimistic, vision of future westward migration from Poland and its potential consequences is not entirely justified. The purpose of this chapter is to compare different scientific attempts to estimate the so-called migratory potential of Poland using Polish research results. I attempt to show that there is another method of looking at future migration streams, based not only on the models or on polls but on an analysis of mechanisms and factors underlying mobility as well. Several factors regarding especially, contemporary Polish migration to Germany, such as institutional barriers, networks and the importance of labour market structure, prove that the scale of future migration flows from Poland has been overestimated.

4.2. Basic Data on Contemporary Migration from Poland

Before I start to discuss different attempts to estimate the migratory potential from Poland, it would be very useful to give an overview of Polish migration from the end of the World War II through the 1990s.

The first post-war years were a period of mass movements because of the redrawing of state borders and of international agreements. As a result, about four million people departed Poland (mainly the so-called ethnic Germans, that is people with German descent, Ukrainians and Jews) and at the same time about 3.7 million flowed into Poland (mainly of Polish or Jewish descent). Figure 4.1 shows that, after this relatively short period of mass movements, the number of departures and emigrants decreased dramatically and remained at very low level because of political restrictions imposed by the Polish government.

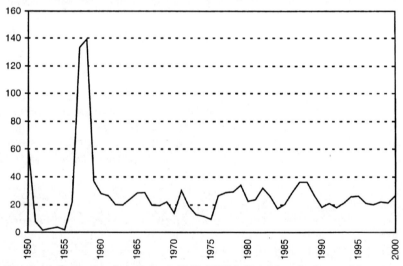

Figure 4.1 Emigration from Poland, 1950–2000 (official data, in thousands)
Source: Own elaboration on the basis of data from Central Statistical Office

The situation began to change in the mid-1950s and especially at the end of 1960s. According to official statistics, a total of over four million residents departed Poland between 1971 and 1980. The number of people taking up employment abroad and petty traders amounted to 100,000–200,000 annually (Stola, 2001). The total number of long-term migrants from Poland in the next decade (1980s) is estimated to be between 1.1 and 1.3 million people, or about 3 per cent of the total population. A large number of people (estimated at over one million) who spent fewer than 12 months abroad should also be taken into account (Frejka, Okólski and Sword, 1998). Undoubtedly, the major destination country in the post-war period was Germany (about 60 per cent of all emigrants).

There exist no unambiguous and exhaustive data on migration from Poland in the 1990s. Official data on migration portray only a small fraction of the phenomenon, that is departures related to a permanent change in residence,[2] but on the other hand this kind of migration (settlement migration) is depicted more finely than earlier. Before 1989, emigration was treated as illegal and so there was a strong disincentive to reveal the real purpose or nature of the departure. Figure 4.1 shows a clear stabilization of the number of departures associated with a declared change in the place of residence at between 20,000 and 25,000 annually. In total, over 216,000 people left Poland between 1990 and 1999 with the intention to settle abroad,[3] which obviously says nothing about the real scale of migration from Poland (Central Statistical Office, various years).

More reliable data concerning migrants staying abroad in the 1990s may be obtained from registries and surveys. From the 1995 Microcensus, a figure of about 900,000 permanent residents of Poland who temporarily, that is over two months, had stayed outside of national borders was derived, which equals about 2 per cent of the total population. A cyclically conducted Labour Force Survey (LFS) indicates that 130,000–210,000 adult people stayed abroad during each year between 1993 and 2000. Figure 4.2 shows that the number peaked in 1994 and has since markedly fallen off (but has been steadily rising in last two years). Moreover, LFS has proven that between 70 and 80 per cent of migrants undertake work during their stay abroad (Central Statistical Office, 1998).

A similar scale of population mobility was shown in the results of the 1997 national 'Conditions of Living in Poland' survey as well. It indicated that at the moment the survey was carried out there were about 200,000 people (0.5 per cent of the total population) who had been staying abroad for over two months. As data from all of these sources indicate, Germany held the most significant position

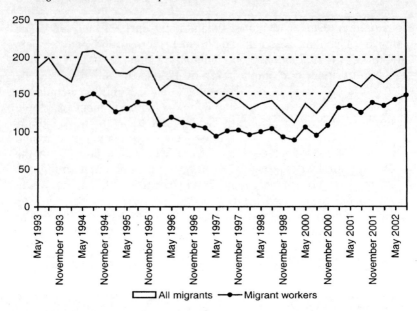

Figure 4.2 Polish citizens staying abroad for longer than two months who at the time of each Labour Force Survey were members of households in Poland, 1993–2002 (in thousands)[a]

[a] No data on migrant workers available before May 1994

Source: Own elaboration on the basis of data from the Central Statistical Office

amongst destination countries (about 40–50 per cent of all migrants) (Central Statistical Office, 1998, 2000).

Last but not least, one should take into account about 300,000–350,000 Poles, who each year legally take up work abroad on the basis of bilateral international agreements. An overwhelming majority of these are seasonal workers (80–90 per cent of all workers of this kind), and significantly more than half are employed in Germany (over 200,000 Polish seasonal workers annually have been employed there since 1996) (Okólski, 2000). Regardless of earlier presented data, various studies estimate the scale of irregular employment of Polish migrants in western host countries at a minimum of 150,000–200,000 annually.

In general, it is worth emphasizing that nowadays migrations from Poland differ from those in 1970s and 1980s in several aspects. The most important in the context of this chapter are the following differences.

▪ The shift from permanent to temporary migration. According to the 1997 'Conditions of Living in Poland' survey, practically

50 per cent of all migrants' stays were under a year and 30 per cent of them lasted fewer than six months. Prior to the 1990s trips abroad often took a final, definite nature. However, along with the transformation of the socio-economic system residents of Poland were granted not only the opportunity for free movement abroad but also for free return. As a consequence, settlement migration has become only a small part of all movements.

- The predominance of economics-driven labour migration. Since 1989, economic factors have been the most important causes determining scale and nature of contemporary mobility.
- Strong territorial concentration of migrants with reference to sending regions and host countries. Important 'emigration centres' are located in peripheral regions of Poland (Silesia, Podlasie). The migrants reach especially Western European countries, with Germany as the most significant destination country.

4.3. Selected Estimates on Migratory Potential from Poland and other CEE Countries

As mentioned in the introduction, in recent years one can find in the literature different kinds of estimations of the migratory potential from Poland and other Central and Eastern European (CEE) countries. The first category comprises model-based estimates, which estimate the scale of future migratory streams based on analysis of factors influencing current migratory movements and trends. The second kind, the so-called survey-based approach, estimates migratory potential on the basis of the responses of a representative sample of a population to a set of questions about their propensity for mobility (their declaration of a willingness to migrate).

This chapter will now turn to first discussing the most important forecasts based on econometric models. Later, surveys and survey-based forecasts will be presented and discussed.

4.3.1. Model-based studies

An analysis done for the European Commission and presented by Boeri, Brücker et al. (2000) may serve as a perfect example of a model-based study. Its aim was to estimate the potential economic consequences of EU enlargement. As a part of this analysis, estimates of future outflow from candidate countries, including Poland, were presented. The econometric model was based on the premises that, one, there exists a large income differential gap between EU and CEE countries and, two, that a rapid convergence of per capita income is rather unlikely. As a consequence, a distinct increase in migration from this region is expected given EU expansion.

It was also assumed that income disparity would play a key role in stimulation of migratory streams to EU countries. Nevertheless, a range of other variables were also considered, including unemployment rates (as a reflection of labour market situation), quality of life indices, the presence of a migrants' network (related variables concerning the resources of migrants already living or staying within the EU) and a set of non-economic variables (that is existence of guest-worker agreements, country-specific effects such as common language, culture and so on). The model was calibrated based on data pertaining to immigration to Germany in the previous 30 years (1967–98) and presented according to various estimates on factors surrounding convergence.[4]

For the basis scenario, wherein a per capita GNP convergence rate of 2 per cent annually and the maintenance of the current unemployment rates were assumed, the analysis led to an estimate of the long-term immigration potential from the ten CEE countries[5] of about 1 per cent of the EU population, which would represent about 4 per cent of the population of the countries of origin.[6] The greatest number of emigrants will be reached in 30 years. The initial inflow of new residents from Central and Eastern Europe to the present-day EU countries is estimated at about 335,000 annually, with the

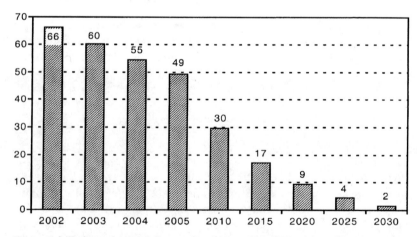

Figure 4.3 Estimated annual flows of emigrants from Poland into Germany (basis scenario, in thousands)
Source: Own elaboration on the basis of Boeri, Brücker et al. (2000)

number of immigrants peaking in 2030 at 3.9 million (estimated number of immigrants for 2010 and 2020: 1.9 million and 2.4 million).

The data concerning migration potential from Poland will be presented only for Germany, since it is the most important destination country. It is estimated that the initial inflow of migrants from Poland to Germany will be about 65,000 people annually and will gradually decrease to a very low level (about 1500 immigrants in 2030). Figures on the flow of people from Poland to Germany for the basis scenario show that the number of people from Poland residing permanently in Germany would be expected to rise from 277,000 in 1999 to 905,000 in 2030. Even this latter number does not give, in fact, any justification for a dramatic discussion on the 'new wave of Polish emigration'.

A similar analysis, but devoted exclusively to future migration from Poland, was presented by Orłowski and Zienkowski (1998). They used a model based on the accession of Greece (1981), Spain and Portugal (1986) for their analyses.[7] It was assumed that, despite certain differences (cultural, societal, social), the model for the three Southern European countries may be accepted, especially since there exist similar income differentials and these countries had already been supplying substantial numbers of workers to the EU labour market, as Poland does now.

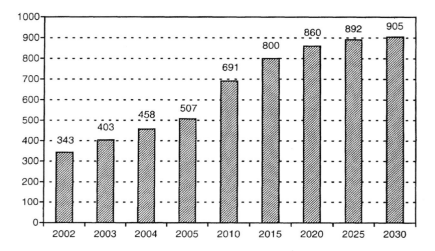

Figure 4.4 Estimated number of emigrants from Poland residing in Germany (basis scenario, in thousands)
Source: Own elaboration on the basis of Boeri, Brücker et al. (2000)

The models made use of the following variables: GNP per capita in dollars according to free market exchange rates and purchasing power parity, geographic distance, absorption capacity (size of labour market), estimated GNP growth rate as an approximation of development prospects, and the labour market situation (unemployment rate). It turned out that variables pertaining to the income differentials were key. Therefore, forecasts were made for each of three scenarios:

1   Pessimistic — low GNP growth rate in Poland and the consequent persistence of income differences between Poland and the EU without a real appreciation of the Polish złoty;
2   Basis — a relatively slow increase in Polish GNP of about 4 per cent annually plus a real appreciation in the złoty of about 3 per cent yearly;
3   Optimistic — a rapid increase in Polish GNP of about 7 per cent annually, which would lead to an increase in the value of the złoty by about 5 per cent a year.

All three scenarios assume that EU economic growth will amount to 2 per cent annually. The goal was to estimate the increase in the number of Poles living in the EU ten to 12 years after Poland's accession, presuming that the interim period will span five to eight years. The figures illustrate that, depending on the scenario, diametrically different assessments of the migratory potential from Poland to the EU and Germany are possible.

The authors consider variants two and three realistic. Based on their estimates for the basis scenario, one could expect a moderate outflow from Poland to the EU countries. The estimated number of Poles in the EU 10–12 years after accession amounts to 770,000 persons, of which about 280,000 will be in Germany.

Even the two models presented above show how different data can be obtained under different assumptions. In Table 4.1, the results of other selected attempts to estimate migration potential from Poland to the EU countries were collected.

According to a model estimated by Franzmeyer and Brücker (1997), the annual outflow from Poland should achieve a level of about 500,000 persons annually. Marek Kupiszewski stressed that this number equals about a half of all Polish migration in the 1980s and one has to remember that the 1980s were a period of mass movements which took place under totally different conditions than now (in Poland and in target countries). Moreover, according to the upper scenario of this estimate, we could expect a cumulative outflow of about ten million people, that is one quarter of Poland's

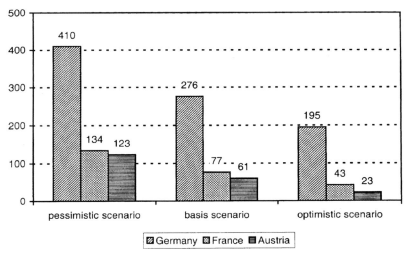

Figure 4.5 Estimated number of emigrants from Poland in selected EU countries 10–12 years after accession (in thousands)
Source: Own elaboration on the basis of Orłowski and Zienkowski (1998)

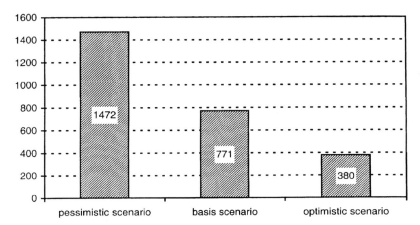

Figure 4.6 Estimated number of emigrants from Poland in the EU countries 10–12 years after accession (in thousands)
Source: Own elaboration on the basis Orłowski and Zienkowski (1998)

total population (Kupiszewski, 2001). Similar numbers were generated by the model used by Sinn et al. (2000). Based on these data, one could expect a 48–50 times greater annual outflow from Poland than the average for the years 1993–97. It is not so surprising when we take into consideration that the model was calibrated by using data concerning inflow of Turks to Germany, amongst others.

Generally, the presented data and the results of different analyses illustrate the difficulties in estimating so-called migration potential. The outcomes are very sensitive to assumptions made and to the data used for calibration of econometric models. In that sense it is rather problematic that most models made use of quite long time-series data for Germany — a country with a very rich immigration history but, more importantly, which has led many immigration-supporting programs as well (for instance its guest-worker system). An accurate, predictive model based on past German immigration experience seems to be very implausible under current and likely conditions. From my comparison of the different models presented, I argue that a scenario that predicts a total outflow of about 700,000–900,000 people from Poland to present-day EU member states in the next 30 years seems to be relatively likely. This sum total should also be treated as a point of reference for further discussion.

Table 4.1 Expected outflow from Poland to the EU countries — selected estimates (in thousands)

Source	Scenarios	Cumulative outflow for year 2030 (Thousands of long-term/permanent migrants)
Franzmeyer and Brücker 1997	Lower scenario	5,297
	Medium scenario	7,485
	Upper scenario	9,788
Boeri, Brücker et al. 2000	–	961
Brücker, Trübswetter and Weise 2000	–	961
Sinn et al. 2000	0% convergence scenario	3,016[a]
	2% convergence scenario	2,419[a]
Fertig and Schmidt 2000	Basis model for an average sending country	255[b]
	Model for an average sending country with respect to age structure	208[b]
	Basis model for a 'typical emigration country'	890[b]
	Model for a 'typical emigration country' with respect to age structure of the sending country	689[b]

[a] Estimates for year 2020
[b] Estimates for year 2017
Source: Kupiszewski (2001, p. 94)

4.3.2. Survey-based studies

As mentioned, the second kind of research is based on survey results and an assessment of the migration intentions of a population. In 1998, Wallace surveyed a representative sample from 11 Central and Eastern European countries. The estimated migratory potential varied heavily from country to country: between 7 and 26 per cent of respondents in different countries from this region declared a willingness to emigrate permanently, between 18 and 57 per cent wished to go abroad to work for a few years and between 13 and 68 per cent would go abroad for short-term migration. The highest level of migratory potential was observed in the Federal Republic of Yugoslavia, Croatia and Romania. Poland was placed in the middle of the sample. Wallace found that about 46 per cent of respondents in Poland would like to work abroad for a few weeks; this was the largest group. Of the Polish sample, 37 per cent claimed to be willing to work abroad for several months, 18 per cent declared a desire to work abroad for over a year and 14 per cent stated a willingness to move abroad permanently (Wallace, 1998).[8] By far the most (36 per cent) would choose Germany as their destination, although that country is favoured mostly for work-related, non-permanent migration.

Such high numbers obviously give rise to questions about what extent they reflect genuine and realistic intentions rather than wishes and vague expectations.[9] Fassman and Hinterman (1997) elected to take a somewhat different approach when they polled a sample of Poles, Czechs, Slovaks and Hungarians. They differentiated between potential migration based on unsubstantiated self-declarations (the 'general migratory potential') and the migratory potential of those who had made certain steps towards going abroad, which they called the real migratory potential. Their results showed, as can be expected, an immense contrast. The general migratory potential of the four countries was estimated to be 9,560,000 persons whereas the real migratory potential was estimated at about 770,000 persons aged over 14. In the case of Poland, the general migratory potential was estimated to be 16.6 per cent of the populace (aged over 14), or about five million people, whereas the real migratory potential was estimated at 1.33 per cent, or only 400,000 people. Similarly to Wallace's study, about 37 per cent of them would choose Germany as their destination, meaning that potential migration to that country amounts to between 147,303 and 1,870,000 people, depending which notion of potential is being discussed. Finally, Polish migratory potential is strongly regionally differentiated, as shown on Map 4.A1 in the Appendix.

In this context, I would like to quote the data from very recent surveys done by Polish institutions. A reputable survey conducted in May 2002 dealt, in part, with Polish citizens' migration plans (Ipsos Demoskop, 2002). About 22 per cent of all respondents (aged 15 to 75) declared a readiness to settle abroad during the few next years, most of them (about 60 per cent) in Germany. This number could imply a huge migration potential. To assess the likelihood of the plans and vagueness of the declarations, the respondents were also asked for more precise responses concerning their future mobility. About 12 per cent of respondents declared a willingness to go abroad for work or settlement purposes in the next 12 months and only 5 per cent had already taken any measures to prepare for the trip abroad. This number can be used as the real migratory potential of Poles. A similar analysis was prepared for a leading Polish newspaper in September 2002 (*Gazeta Wyborcza*, 2002). The results are quite comparable. About 5 per cent of respondents stated their determination to take up employment in an EU country (after the accession). Only 3 per cent of all surveyed intended to settle abroad.

4.4. Discussion

Both presented approaches to international mobility analyses are controversial. In the model-based approach, controversy is due mainly to the use of risky hypotheses. Furthermore, values for independent variables are unknown and must be estimated and, in consequence, it becomes necessary to formulate various scenarios for the development of the situation. This can mean that the derived predictions often vary enormously and it is not always possible to conclude which are the most plausible (see Table 4.1). Such analyses are, therefore, of questionable value. Besides that, they are exemplary of a fairly mechanistic approach to population mobility and say little of the mechanisms behind this process and its dynamics.

Serious criticisms have been levelled against the second method as well, which is supposed to measure desire or willingness to migrate rather than actual plans to do so. The doubt has been substantiated conclusively by Fassman and Hinterman (1997). The research experience gathered by the Centre of Migration Research at the Institute for Social Studies (Warsaw University) has also shown that an analysis of the conditions underlying mobility is possible only after the fact and that there exists a large difference between declarations and actual preparations for going abroad.

I would like to emphasize that this chapter does not represent a debate about the studies quoted and their results. The arguments I am about to give are rather a discussion with a certain school of thinking and analysing migratory phenomena. Contemporary experience makes it possible to suggest that international mobility is too complex a process for the formulation of reliable migration forecasts. Thus, a third method of looking at future migration from Poland, based on analysis of mechanisms and factors underlying current migratory streams, seems reasonable (see Okólski, 2001). All these methods should be treated as complementary ways to understand human mobility.

Having in mind that even the forecast results mentioned earlier in no way justify the heated atmosphere around the negotiations between Poland and the EU, I would like to put forward some further points that should throw a somewhat different light on contemporary and future migrations by residents of Poland.[10] I am going to concentrate mainly on phenomena relating to Germany, the most popular destination for migrants from Poland.

4.4.1. The mobility assumption

Neoclassical migration theory is founded on the presumption that people are basically mobile. However, it appears hard to acknowledge that as a universal paradigm: a population's mobility is a function of many different factors, including historical, cultural and structural ones. Many researchers have pointed out the possible benefits associated with non-mobility; for example, the *insider advantage approach* proposed by Fisher, Martin and Straubhaar (1998). The question should be asked whether the assumption that the Polish population is 'mobile' is warranted.[11] (Some researchers looking into issues around the Eastward expansion of the EU are checking this assumption.) I believe it is rather not. Instead, I think that only a small portion of the population exhibits a propensity for mobility.

Firstly, where mobility exists, there should be a tendency to equalize differences on the domestic, as well as international, labour market. Yet Poland is a country featuring very disparate regional differences (see Appendix, Map 4.A2). The differences cover elements considered fundamental pro-migration factors — variances in per capita incomes and unemployment rates. The variances are supposed to imply substantial internal migration and thereby the gradual elimination of those differences. The reality, however, is that those phenomena do not exist to any meaningful extent and that the current differences have become entrenched and 'petrified'. This means that either the preconditions for mobility are quite a bit more complex or that the financial stimulus must be especially strong to overcome a dispropensity for mobility.

Such a hypothesis can be supported by different data. In one of the most recent studies conducted by the Centre for Migration Research, seasonal workers employed in Germany were asked about their migration plans (Jaźwińska and Kaczmarczyk, 2002). It turned out that even that group, which, after all, has experience with migration and employment abroad, did not declare a high inclination for mobility. The research shows that about 36 per cent of respondents state their intention to go abroad again for more seasonal work, another eight per cent for other work and only three per cent intend to settle outside of Poland. It is worth emphasizing that it is this latter category that is being estimated in the studies already cited.

The studies I have cited estimate the potential number of migrants using the classical definition of them, that is people intending to settle outside of their state boundaries. Taking this approach is not entirely comprehensible in light of current trends in Poles' mobility. As I have tried to show, most migration from Poland is short-term or even 'shuttle' in nature. It is important to remember that short-term mobility may have different roots than permanent migration. Because short-term migrants keep the 'go back option' open and retain strong connections with the sending community, the constellation of causes and costs is different than in the case of settlement migration.

4.4.2. The wage argument

The basic problem in estimating the migratory potential is due, in most cases, to quantitative, macro-analytic approaches that are based on a simple, orthodox version of economics (for example without taking into account market imperfections).[12] Generally, economic orthodoxy postulates labour flows as an expression of a tendency to balance out labour productivity and prices (wages). Workers are paid according to their marginal productivity and the whole process goes on until values find equilibrium in a barrier-free arena. Human migration is also considered instrumentally as a means to even out differences and imbalances on the labour market. However, it is possible to forward at least a few arguments that question such a simplistic, income-oriented perception of international mobility.

Contemporary 'migration theories' more and more often go beyond neo-classical economics. Of course, they accept that imbalances in wages are one of the pre-conditions for mobility, but the theories do not assume them to be a sufficient cause for it. Statistics indicate that the scale of different kinds of migration from Poland has declined despite the persistence of significant differences in wages and per capita gross national income. Numerous empirical studies support this; quoting Wallace (1999): 'Being poor is not enough to become a migrant'. This means that the presence of other causes, ones associated with demographic variables, family situation, and so on, is also needed.

Note also that it would be necessary to specify a minimum gap between domestic and foreign wages that would compensate for non-material costs of mobility, which are very difficult to include in a quantitative model. One Polish researcher studying present-day migration from the Opole region to Germany tried to determine this minimum by looking at subjects' responses on the minimum wages they would accept to work in Germany and the so-called 're-emigration' wages, that is the earnings that would induce them back home to Poland. He discovered that migrants were willing to accept even 2.24 times less pay in order to return to their places of origin (Jończy, 2000). That presumably indicates that the stimulus from wage differentials must be sufficiently strong to lead to migration/emigration decisions.

To further undermine the absolute prominence of the 'wage argument', there is also the fact that even a total equalization of wages would not necessarily halt migration. New Economics of Labour Migration representatives have noted that migrant flows may be the result of following factors.

- For one thing, among the multitude of goals migrants have, a frequently sufficient motive behind migration may be the desire to diversify risk in a household. For example, one adult from a family whose members do not enjoy job security may opt to go abroad to look for work rather than put all the family's eggs in the same local, depressed labour market basket. This argument seems very well founded in the case of CEE countries. Their economies during the transition period have been characterized by significant market failures and, in consequence, a high level of risk. Migration can be treated as a means to reduce such risks.
- Secondly, as suggested by Stark and Taylor (1991) and confirmed by research in Poland and other places, people rarely base their decisions on an evaluation of absolute income alone but also weigh other considerations, for example income *relative to* other people in his or her own local community. From this perspective, increasing income differentials in Poland and other CEE countries can be perceived as an important pro-migratory factor.

Last but not least, the barriers and obstacles curtailing the scale of labour flow or of other migrant flows must not be forgotten. These obstacles are not only formal ones, such as international borders, visa and/or work permit requirements, but also informal barriers, like foreign culture and languages. As Mancur Olson has noted, a border is more than a line separating two state organisms, but a real barrier standing between separate institutional systems. Poland's accession to the EU brings with it a lifting of formal barriers but, at least in the short term, will not bear a large effect on informal barriers, amongst which language is certainly a major one. It must be remembered that Poland and Germany are countries that are close geographically but culturally divergent. This is shown even by the example of ethnic Germans from Poland, who frequently encountered serious problems with finding their niche in Germany and on the German labour market.

4.4.3. Beyond the neoclassical economic theory — the demand side

It is often forgotten that labour migration is primarily a function of demand. 'There cannot be any emigration without immigration opportunities elsewhere ... international migration is, explicitly or implicitly, determined by the economic demand for foreigners' (Böhning 1981, p. 32). It should be emphasized that migration potential is not just a function of structural and/or demographic factors in the country of origin but is, and perhaps is mainly, of similar factors in the destination country. The thesis that I would like to forward is this: contemporary earnings-oriented migrations from Poland are, in large part, generated by the demand for labour in Western European countries. To substantiate this, I would like to draw on two illustrations.

It has already been pointed out that the 1980s was a period of invigoration of both settlement and short-term migration by residents of Poland (see Chapter 4.2). The scale becomes surprising when we consider that this occurred despite strict mobility barriers (for example exit visas) imposed by the Polish regime of the time. However, it was mainly the 'friendly' immigration policies of destination countries and the absorbency of Western European labour markets that drove the migration dynamics. Polish migration to the most 'popular' destination country — Germany — was driven by, on the one hand, German policy on ethnic Germans[13] (so-called *Aussiedlers*) and, on the other hand, asylum policies that favoured migrants from the Soviet bloc.

Since the beginning of the 1970s, there has been no real way to analyse labour migration without referring to Piore (1979) and his dual labour market theory. The theory is founded on the assumption that the structure of the labour markets in destination countries has a decisive influence on migration processes. Piore noticed that one of the most prominent traits of highly-developed economies is their generation of two classes of jobs. The secondary sector is associated generally with smallish enterprises operating on local and regional markets, which offer jobs of relatively low pay, low social status and low security. Nationals rarely accept the positions, but they do meet migrants' expectations, especially those of temporary migrants who are willing to accept the rules and conditions of the sector. A wide range of authors (for example Biller, 1989; Szydlik, 1996) have noted that near-ideal conditions for the formation of a secondary market arose on the German labour market, which was/is key to migrants from Poland:

- there was a demand for labour that exceeded domestic supply,
- the state admitted a foreign labour force onto the market but simultaneously restricted its rights (*Gastarbeiting*),
- employers were given leeway to differentiate employment structures.

Empirical studies from the 1980s and 1990s bear this out. The research found concentrations of foreigners in such sectors as construction, hotelling, food services, and trade, and also showed that foreign workers tended to occupy positions requiring unskilled or semi-skilled labour (often irrespective of their qualifications). The high rate of unemployment facing foreigners on the German labour market illustrates the peculiar situation they find themselves in: whereas the unemployment rates of foreigners and Germans were comparable in 1977 (4.9 vs. 4.4 per cent), the difference had jumped by about 8 per cent by 1997 (16 vs. 8.5 per cent).

This is also and surprisingly true for ethnic German migrants, who rarely attain a position befitting their expectations and abilities. However, it would be hard to call them victims of discrimination; German law indeed favoured them for a long time by providing them with social benefits and housing. Research from the 1990s has shown that almost 70 per cent of these ethnic German migrants were employed as unskilled labour (often under their qualifications) and their earnings were roughly 15 per cent lower than Germans' working at analogous positions (Münz and Ohliger, 1997; Koller, 1997).

The case of a very numerous group of earnings-oriented migrants from Poland — seasonal workers — is most relevant to my discussion; their lot is clearly consistent with the conditions that Piore described. Such seasonal work is characterized by its generally not requiring any qualifications and involves simple, unmechanized tasks. Research conducted last year among seasonal workers from Warsaw and its environs (Jaźwińska and Kaczmarczyk, 2002) found that people migrating to do such work feature a relatively high level of education, although the seasonal work is entirely unrelated to their qualifications.[14] Employment is typically unstable, with about a quarter of the contracts lasting less than foreseen.

The vast majority of seasonal workers (85–90 per cent) find themselves working in agriculture, that is to say a sector prone to drastic changes and interested in attracting a cheap labour force, which will be employed only for a temporary period of increased labour demand. Enterprises that hire Polish seasonal workers are, for the most part, small or modest operations — our research indicates about 70 per cent of them employed fewer than 25 people. Most of them relied heavily on foreign labour (80 per cent). There is one well-known, 1997, instance when the German federal government wanted to decrease the number of seasonal workers from Poland due to growing domestic unemployment. The government's initiative was a complete failure: they were unable to find enough people willing to work and German agriculturalists bore large financial losses (Marek, 2000).

Finally, in the context of the dual labour market theory, it is also worth emphasizing that the principle of free flow of people requires the banning of discrimination in work conditions and compensation. This, in turn, means that Poles will stop being such attractive workers in many sectors of the EU labour market and may significantly reduce the demand for Polish workers (and therefore the scale of Polish labour migration).

4.4.4. Demographic pressure

The next argument raised by proponents of restrictions on migration between the EU and Poland concerns the demographic pressure that is supposed to additionally inflate the migratory potential as huge numbers of people enter productivity age in Poland. Their point seems well taken because, due to the high unemployment rate in Poland (approximately 18 per cent in February 2002), these people could very well end up in the Western European labour market. Fears of this are, on closer examination, unfounded. The demographic forecast for Poland over the years 2000–20 does indicate a stable growth in the numbers of working-age people, but that will be practically exclusively a result of an increase in the numbers of people aged 50 and over.

The Figure 4.7 shows that changes in the other cohorts will be negative from 2006 on. A wide range of emigration studies, including ones on Poles' mobility in the 1990s done by the CMR, has shown that people aged 35–45 have the greatest mobility propensity (see Frejka, Okólski and Sword, 1998; Jaźwińska and Okólski, 2001). Over the next 15 years, the number of people under 45 years old is going to fall by about 500,000. This signals that the demographic potential of Poland is 'exportable' to EU countries to only a small extent unless there is a drastic change to migration trends, which is unlikely.

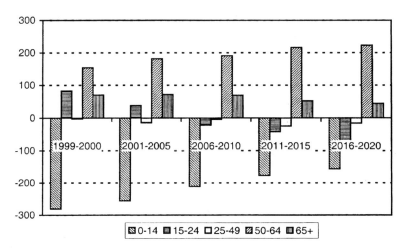

Figure 4.7 Changes in Polish population structure, by age groups, forecasts for years 1999–2020 (in thousands)
Source: Own elaboration on the basis of Sztanderska (1999)

4.4.5. Internal dynamics of migration — migration networks

An ever-greater role is being attributed to networks responsible for the so-called internal dynamics of migration. Thanks to the networks, the migration process diverges from its initial roots and *raison d'etre* and takes on a life of its own. In doing so, it becomes part of families' strategies and social life on a local scale. This observation has been confirmed in research on migration potential and was presented by Fassman et al. Map 4.A1 (see Appendix) incontrovertibly shows that the areas of highest potential are by no means the ones featuring the lowest levels of economic development, but rather stand out as having a tradition of migration or ties with potential destination countries (Silesia and Podlasie are classic examples).

The existence of networks causes that the income argument may, in practice, be of secondary importance and that the migration process itself is characterized by a good deal of inertia. Networks may result in continuing migration even when the wage gap between the countries of origin and destination narrows. On the other hand, it is difficult to expect future drastic changes in the magnitude of mobility (including a decrease in it) especially since the extent of illegal migration proves that current administrative and legal barriers are often illusory.

4.5. Conclusions

The arguments I have put forward have been intended to show, on one hand, that earnings-oriented migration from Poland has reached such a point that, due to present dynamics and the main characteristics of migration, it would be hard to foresee a significant increase in its scale. Factors causing this include improving living conditions in Poland and demographic, social and cultural conditions. The presented arguments concentrated mainly on the mechanisms of mobility rather than on criticisms of migratory potential estimates. In my opinion, both approaches are non-rival and should be treated as complementary.

On the other hand, most of the analyses quoted do not justify concerns associated with EU enlargement and its consequences for Western European labour markets. It could be assumed that the future outflow from accession countries is going to be rather moderate and will not cause drastic changes on the EU markets. Moreover, once we realize that the vast majority of contemporary migration from Poland represents short-term mobility, that those leaving for such work are characterized by their holding average qualifications and skills but frequently without knowing the language, and performing only simple jobs abroad, there arises the question of what kind of threat such migration may amount to. Instead, one may emphasize that EU countries can take advantage of such migration to fill gaps in their own labour market supply while not being burdened with the costs associated with the integration of permanent or long-term migrants.

Finally, I tried to emphasize the importance of labour demand on Western European labour markets, which diminishes barriers to labour mobility to secondary significance. In such a context, the anticipated interim period will not make, in reality, much sense. The introduction of such a period might only lead to an increase in illegal migration, for example from ex-Soviet countries, whose citizens more and more often appear in sectors once associated with workers from Poland that are heavily reliant on foreign labour.

Notes

1   We could simply define migration potential as a number of people willing to migrate from one country/region to another. The migration potential is solely a macro-structural phenomenon, but the necessary condition for the existence of migration potential is propensity to migrate at the micro level, which is determined by utility functions at an individual level (Straubhaar, 1993).

2   Because of migrant definition employed. In official statistics, a migrant is defined as a person who de-listed himself from his place of permanent residence in Poland.

3   It is 50,000 fewer than in the preceding decade.

4   Data and forecasts for the other EU countries are extrapolations on the basis of the present distribution of immigrants within EU.

5   Bulgaria, Czech Republic, Estonia, Hungary, Latvia, Lithuania, Poland, Romania, Slovak Republic, Slovenia.

6   It is worthy to present some data on the migration scale from these countries to date. The annual net immigration from ten CEECs into the EU peaked in 1990 (at more than 300,000 people), but than declined sharply. The number of residents from these countries in the EU was estimated at 850,000 (mainly in Germany — about 560,000). Nevertheless, EUROSTAT LFS indicated around 250,000 foreign workers from CEE countries are employed in the EU (Boeri, Brücker et al., 2000).

7   The German experience was also tested for its applicability, but in the case of German unification there were no legal or cultural barriers that could restrict the scale of population movements; this is, of course, quite different from Poland's current situation.

8   The sum is more than 100 per cent due to non-exclusive categories.

9   After all, towards the end of the 1990s a similar survey was conducted in one of Warsaw secondary schools. It indicated that 90 per cent of the students surveyed wanted to go abroad to earn money!

10   Although different forecasting varies depending on methodology and the assumptions made, the research suggests that there will be no dramatic increase in migration. Therefore, we shouldn't expect a significant impact on EU labour markets: according to Boeri, Brücker et al. (2000) in the case of Germany, we might expect 0.65 per cent wage reduction for every percentage rise in foreigner labour's share in a sector and a 0.2 per cent increase in the risk of unemployment for every 1 per cent increase in foreigners' proportion of the total population.

11   That is to say: what is the likelihood that migration potential, especially as estimated through survey responses, will turn into an actual flow of migrants.
12   However, it must be admitted that the simplifications have been adopted, in part, out of necessity.
13   Poland-born people of German ethnicity. About 1.4 million of them left Poland in the years 1950–98.
14   Over 90 per cent of those polled either spoke no German or spoke it only poorly. However, this did not present a problem during their work to the vast majority (90 per cent); this is indicative of its simple nature.

References

Biller, M. *Arbeitsmarktsegmentation und Ausländerbeschäftigung. Ein Beitrag zur Soziologie des Arbeitsmarktes mit einer Fallstudie aus der Automobilindustrie* (Frankfurt, New York: Campus Verlag, 1989).
Böhning, W. R. 'Elements of Theory of International Migration to Industrial Nation States', in M. M. Kritz, C. B. Keely, S. M. Tomasi, *Global Trends in Migration. Theory and Research on International Population Movements* (New York: Center of Migration Studies, 1981), pp. 28–43.
Boeri, T., H. Brücker et al., *The Impact of Eastern Enlargement on Employment and Wages in the EU Member States* (Berlin, Milano: European Integration Consortium: DIW, CEPR, FIEF, IAS, IGIER, 2000).
Brücker, H., P. Trübswetter, C. Weise, 'EU-Osterweiterung: Keine massive Zuwanderung zu erwarten', *Wochenbericht*, No. 21 (Berlin: DIW, 2000).
Central Statistical Office, *Migracje zagraniczne ludności Polski w latach 1988–1997* (Warsaw, 1998).
Central Statistical Office, *Migracje zagraniczne ludności Polski. Aneks* (Warsaw: Central Statistical Office, 2000).
Central Statistical Office, *Statistical Yearbook of Poland* (Warsaw: Central Statistical Office, various years).
Fassman, H., Ch. Hintermann, 'Migrationspotential Ostmitteleuropa. Struktur und Motivation potentieller Migranten aus Polen, der Slovakei, Tschechien und Ungarn', *ISR-Forschungsbericht*, No. 15 (Vienna: Austrian Academy of Sciences, 1997).
Fertig, M., C. M. Schmidt, 'Aggregate-level migration studies as a tool for forecasting future migration streams', *IZA Discussion Paper*, No. 183 (Bonn: Institute for the Study of Labor, 2000).
Fischer, P., R. Martin, T. Straubhaar, 'Should I Stay or Should I Go?', in T. Hammar, G. Brochmann, K. Tamas, T. Faist (eds), *International Migration, Immobility and Development. Multidisciplinary Perspectives* (Oxford: Berg, 1998), pp. 49–90.
Franzmeyer, F., H. Brücker, 'Europäische Union: Osterweiterung und Arbeitskräftemigration', *Wochenbericht*, No. 5 (Berlin: DIW, 1997).
Frejka, T., M. Okólski, K. Sword, *In-depth studies on migration in Central and Eastern Europe: the case of Poland* (New York, Geneva: UN Population Fund, 1998).
Gazeta Wyborcza, 'Only 5 per cent of Poles will seek work abroad after accession to the European Union', (October 2002).
Ipsos Demoskop, 'Omnibus survey', (May 2002).
Jaźwińska, E., P. Kaczmarczyk, 'Warszawscy pracownicy sezonowi w Niemczech', in A. Grzymała-Kazłowska, K. Iglicka, E. Jaźwińska, P. Kaczmarczyk,

Paweł Kaczmarczyk 87

E. Kępińska, M. Okólski, A. Weinar 'Wpływ migracji zagranicznych w Warszawie na sytuację na stołecznym rynku pracy', *ISS Working Papers, Migration Series*, No. 44 (Warsaw: Institute for Social Studies, Warsaw University, 2002), pp. 43–72.

Jaźwińska, E., M. Okólski, *Ludzie na huśtawce. Migracje między peryferiami Polski i Zachodu* (Warsaw: Scholar, 2001).

Jończy, R., 'Migracje zarobkowe z rejonu opolskiego do Niemiec. Aspekty ekonomiczne', in A. Rajkiewicz (ed.), *Zewnętrzne migracje zarobkowe we współczesnej Polsce. Wybrane zagadnienia* (Włocławek, Warsaw: Wyższa Szkoła Humanistyczno-Ekonomiczna, IPiSS, 2000), pp. 79–105.

Koller, B., 'Aussiedler der großen Zuwanderungswellen — was ist aus ihnen geworden? Die Eingliederungssituation von Aussiedlerinnen und Aussiedlern auf dem Arbeitsmarkt in Deutschland', in *Mitteilungen aus der Arbeitsmarkt- und Berufsforschung*, No. 4 (1997), pp. 766–89.

Kupiszewski, M., 'Demograficzne aspekty wybranych prognoz migracji zagranicznych', in A. Stępniak (ed.), *Swobodny przepływ pracowników w kontekście wejścia Polski do Unii Europejskiej* (Warsaw: UKIE, 2001), pp. 73–98.

Marek, E., 'Sezonowe zatrudnianie pracowników za granicą', in A. Rajkiewicz, (ed.), *Zewnętrzne migracje zarobkowe we współczesnej Polsce. Wybrane zagadnienia* (Włocławek, Warsaw: Wyższa Szkoła Humanistyczno-Ekonomiczna, IPiSS, 2000), pp. 19–39.

Münz, R., R. Ohliger, 'Deutsche Minderheiten in Ostmittel- und Osteuropa, Aussiedler in Deutschland. Eine Analyse ethnisch privilegierter Migration', *Demographie aktuell*, No. 9 (Berlin: Humboldt University, 1997).

Okólski, M., 'Recent trends in international migration — Poland 2000', *ISS Working Papers, Migration Series*, No. 39 (Warsaw: Institute for Social Studies, Warsaw University, 2000).

Okólski, M., 'O rzeczową argumentację w kwestii swobodnego przepływu pracowników', in A. Stępniak (ed.), *Swobodny przepływ pracowników w kontekście wejścia Polski do Unii Europejskiej* (Warsaw: UKIE, 2001), pp. 19–40.

Orłowski, W. M., L. Zienkowski, 'Skala potencjalnej migracji z Polski a członkostwo w Unii Europejskiej', in: P. Korcelli (ed.), *Przemiany w zakresie migracji ludności jako konsekwencja przystąpienia Polski do UE* (Warsaw: PAN, 1998), pp. 55–66.

Piore, M., *Birds of Passage. Migrant Labor and Industrial Societies* (Cambridge: Cambridge University Press, 1979).

Sinn, H. W., et al., *EU-Erweiterung und Arbeitskraeftemigration: Wege zu einer Schriftweisen Annaeherung der Arbeitsmaerkte* (München: Institut für Wirtschaftsforschung, 2000).

Stark, O., E. Taylor, 'Migraton incentives, migration types: The role of relative deprivation', *The Economic Journal*, Vol. 101, No. 408 (1991), pp. 1163–78.

Stola, D., 'Międzynarodowa mobilność zarobkowa w PRL', in E. Jaźwińska, M. Okólski (eds), *Ludzie na huśtawce. Migracje między peryferiami Polski i Zachodu* (Warsaw: Scholar, 2001), pp. 62–100.

Straubhaar, T., 'Migration Pressure', *International Migration*, Vol. 31, No. 1 (1993), pp. 5–42.

Sztanderska, U., 'Bagkround Study on Labour Market and Employment in Poland' (Turin, 1999), unpublished.

Szydlik, M., 'Ethnische Ungleichheit auf dem deutschen Arbeitsmarkt', *Kölner Zeitschrift für Soziologie und Sozialpsychologie*, Vol. 48, No. 4 (1996), pp. 658–76.

Wallace, C., *Migration Potential in Central and Eastern Europe* (Geneva: IOM, 1998).

Wallace, C., 'Economic Hardship, Migration, and Survival Strategies in East-Central Europe', *Sociological Series*, No. 35 (Vienna: Institute for Advanced Studies, 1999).

Appendix

Migration potential as a per cent of inhabitants at the age 14 and more

☐ no data
■ 31 to 40
▨ 21 to 31
▧ 11 to 21
☐ 0 to 11

Map 4.A1 Migration potential in selected Polish regions
Source: Fassman, Hintermann (1997)

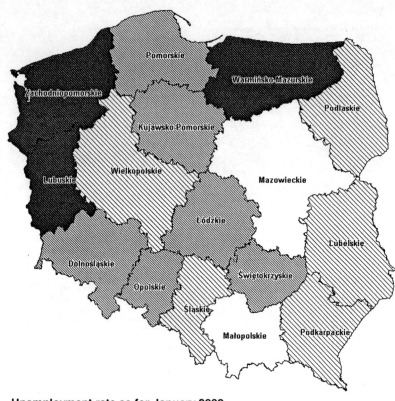

Unemployment rate as for January 2002

- 23   to 29.3
- 18   to 23
- 15   to 18
- 13.4 to 15

Map 4.A2 Unemployment rate in Polish regions
Source: Own elaboration on the basis of data from Central Statistical Office

Part II

The Struggle for Recognition:
New and Old Minorities in Europe

5

Multiculturalism and Political Integration in Modern Nation States[1]

John Rex

Multiculturalism has been a central question in the political concerns of European countries since 1945. However, it is an umbrella term that covers a number of different issues; which issue predominates varies according to political circumstances. The multiculturalism discussion reflected concern about immigration and the ways in which immigrants might settle in Western Europe in the 1950s and 1960s. After the 1989 break-up of the Communist bloc and the resurgence of ethnic nationalism in Europe's eastern regions, it centred around questions of devolution of power from central national governments to regionally-based, sub-national groups and the possibilities of power sharing at the centre. Thirdly, the multiculturalism debate has had to deal with the growing numbers of political refugees and asylum seekers in Western Europe. Fourthly, and most recently, in the wake of terrorist attacks on America, the debate has been concerned with actual, potential or perceived dangers posed by unassimilated immigrant groups.

It is not the intention of this article to delve into each of the structures and processes in all the different political situations it mentions. Rather, it seeks to place these situations within an overall conceptual framework and, in doing so, to produce a general theory of multiculturalism.

5.1. Multiculturalism in Popular Discourse

There are few terms used more widely in popular discourse, in the media and in politics than *multiculturalism*. Until recently, it carried a positive connotation as a feature of national societies and cities. Politicians and even monarchs would say 'We now live in a multicultural society' and cities would boast that they were

93

'multicultural' or, sometimes, '*cosmopolitan*'. We may refer to such usages as soft versions of multiculturalism.

In recent times, given ethnic conflicts where societies broke up and what was called *ethnic cleansing* occurred (as in the former Yugoslavia), or where violent ethnic conflicts broke out within states and cities (such conflicts were globally commonplace), multiculturalism was seen in a very much more negative light. In the United Kingdom, for example, violent conflict between Asian and native British citizens was diagnosed as due to multiculturalism. Economic migrants or political migrants and refugees were seen as endangering the unity of society. As a result, this unity was seen as needing to be defended against multiculturalism.

5.2. Philosophical and Social Science Views of Multiculturalism

During the past 25 years, multiculturalism has also been debated by philosophers and social scientists. In political philosophy, the issue arose while attempting to define the nature of a good, liberal society. Such a society, it was thought, would guarantee the rights of individuals (see, for instance, Walzer and Miller, 1995). A common question now asked is whether similar rights should be extended to groups. *Prima facie*, it seems that the very recognition of groups would involve a denial of individual rights. Charles Taylor (1994), however, saw what he called *recognition* as essential to the concept of rights, and individuals could be recognized as members of groups. Will Kymlicka (1995) raised similar issues in writing about multi-cultural citizenship. Both of these writers, being Canadian, had to deal with the special problem of Quebec's demands for a separate political identity while discussing the identity of disparate groups of immigrants and their descendants. A related question arose in Europe, where Rainer Baubock (1992) posited the idea of a transnational citizenship alongside that of state citizenship.

All of these approaches imply a positive evaluation of multi-culturalism. So too does that of the British Indian political philosopher, Bhiku Parekh (2000). Parekh discusses the possibility of culturally distinct groups co-existing in a single society. He believes that they can and, furthermore, that the multicultural nature of such a society should be welcomed and celebrated. Monocultural societies for him are no longer likely in the modern world as a result of migration. Far more likely are societies in which multiple cultures coexist; it is important for him that they should all have equal respect. Parekh coupled this theoretical work with his leadership of the Commission for a Multiracial Britain, which sought to spell out the policies and institutions necessary to create a society in which racial discrimination, exploitation, and oppression were prevented (Runnymede Trust, 2000).

5.3. An Alternative Theory of Multiculturalism

Brian M. Barry (1999) sharply critiques the theories on multiculturalism discussed above. He sets out to defend the values of a liberal society, which he believes stands in contrast to what these theories advocate. He believes that they are wrong in seeing the various groups discussed as only *culturally* different; instead, he focuses upon their political relations. When the groups' differences are thus understood, they present a real problem that liberal political theory has to face.

In discussing Barry's work (Rex, 2001), I have argued that there is a limited version of multiculturalism that can be upheld even if his basic criticism is accepted. I base this on Thomas H. Marshall's (1951) theory of citizenship and a British definition of the term *integration* as it should appropriately be applied to immigrant ethnic minorities (see Rex and Tomlinson, 1979).

5.3.1. Social citizenship and the welfare state

Marshall was not directly concerned with immigrant ethnic minorities. Rather, his theory sought to show how the concept of citizenship has transcended class loyalties and class conflict. The first stage of this transcendence is in the legal sphere within which all individuals, regardless of class, are formally equal before the law. The second is political. Under universal franchise, all individuals participate in selecting the government. The third, gradually being achieved in the post-1945 world, is social: assurance of a minimum income in times of unemployment and ill health, free collective bargaining, minimum standards of housing and education and free health care for all at the point of delivery. Marshall based these ideas on William Beveridge's book, 'Full Employment in a Free Society' (1944), and on the Report on Social Insurance and Allied Services (Beveridge, 1942). Together, Beveridge and Marshall laid the foundation of what came to be called the Welfare State.[2]

I have expressed some doubt as to whether citizenship would totally and permanently transcend class (Rex, 1961). I argued that it would so long as there were a balance of class forces but that, if this balance were destroyed, class conflict might well resume. This was an important issue in Britain during the term of the 1964 Labour government and later during Conservative administrations between 1979 and 1993. The Labour government issued a White Paper entitled 'In Place of Strife' (Department of Labour and Productivity, 1969), which envisaged co-operation between trade unions and employers' organizations in government-sponsored institutions. The Conservative government of the eighties subsequently greatly weakened workers' rights and envisaged a much more limited welfare state, which involved little more than social insurance and a free health service. Nonetheless, a later Conservative government declared itself in favour of a *classless society*.

What has been discussed here is the evolution of social policy and political institutions in Britain, but very similar ideas were operative in most West European countries. Frank-Olaf Radtke (1994), for instance, spoke of the social democratic welfare state as one in which a plurality of conflicting interests had led to a negotiated compromise.

All of the above discussion indicates the possibility of class conflict and class compromise. None of it refers to the place of ethnic groups, which is at the centre of discussions about multi-cultural societies. To this question we must now turn.

5.3.2. The integration of immigrant ethnic minorities

There have been three basic European responses to the arrival of immigrant ethnic minorities in the post-1945 period. The first is that of assimilationism, which is most strongly affirmed in France. The second is German-speaking countries' *gastarbeiter* system, under which immigrant workers are denied political citizenship. The third is represented by a sort of multiculturalism commonly thought to be exemplified by Sweden, the Netherlands and the United Kingdom.

In Sweden, provision was explicitly made for ethnic minorities during the inception of the Welfare State. The problem facing Swedish government, however, was whom to choose to represent immigrant minorities. The government was accused of choosing traditional leaders, usually elderly men. Their critics, such as Carl-Ulrik Schierup and Aleksandra Alund (1990), argued that, in reality, younger members of these communities remained unrepresented. They also argued that the representatives tended to form cross-ethnic alliances and alliances with dissident Swedish youth, thereby creating new syncretic cultures.

The historical Dutch response to cultural diversity has been what is called *pillarization*. This was the establishment of separate educational systems, separate trade unions and separate media for Catholics and Protestants. This policy was extended to deal with ethnic minorities. One important critic of this policy, Jan Rath (1991), suggested, however, that the policy of so-called *'minorization'* by no means necessarily ensured that minorities would be subject to equal treatment. As he saw it, minorization could mean the singling out of those deemed minorities for unequal treatment.

In the United Kingdom, after a brief policy of assimilation in education in 1964, the government accepted the notion of *integration*. This was defined by the Home Secretary, Roy Jenkins, as 'not a flattening process of uniformity but cultural diversity, coupled with equal opportunity in an atmosphere of mutual tolerance' (Joppke, 1999, p. 225).

What is significant about this definition is that it dissociates itself from any forms of multiculturalism that permit the unequal treatment of minorities. In fact, it relates the notion of integration to Marshall's notion of social citizenship.

I have suggested that Jenkins' definition also suggests the existence of two cultural or institutional domains. On the one hand, there is a public political culture centred around the idea of a welfare state in which everyone has a minimum degree of equality. On the other, there are the separate cultures of the different ethnic communities, including of the host community. In each culture, community members speak their own language amongst themselves, practise their own religion and maintain their own family practices.

This, however, is only a general starting point for a definition of an egalitarian multicultural society. In practice, it raises many difficult questions and is contested by a number of different groups.

A first question is that of why separate communal cultures should continue to exist. Three lines of argument have been used in response. The first is that the distinct cultures should be allowed to exist since they may be intrinsically valuable. This is implied by the notion of mutual tolerance. The second is that they provide individuals with a moral and emotional home base, which is essential for their personal psychological stability. Emile Durkheim, in his classic work 'The Division of Labour' (1933), argued that such stability was only possible under conditions of organic solidarity if there were some collective unit between the individual family and the state. He thought that this might be achieved through the development of guilds. This is obviously unlikely in modern times but clearly ethnic minority groups can perform a similar role. This is true also for the members of the host society. Quite apart from their participation in the public political institutions of the welfare state, they too have their own culture and organizations in which they feel at home. The third reason for preserving ethno-cultural groups is that they allow collective, political action to protect their members.

5.3.3. Problems of the two domains thesis

Everything said so far provides only a starting point for an analysis of multiculturalism. We must now consider some of the problems in the two domains thesis. These include: problems within the educational system, the attempt to extend the values of the public political culture into the private communal sphere and the inverse claim that the values of the private communal cultures should be extended into to the public realm and, lastly the different issue of immigrant groups' degree of commitment or lack thereof to living in a host society and accepting its values.

5.3.3.1. The problem of multicultural education

The one institution that clearly straddles both the private and public spheres is the educational system. Here we can distinguish, with some oversimplification, between primary and secondary schools.

Primary schools share at least one function with families. Un-socialized babies are the barbarian invaders of the social system. They have to learn and accept a complex set of norms if they are to become full, social beings. These their parents teach them; later so do primary schools. In the primary schools, they also become bilingual. Ideally, they start to learn in their home language or dialect but they also have to learn the language of the host society and even use it as their main language at school.

In secondary education, students are prepared to enter a wider world governed by norms of a different kind. These norms involve individualism and competition, even though these may be tempered by or subjugated to some conception of common citizenship. Secondary school students are to be prepared for the world of work; besides learning relevant norms, they must also acquire skills.[3] One should now ask whether there is any place within schools for the perpetuation of different languages and cultures other than that of the host society.

One view, which has considerable currency in many countries, is that the perpetuation of these languages in schools increases students' self-esteem and enhances their performance. The view has been robustly criticized by a West Indian schoolteacher, Maureen

Stone (1985), in England. She argued that the relation between low self-esteem and poor performance had never been proven. She therefore believed that any supplementary education should be devoted to basic skills and not to education in different cultures. In saying this, she acknowledged that schools are concerned with the wider world and participation in the public realm. Another author, Jennifer Williams (1967), pointed out that where multicultural education was taught in schools, it was taught in the low-status, uncertificated parts of the syllabus. Despite these criticisms (or due to them) there have been some attempts in Britain to foster the study of minority languages and cultures in the high-status, certificated parts of the syllabus. Those who support such developments clearly favour the creation of a multicultural society in which a variety of cultural traditions is respected.

5.3.3.2. *The public and private domains reconsidered*

The sharp distinction between public and private domains, which was our starting point, is disputed from both sides. It is disputed by some who believe that there are certain values in the public sphere that apply or should apply in the private as well. Contrarily, there are those who believe that the privately held values of an ethnic community are also applicable and indeed found in the public domain. Furthermore, some immigrant ethnic communities are transnational in character and may have conflicting commitments or loyalties elsewhere.

Many Westerners who argue for extending the values of the public domain into the private sphere often do so in the name of human rights. For them, these rights go beyond the values of the Welfare State and suggest that our conception of the public sphere must itself be revised. This is particularly true of feminist claims. Host-society feminists reserve the right to decry the private family practices of immigrant communities. For example, they may suggest that women of certain communities are oppressed by their menfolk and that many are victims of arranged and forced marriages. Apologists for immigrant communities may reply to both accusations. They point out that the oppression of women is the product not of their culture *per se* but of the village practices that they bring with them. These they agree should be altered and they are prepared to co-operate in altering them. Furthermore, they defend what they are doing as protecting their women and children from a society which is sexually promiscuous and whose icons include the pornographic magazine and the sex shop. This could be, and sometimes is, a basis for dialogue with more sophisticated host-society feminists who recognize these problems from a feminist point of view. In so far as arranged marriages are concerned, some apologists argue that these need not and should not be forced and that the normal random mating practices of Western Europe are not necessarily preferable to arrangements in which the family of a bride frequently ensures that she is supported with a significant wedding gift. In modern conditions, this might involve a contribution towards the cost of a house or a car. Love, which Westerners claim is essential to marriage, is something that may be more lasting in arranged marriages than it commonly is in the West.

The opposite objection to the notion of two discrete domains comes from immigrant communities. Some would say that their culture must necessarily not be restricted simply to the private sphere. This is what many Muslims assert when they say that Islam is a whole way of life. That said, they sometimes see that the values of the Welfare State or those advocated in the name of human rights are integral to their own beliefs. If this is so, then we cannot simply regard the political culture of the public domain as purely secular. However, the same or similar values may be shared among different communities. The two domain thesis requires rethinking in order to leave open a space for dialogue.

In estimating the possibilities of minority communities' integration, we should also avoid the essentialist view that such cultures are unchanging and uniform. In fact, I have suggested they have three points of cultural reference. The first is to the homeland, which is itself undergoing change; the second is to the land of present settlement; and the third is to possible countries of onward migration. This raises the whole problem of the nature of transnational migrant communities, which I have discussed elsewhere (Rex, 1996). The host countries may modernize immigrant communities' perspectives and socio-political stances, since it is in their members' interest to fight for equality and equal treatment, even while being bound together by the use of their mother tongue amongst themselves and dealing with major lifetime events such as births, marriage and death in their own religious ceremonies. Furthermore, the communities themselves may not remain perfectly intact; some of the second, third and later generations may well 'defect' from their communities and culture and assimilate. All of these factors suggest that the problem of integrating immigrant communities may be a more temporary and simple one than many of the advocates and opponents of multiculturalism believe.

We have already seen that the culture and institutions of the public domain consist of more than equality guarantors in the Welfare State. The public domain's concord includes concepts of human rights, as we have seen, but it also includes everything implicit in participating in a modern economy and polity, including accepting its criminal and civil law.[4] This is something immigrants accept because it is essential to the migrant enterprise.

The next contentious area of the two domains thesis is the question of whether there exist some new, emergent and shared areas of private and civic life, where elements of non-native cultures have embedded themselves firmly in local mainstream society. The most obvious of these is cuisine. Chicken Tikka Masala is the most-purchased packed meal in British supermarkets and it is true that in all modern societies a shared interest in a new, international range of dishes has developed. Another, rather different, overlap occurs in literature in particular but probably most of the creative arts. Much contemporary highbrow and popular literature deals with many immigrant and multi-cultural problems. Similarly, music also obviously crosses borders. Obviously, there is a case for presuming a domain of shared culture. However, this does not necessarily mean that the separation between the domains discussed is non-existent or that shared cuisine and reciprocal creative arts necessarily foreshadow a new, shared mass culture.

Finally, we should notice that the emergence of some shared intermediary institutions in particular societies goes along with the globalization of culture, at least among elites.

5.4. Sub-National Societies and the Possibility of Devolution

5.4.1. *Sub-nationalism and the process of peaceful devolution*

Arguments about multiculturalism usually confuse the problems we have been discussing — those of the integration of immigrants and their descendents — with problems of a different kind. These are those of the place of sub-national units such as the Welsh, Scots and Irish in the UK or the Catalans and Basques in Spain. Besides these cases are the different issues faced by such bi-national states as Belgium and Canada. In each case, sub-national membership may be based either on linguistic, religious or cultural heritage or simply place of residence. Catalonian nationality is ascribed to all those who live in the Catalonian region; Scottish nationality and the right to vote in Scottish parliamentary elections is attributed to all those who live in Scotland. Slightly different situations occur in Belgium and Francophone Canada. In Belgium, Walloonia is French speaking and Flanders Flemish speaking, while Brussels is bilingual. Government at a national level is shared by the two groups, but is in the hands of the French speaking in Walloonia and Flemish speakers in Flanders. In Canada, claims of distinct nationhood are common in Quebec, the one province with a French-speaking majority, but not by other Francophones in Manitoba and some other provinces.

Devolution may involve the concession of more or fewer powers to the sub-nations. The greatest degree of devolution in the United Kingdom is accorded to Scotland with its Scottish Parliament, while the Welsh Assembly has far more limited powers. The situation in Catalonia is similar to Scotland's and in both cases the sub-federal government is subordinate to that in Madrid or London. In both cases as well as in places where devolution has been more limited, there are minority, secessionist parties (for a discussion of these cases, see Guibernau and Rex, 1997).

Similar problems are to be found in other parts of the present-day European Union. France, for instance, is contending with devolution in Corsica. Italy faces similar problems, both in dealing with its regions and the islands of Sicily and Sardinia. Greece has a problem with its island dependencies of Corfu and Crete and along its northern border with Macedonia and Thrace.

Moreover, there are devolution issues in some imminent entrants to the European Union, some of which also have border problems. This is true of the Czech Republic, Slovakia and Hungary, all of which have had to deal with devolution, and it is even more true of countries that might later join, such as Romania and Bulgaria. As well, among prospective entrants there are places like the Baltic Republics and Cyprus that are experiencing very special difficulties. In the Baltic republics, there are large Russian minorities, which used to be ruling minorities, whereas in the case of Cyprus the recognized Greek Cypriot territory will be required to have negotiated at least a loose federation with the unrecognized Turkish part of the island.

5.4.2. *The problem of incorporation into supranational units*

A new situation is arising with the emergence of supra-national units like the European Union. Now, regions may deal with the supra-national government directly. True, ultimate power in the EU lies with the Council of Ministers drawn from its central governments, but there are many ways in which the EU deals directly with the regions. This raises the possibility that radical groups in sub-federal territories may not simply seek secession from their own countries but may seek to turn the EU into a union of regions rather than of nation states.

The Soviet Union also had to deal with the problem of devolution and self-government. Although the Communist Party controlled the whole society, Soviet policy allowed varying degrees of autonomy among particular departments in different kinds of autonomous regions (Connor, Walker, 1994). Tartarstan represented a case in which a very workable type of cooperation was worked out between the regional and central Soviet government (Yemelianova, 1999). As in the West, however, there were a variety of political and religious groups who sought more independence; some of them had international bonds outside the Soviet Union.

5.4.3. *Cases of armed ethnic conflict*

In the cases discussed so far, we have been assuming that some degree of peaceful devolution is possible and that there are very few violent extremists. This, unfortunately, has not been the case with some Basques in Spain or Republicans in Northern Ireland. There, political parties have emerged which engage in violent armed struggle; members of those movements are deemed terrorists by the central governments concerned. Since the two hotspots share some similarities, it is not surprising that there have been contacts between the Basque separatist organization (ETA) and the Provisional IRA. Nonetheless, there are differences between the two cases. In Spain, the conflict is between one ethnic group and the Spanish state. In Northern Ireland, there are two ethnic groups in conflict with one another, one seeking the unification of Northern Ireland and the Irish Republic, the other professing loyalty to, and demanding continuing union with, the United Kingdom.

What the two groups have in common is their use of violence. Moreover, in both cases there is the problem of their relationship with parties that share their aims but oppose the use of violence. The relationship is a complex one in which moderate parties give some protection to the more radical and violent ones.

The Spanish government's response has been to take strong measures against violence but also to offer some degree of devolution. In the Northern Ireland case, the British government has had to use its own army to oppose two groups of paramilitaries, even though one fights in the name of loyalism. Not surprisingly, the British army is often accused of devoting most of its energies to fighting the republican paramilitaries. Here too there has been an offer of eventual devolution, but this has to follow the delicately and carefully constructed Peace Process.

5.4.4. Armed conflict in post-communist societies

This article is titled Multiculturalism and Political Integration in Modern Nation States. Thus far, however, we have referred only to one type of modern state, namely free- or mixed-market parliamentary democracies inclining towards some kind of welfare state. Communist countries represent another type of modern nation state. As we have seen, such states had dealt with the possibility of ethnic conflict relatively successfully until Communism as an economic and social system began to collapse in 1989. At this point, many groups sought secession from the state and engaged in violent conflict with the successor states and among one another.

The experience of the former Yugoslavia in this respect has been central to the study of ethnic conflict and the prospects of multiculturalism. Under Tito, Serbs, Croats, Bosnians, Montenegrins, Herzegovinians, Slovenians and Macedonians were held together by a federal Communist government, albeit through a subtle balancing of ethnic forces at local levels. With the collapse of Communism, however, ethnic groups warred amongst themselves, culminating in ethnic cleansing in Croatia and Bosnia-Herzegovina. The Bosnian and Kosovan wars led to outside intervention by the international community, which then sought to promote new constitutions based on some notion of multicultural balance. These new constitutions required outside force but the outside powers wanted to withdraw. It was easy enough to suggest new multicultural constitutions but harder to put them into practice. The various ethnic groups that were required to implement the new constitutions sat down at the conference table with their guns still smoking. Some of the problems involved were made explicit in The Kosovo Report (Independent International Commission on Kosovo, 2000), which recommended independence for Kosovo on condition that it becomes fully multicultural.

Less well known are the problems that have faced successively the Soviet Union, the Commonwealth of Independent States and the Russian Federation. There, the various ethnic political and religious groups that had always resisted the central (Moscow) government became able to pursue secessionist liberation struggles and were inevitably dubbed as terrorists by the central governments involved. The war in Chechnya is the best known of these conflicts but there were many others in Georgia, Azerbaijan and Armenia and in former Central Asian territories. Such conflicts involve complex alliances between religious sects and political parties, coupled with involvement or intervention from allies in neighbouring states (Yemenialova, 2001).

5.5. The Prospects of Multiculturalism after the American-Led War Against Terrorism

Following the September 11 attacks on New York and Washington, a new political climate emerged that was fearful of multiculturalism. The diversity of cultures, and Islam in particular, appeared to provide a base for more terrorist attacks.

An attempt was made by the United States to establish a coalition of nations against terrorism to destroy terrorist bases worldwide. Against this, there was little chance for those opposing this coalition to find a multicultural solution. Rather, they established their own international networks of opposition and regarded any party, sect, or nation not joining these networks as allies of the US-led coalition. The war against terrorism continued in 2002, thereby making the notion of tolerant and co-operative multiculturalism an impossible and unrealisable ideal, except in so far as the coalition or the international protest movements uses it to strengthen their own unity.

Within this framework, the United Kingdom's commitment to multiculturalism was weakened when it faced more local but violent conflicts between white natives and Asians in some northern cities and between local people and asylum seekers in Glasgow and other places. At the beginning of 2002, there was considerable confused debate amongst politicians and the press about the dangers of multiculturalism, which was identified with segregated forms of housing and education. There was a new emphasis on the importance of immigrants and their children to learn English as rapidly as possible and learning about the duties supposedly entailed by their British citizenship. Thus, whereas the United Kingdom had been a place where multiculturalism could be sympathetically discussed and shown to be compatible with a modern society and the welfare state, it was now seen as a danger. The predominant view now is one far more like the assimilationist French approach. In this new climate, any residual multiculturalism will have to be shown to be compatible with an essentially unitary society. Even if multi-culturalism as defended in this article is compatible with such a policy, it will be difficult for it to get a hearing.

5.6. Conclusion

This article has brought up a number of topics including nationalism
and devolution in West Europe, South-East Europe and countries of
the former Soviet Union as well as dealing with the settlement of
immigrant minorities, who do not make the same claims as sub-
nationalities do. It has been necessary to do this due to the nature of
the public debate, regardless of whether the discourse is sympathetic
or hostile to the multiculturalist idea. The article has recognized
throughout that national and immigrant minorities cannot be simply
the objects of policy determined and imposed from above. A viable
multicultural policy will be one that recognizes conflicts of ideas and
interests among different groups and shows the way in which such
conflict can lead to negotiation and compromise.

Notes

1   A version of this article first published in Spanish as 'Multiculturalismo
     e integración política en el Estado naciónal moderno', in *Isegoría: Revista
     de Filosofía Moral y Política*, No. 26, 6 June 2002, published by the Instituto
     de Filosofía of the Consejo Superior de Investigaciones Científicas, Madrid.
2   Of course there are a number of alternative types of Welfare State as Esping-
     Andersen has shown (Esping-Andersen, 1990), but the British version has
     been widely influential.
3   Secondary schools also clearly prepare their students for a socially-stratified
     world and the schools themselves may be stratified. In England, there has
     been prolonged debate about whether there should be a tripartite system of
     schools or whether all children should study in the same comprehensive
     schools. Similar arguments occur in other European countries, although the
     problem may be resolved in different ways there.
4   There are of course minorities, especially in Muslim communities, who
     would support schools preparing their students for living in a separate society
     and there are even those who would wish to find ways of applying Sharia law
     in domestic matters. It is to be doubted, however, whether even those who
     live in communities with these aims do not also adjust to living in a modern
     economy and polity for most of their lives.

References

Barry, B., *Culture and Equality: An Egalitarian Critique of Multiculturalism*
   (Cambridge: Polity Press, 1999).
Baubock, R., *Transnational Citizenship* (Aldershot: Edward Elgar, 1992).
Beveridge, W., *Full Employment in a Free Society* (London: G Allen, 1944).
Beveridge, W., *Social Insurance and Allied Services* (London: Her Majesty's
   Stationery Office, 1942).
Connor, W., *Ethnonationalism: The Quest for Understanding* (Princeton NJ:
   Princeton University Press, 1994).

Department of Employment and Productivity, In Place of Strife: A Policy for Industrial Relations, *Command Paper*, No. 3888 (London: Her Majesty's Stationery Office, 1969).

Durkheim, E., *The Division of Labour* (Glencoe, Illinois: Free Press, 1933).

Esping-Andersen, G., *The Three Worlds of Welfare Capitalism* (Cambridge: Polity Press, 1990).

Guibernau, M., J. Rex, *The Ethnicity Reader: Nationalism, Multiculturalism and Migration* (Cambridge: Polity Press, 1997).

Independent International Commission on Kosovo, *The Kosovo Report: Conflict, International Response, Lessons Learned* (Oxford: Oxford University Press, 2000).

Joppke, C., *Immigration and the Nation-State: The United States, Germany, and Great Britain* (Oxford: Oxford University Press, 1999).

Kymlicka, W., *Multicultural Citizenship* (Oxford: Oxford University Press, 1995).

Marshall, T., *Citizenship and Social Class* (Cambridge: Cambridge University Press, 1951).

Montagu, A., *Statement on Race: An Annotated Elaboration and Exposition of the Four Statements on Race Issued by the United Nations Educational, Scientific and Cultural Organisation*, Third Edition (Oxford: Oxford University Press, 1972).

Parekh, B., *Rethinking Multiculturalism: Cultural Diversity and Political Theory* (Cambridge, MA: Harvard University Press, 2000).

Radtke, F-O., 'The Formation of Ethnic Minorities and the Transformation of Social into Ethnic Conflicts in the So-called Multicultural Society — The German Case', in J. Rex, B. Drury (eds), *Ethnic Mobilisation in a Multicultural Europe* (Aldershot: Avebury, 1994), pp. 30–7.

Rath, J., 'Minosering: De Social Constructe van Ethnische Minderheden', Ph.D. Thesis, (Utrecht: University of Utrecht, 1991).

Rex, J., 'Review of Barry B.', *Innovation in Social Science*, Vol. 14, No. 3 (Abingdon, 2001), pp. 277–8.

Rex, J., *Ethnic Minorities in the Modern Nation State: Working Papers in the Theory of Multiculturalism* (Aldershot, New York: Macmillan and St Martin's Press, 1996).

Rex, J., *Key Problems in Sociological Theory* (London: Routledge and Paul Kegan, 1961).

Rex, J., S. Tomlinson, *Colonial Immigrants in a British City: A Class Analysis* (London: Routledge and Kegan Paul, 1979).

Runnymede Trust, 'The Future of Multi-ethnic Britain', *The Parekh Report* (London: Runnymede Trust, 2000).

Schierup, C-U., A. Alund, *Paradoxes of Multiculturalism* (Aldershot: Avebury, 1990).

Stone, M.,The Education of the Black Child: The Myth of Multicultural Education (London: Fontana Press, 1985).

Taylor, C., 'Multiculturalism and "The Politics of Recognition"', in A. Guttman (ed.), *Multiculturalism: Examining the Politics of Recognition* (Princeton NJ: Princeton University Press, 1994).

Walzer, M., D. Miller, *Pluralism Justice and Democracy* (Oxford: Oxford University Press, 1995).

Williams, J., 'The Young Generation', in J. Rex, R. Moore (eds), *Race Community and Conflict* (Oxford: Oxford University Press, 1967), pp. 230–57.

Yemenialova, G., 'Islam and Nation Building in Tatarstan and Dagestan', *Nationality Papers*, Vol. 27, No. 4 (Abingdon, Oxfordshire: Carfax Publishing, 1999), pp. 605–30.

Yemenialova, G., 'Sufism and Politics in the North Caucasus', *Nationality Papers*, Vol. 29, No. 4 (Abingdon, Oxfordshire: Carfax Publishing, 2001), pp. 661–88.

6
Politics and Policies of French Citizenship, Ethnic Minorities and the European Agenda

Christophe Bertossi

6.1. Introduction

There is a strong dispute amongst academics about the impact European institutional integration may have on classical nation-based models of democracy. This is a debate on the nation-state versus supranational or post-national paradigms. Moreover, the debate assumes that various nations' models of integration and citizenship feature stable characteristics (French Republicanism, British communitarianism, Dutch multiculturalism, German ethno-cultural nationalism, and so on).

I believe these two questions (of nation-state vs. its alternatives and various nations' models for integration and citizenship) have been mooted by the realities of contemporary Europe. That is, matters of citizenship are undergoing transformation in Europe. This goes beyond the nation-state and beyond cultural paradigms for the integration of migrants into particular European societies.

In order to clarify these perspectives, this chapter proposes an analytical understanding of the French citizenship policy, multiculturalism and the way politics and policy have been influenced by the European Union agenda. The chapter's main goal is to outline how far recent evolutions of the French agenda on those issues have fit in two main processes. One concerns ethnic and migrant mobilizations that have challenged the classical paradigm of French citizenship. The second is the import and adoption of 'pluralist' integration policies from other European societies. Such pluralism promotes anti-discrimination as a *sine qua non* for liberal, equality-based societies.

Before discussion about parallel developments in a criticism of French Republicanism's classical paradigms, it is important to understand the ideological and philosophical bases cited as the grounds of French democracy. From the description of the so-called model of citizenship *à la française*, I shall attempt to assess how much French policies have changed in the context of an integrated Europe.

6.2. Civic Integration and the Republic

French political policies of citizenship have been based exclusively on the principle of individuals' uniqueness. Ethnic, regional or religious categorizations have been ignored. *Only* individuals are citizens, citizens are *equal*, therefore *all* individuals are equal citizens. This syllogism has grounded French citizenship for the last two centuries.

How can the needs of ethno-cultural and religious diversity be accommodated by such an underlying notion of equality? Formally, the ideological scaffolding behind French citizenship provides a sharp solution: the transformation of individuals into citizens parallels the melting of cultural and religious 'identities' into the common national identity. As Clermont-Tonnerre famously stated: 'nothing to the Jew as a Jew, everything to the Jew as a citizen'. Republican legitimacy is therefore based on the primacy of civic individualism and national modernity (Leca, 1990; Bertossi, 2001).

This Republican understanding of citizenship is rooted in the 1789 French Revolution and its aftermath. It was enhanced by the nineteenth century's politics and policies on nationality and immigration, by which French citizenship became based on three principles at the end of the century: *ius sanguinis* in 1804 (blood right to citizenship), dual *ius soli* in 1851 (a conditional birthright[1] based on place of birth) and automatic *ius soli* in 1889 (simple birthright). The underlying philosophy that shapes these principles is that socialization in France, through school, trade unions, associations, and/or the military service, leads to one's full-fledged integration into the national/civic *habitus* that embodies French citizenship. This ideology concerns foreigners, but not exclusively so. As Eugen Weber shows, it also dealt with the transformation of peasants into Frenchmen (Weber, 1976).

However, there has never been a stable and permanent republican structure in France's modern history. The rights of citizenship and nationality have not always been equated. During the colonial period, for example, nationality was not synonymous with citizenship. Specific colonial statuses were created, such as 'French colonial nationals' and the implementation of a second electoral body in Algeria (reserved for Muslims).

That said, formal nationality was not a precondition for full-fledged citizenship during the process of suffrage extension. Until 1848, suffrage was based on mental capacity and tax quotas. Similarly, women were not entitled to vote until 1945, nor could youths under 21 until 1974 (when voting age was lowered to 18). What is also striking in regard to the formal Republican ideology is that, from the very end of the nineteenth century on, new French nationals were not becoming new citizens at once. They had to wait five years before getting the right to vote and ten years for eligibility to become a citizen. This 'dual naturalization' was phased out in 1973 (right to vote) and 1983 (eligibility).

It is also important to consider that the political heritage of 1789 was suspended between 1940 and 1944 by Pétain's *Révolution Nationale* and the Regime of Vichy. Nationality was restrictively manipulated. More than 15,000 French citizens had their French nationality nullified during the period. This affected mostly French Jews (about 6000) (Weil and Hansen, 1999). French nationals who fled from France in 1940 (between 20 May and 30 June) without authorization had their nationality revoked (Act of 23 July 1940). At the end of World War II, the Vichy's regime was abolished and new legislation reinstated the main principles of the nineteenth century Republican doctrine.

In the 1950s through the 1970s, immigration was used to cope with a labour shortage until borders were closed in 1974. Since then, the supposition that migrants would return to their country of origin paralleled the refusal to come to terms with ethnic minorities' settlement. The issue of citizenship re-emerged in this context with the mid-1970s economic crisis. Immigration became a public issue. In turn, the very notion of French 'nationhood' was deliberated.

6.3. The 'Problem' of Nationality in the 1980s

As a result, integration was reconceived in the mid-1980s (Feldblum, 1999) as a modernization of the old-fashioned concept of French assimilationism. The debate focused on tolerance towards new-comers' non-European and non-Christian cultural backgrounds. This was embedded in the post-colonial context and the establishment of permanent communities of the non-French.

In the early 1980s, France's post-colonial heritage was reassessed. This mostly concerned Algeria. Algerian independence in 1962 sounded the death knell for the myth of a universalistic French nation. Despite the colonial dichotomy between French citizens and Muslim subjects, Algeria had been integrated into metropolitan France as part of one of three *départements*, namely the metropolitan territorial one, considered to be integral to France. The so-called civic definition of the French nation, which was to be reproduced overseas, failed with the Algerian war of independence (1954–62).

Meanwhile, former colonial subjects became migrant workers. By virtue of the right to family reunification, they started to settle. By the 1980s, they had become part of the political agenda (immigration as a public issue) and the polity (their children having become French nationals by birth). This led to a reassessment of national identity as a condition for citizenship. At the same time, Muslims began to become 'visible' in the public realm (automotive industry strikes in 1983, demands for the construction of places of worship, and so on) (Kepel, 1991). Islam became France's second religion. Subsequently, the boundary between 'one's own' and the 'Other' got blurred: post-colonial migrants and their descendents have settled in metropolitan France, are entitled to the rights of citizenship and have become French nationals. But in contrast, those newcomers, and particularly the Algerians, are politically and socially perceived as *foreign migrants* despite their nationality status.

A new polemic occurred under the same premise by which newcomers did not have what it takes to become 'genuine' citizens. They were seen as being unable or unwilling to accept the burdens of citizenship (obligations in general, but more precisely 'cultural' integration). They were suspected of only claiming French citizenship to reap its benefits. In that perspective, new French nationals were referred to as 'French of papers' or 'French for the papers'. Strongly influenced by the extreme rightwing National Front party, this debate generated a broad consensus on this perspective. It became the core issue of France's mid-1980s political agenda.

6.4. The 1986 Project and the Commission of Nationality

This situation paved the way for reforming the French nationality Code. The reform was carried out by the right-wing government freshly elected in 1986. The project aimed to replace automatic access to French nationality (Article 44 of the Code) by a declaration of will (*manifestion de volonté*). This alluded directly to the claim that new citizens were bogus nationals. The consequences of de-colonization on nationality rules were also addressed: dual *ius soli*

(Article 23 of the Code) was challenged, essentially regarding children from Algerian origins (assessed by the Code as children born in France from foreign parents who were born in France too, Algeria having been part of France before 1962).

However, this first attempt to reform the French nationality Code faced important opposition from groups supporting 'the right to (cultural) difference' (Wihtol de Wenden and Leveau, 2001; Feldblum, 1999). A new generation of associations and groups emerged as a result of foreigners' freedom of association guaranteed by law in October 1981. Associations such as SOS Racisme and France Plus were created in 1983–84. They launched nationwide rallies (*Marche des Beurs* in 1983, 1984 and 1985), inspired by the 1960s Black American civil rights movements.

Parts of the government project were challenged by the Council of State, for they clashed with the Constitution as well as its incorporated Declaration of the Rights of Man and the Citizen. In response, the Prime Minister launched a Commission of Nationality to stem the opposition to the project. Between 1987 and 1988, the Commission undertook public hearings and investigated the under-studied social aspects of migrants' settlement, family reunification, schooling, housing, and policies of nationality and immigration.

Results were published in a two-volume report, entitled 'To Be French Today and Tomorrow' [sic] (Long, 1988). The report defined and crystallized the notion of national integration. This notion met with huge consensus across the political spectrum (except the National Front) and society. It also represented the starting point for an extensive new academic literature on the issues of immigration, citizenship and national identity (Costa-Lascoux, 1989; Etienne, 1989; Schnapper, 1991; Weil, 1991).

Republican ideology was re-focused on a comprehensive basis: national integration, dissolution of minorities into the would-be socio-cultural 'mainstream', relegation of any cultural or religious difference into the private sphere, loyalty and allegiance perceived as *sine qua non* for citizenship. Consequently, French citizenship was re-invented while strict republican features were strengthened and legitimated (opposition between the political and the social, the public and the private, cohesion and diversity, national identity vs. 'others').

The headscarf affair occurred in this context in 1989 when three Muslim schoolgirls refused to take off their *hidjab* in class. Islam was then denounced as a danger towards national identity as the bicentennial of the French revolution was celebrated. The issue of a religious 'threat' to the republican contract was intensified by groups of Christian integrists setting fire to cinemas where Scorcese's *Last Temptation of the Christ* was being screened.

6.5. The 1993 Reform

In this broad drama about French national identity, the reform of the nationality code was finally implemented in 1993 by a newly elected right-wing government. Unlike the 1986 attempt, the 1993 reform did not face any strong resistance. It replaced Article 44 (automatic *ius soli*) with the Manifestation of Will (Article 21–7 of the New Civil Code). From then on, children who were born in France of foreign parents had to declare their will to become French between the age of 16 and 21. Moreover, young people were deprived of that right if they had been sentenced to over six months in prison.

Aside from this restrictive reform of French legal citizenship, the redefinition of integration has had a social cost. The crystallization of national/civic integration in the 1980s–90s was mainly based on conservative Republican philosophy. Namely, it was assumed that being a French national was a sufficient guarantee for fully-fledged citizenship. In these terms, the very notions of discrimination, inequality of opportunity or belonging in the mainstream society were not regarded as legitimate issues for the 'Republican Pact'. On the one hand, there the pact posited that there was no such thing as 'ethnic minorities' in France. On the other, legal equality was equated with full and actual equality. Thus, it was claimed that discrimination did not exist in France. The civic integration's creed was clearly aimed at non-Europeans and non-Christians and the way they could be accommodated. It is striking that the whole debate focused on the Muslim population in general and Algerians in particular, whereas the most common foreign nationality was (and still is) Portuguese.[2] Cultural and religious differences were therefore centre stage of the debate. The issue of controlling immigration flows paralleled this cultural row (the 1993 Immigration Law was passed one month after the Law on Nationality). This sensitive combination appeared clearly in the justification of the new nationality law by one of its instigators:

> I will add — and I know everyone here does think about it — that Islam is not only a religion, but a real rule for social, judicial, philosophical and economic life, which is opposed to our own conceptions, as well as to our own legal principles. Islam — and

I think especially about the threat of fundamentalism — refuses, we have to say, adhesion to our own society. ... Yesterday from European origin, the foreign population is largely from non-European origin today. ... [W]e will face new situations, and integration, again, is more difficult today, because — we have to say this — more and more aliens living in France come from countries which are different than the countries from which they were used to come in the past (Assemblée Nationale, 1993, pp. 347–8).

What is striking is how far the ostensive push for integration became a counter-integrative programme in that perspective. It challenged equality of membership, and therefore of rights, of French *citizens* who were perceived as 'difficult' to accommodate. A report on xenophobia in France in 1995 emphasized the extent of discrimination and the way the latter was legitimated by the new legislation on nationality and immigration (UNCHR, 1996, p. 4).

Despite this, the dominant ideology on citizenship still framed social policies and most of the academic literature until the end of the 1990s. Even when a new discrimination-aware policy emerged in the early 1990s, it faced severe resistance. A survey published in 1991 identified discrimination in two main domains: employment and housing (Tribalat, 1991; 1995). However, there was no statistical tool for researchers and policy-makers to measure the precise nature or extent of discrimination (the census only referred to nationality without any mention of ethnic, cultural or religious backgrounds). The issue of ethnic minorities' access to employment was mostly explained, *inter-alia*, within the mainstream unemployment patterns (Hessel et al., 1988; Haut Conseil à l'Intégration, 1993).

6.6. The Pluralist Challenge to Integration

In such radical developments in the political debate surrounding French citizenship, the very notion of membership in an equality-based society was at issue. Associations of migrants and their children expressed their deep criticism. Issues of equality, identity, democracy, human rights and, moreover, of a citizenship by residency without regard to ethnicity, became tools used by a new generation of migrants' associations for challenging 'integration'.

The anti-nationalist protest movement of the 1980s transformed into a more local and less ambitious movement at the end of the decade (Wihtol de Wenden and Leveau, 2001). New attitudes towards citizenship emerged from this shift in methodology and programme.

A particular group of associations emphasized the notion of 'new citizenship' (Bouamama, 1992). 'New citizenship' values individuals' active commitment to their local environment, rejecting the 'soft' civic attitude of the mainstream population. Broadly speaking, citizenship is considered within the framework of *local* everyday life. As an association leader of Algerian origin puts it:

> Some people do not have French nationality, and yet they may be much more 'citizen-like' than a lot of French natives who are nationals by descent ... They are citizens because they participate in the local social life; because they are militant; because they make associations working for the interest of all; because they are aware of the general interest; because they defend their city with more conviction than the natives do (quoted in Bertossi 2001, p. 202).

Other associations of the non-ethnically French developed the idea by which 'we are from this country, our nationality regardless. Same duties, same rights' (Wihtol de Wenden and Leveau, 1996). All these different critics focused on a key-claim: a citizenship logic must replace a perspective based on nationality and civic/national integration.

One main criticism of national citizenship focused on national identity as a destroyer of cultural differences (and thus as a challenge to democracy), with particular attention to the post-colonial context. Parallel to these statements, Muslims started to initiate another mobilization in the middle of the 1990s, setting up a new agenda: reconciliation between Islam and the Republic, and establishing that Muslims are a full-fledge component of the 'Republican Pact' (Cesari, 1998; Bertossi, 2001, pp. 210–7; see also Ramadan, 1999). The slogan 'Muslim citizens' sums up this new attitude, for 'citizenship is broader than nationality' (*La Medina*, 2000, p. 41). Particularly among some Muslim youth, promotion of the European level is seen as a relevant strategy to bypass the nation-state. Europe is thus seen as a prospect for Islam in France.

6.7. European Citizenship and French Jacobinism

Another challenge to French national Republicanism can be seen in the emergence of a European framework for citizenship. The

European framework stands in opposition to two pillars of French republicanism: the latter's refusal to politically acknowledge cultural diversity in the country as well as the centralized nature of the French state and its denial of possible pluralistic forms (for example regionalism). The close relationship between citizenship and nationality in the French model has been profoundly challenged by the emergence of EU citizenship.

So far, even local (municipal) citizenship for foreign nationals could not possibly fit into the Republican doctrine. Yet this right to local vote was one of the 110 propositions made by François Mitterrand in the 1981 presidential election campaign. This project only reappeared on the political agenda twenty years later, when the National Assembly discussed it in 2000 (without implementing it).

Alternative attempts to bring foreign nationals into local affairs took place in some cities in the 1980s. As early as the mid-1970s, local consultative councils for foreigners were created in Marly and Valenciennes, inspired by similar experiences in Germany, Belgium and the Netherlands. In Mons-en-Baroeul, 'immigrants' were invited to take part in a referendum on the city council's financial issues. In 1985, the city council held an election of 'foreign associate councillors'. In 1987, a similar vote took place in Amiens. Between 1989 and 1992, five other municipalities followed that line of 'associative democracy' (Cerizay, Longjumeau, Les Ullis, Vandoeuvre-Lès-Nancy and Portes-Lès-Valences).

However, these experiments remained on the fringes of legality. What is even more striking is that migrants associations did not reach a clear consensus on the issue. For organizations such as France Plus, any dissociation between nationality and citizenship was understood as too much a sensitive issue. During the 1989 presidential election, its president argued that it was 'dangerous' to give foreigners the local right to vote because it would exacerbate French natives' xenophobic attitudes towards 'migrants' (Arezki Dahmani quoted in Césari 1995, p. 202).

Municipal suffrage for foreign nationals, however, did not arise from national political debate. It has clearly been granted from outside the domestic French political arena, that is from the European development of a EU citizenship.

Article 8 of the Treaty of Maastricht (1992) institutes a residency-based European citizenship at local and supranational level. Whereas Article 8 B-2 (EU citizenship at the European level) remains oddly above the issue of distributing specific political rights to foreign nationals in France, Article 8 B-1 (EU citizenship at the local level), however, is at odds with the Republican constitutional definition of French citizenship (Article 3 and 4 of the 1958 Constitution).

Consequently, on the 3 April 1992, the Constitutional Council ruled that Article 8 B-1 contradicted the French Constitution. Two issues were outlined: firstly, that city councillors participate in national governance and sovereignty insofar as they elect Senators (members of the upper chamber of the French parliament). Secondly, that mayors and deputy mayors act 'in the name of the French people'. Consequently they are to be considered as local agents of national sovereignty. Hence, Article 8 B-1 of the Treaty must be interpreted under this dual restriction: European foreign nationals living in France can have the right to vote and to run in municipal elections, but they cannot be elected as mayors or deputy mayors. When they are city councillors, they cannot vote in senatorial elections (Constitutional Act, 25 June 1995).

Because of these limits, the incorporation of Article 8 of the Treaty of Maastricht was postponed (French declaration to the Council, 24 October 1994). European nationals only got local citizenship in the 2001 municipal elections. However, their voter participation was extremely low (8 per cent nationally). Of over 80,000 city councillors in France (for cities of more than 3500 inhabitants), just 204 European foreigners have been elected. (Notably, 17 Germans, 21 Belgians, 23 Spaniards, 28 Italians, 83 Portuguese, and 16 British have been elected) (*Lettre de la citoyenneté*, 2001). Given this new institutional framework for addressing municipal dissociation between citizenship and nationality, new attempts to promote citizenship by residency have started to emerge. So far, none has been implemented. However, new initiatives of 'associative democracy' have been undertaken in cities such as Strasbourg (1999) and Paris (2001).

6.8. Anti-Discrimination: Core Value of European Citizenship

However, new paradigms of membership in Europe come into play in a less institutional understanding of the notion of citizenship. This perspective goes beyond a possible dissociation between nationality and citizenship. There is a clear trend towards building a European identity, recognizing and inclusive of migrants and multi-ethnicity. Respect for ethno-cultural diversity, religious pluralism, and the fight against all sorts of racism, xenophobia, anti-Semitism, sexism, and so on, are likely to become core values of new models. In so doing, the classical boundary between public and private realms changes.

As a result, anti-discrimination becomes a central *public* issue in which modern definitions of membership in an equality-based society are now possible.

European institutions have acted against racism and xenophobia since the 1980s. The Commission, the Council and the Parliament made a common declaration on that subject in 1986. From the 1990s onwards, numerous resolutions have been passed citing 'respect of human beings' dignity' and the elimination of all forms of discrimination. In 1996, the European Union adopted a joint action to combat racism and xenophobia. This led to the 1997 establishment of the European Monitoring Centre on Racism and Xenophobia in Vienna (EUMC), which opened in April 2000.

Moreover, in 1997, the Treaty of Amsterdam introduced new provisions in EU treaties that address discrimination directly. Article 13 concerns discrimination on the ground of race and ethnic origin, religion and beliefs, sex, disability, age or sexual orientation. The Article supplements existing powers (Article 141 against gender discrimination, Article 137 on exclusion from the labour market). Similarly, the scope of Article 12 (concerning discrimination based on nationality) may be extended after the introduction of the new Title IV[3] (Niessen, 2001, p. 7).

On the basis of Article 13, the Commission adopted a set of proposals leading to two directives: the Council directive implementing the principle of equal treatment irrespective of a person's racial or ethnic origin and the Council directive establishing a general framework for employment equality. The first directive must be incorporated into member states' laws before the 19 July 2003.

6.9. Importing the Anti-Discrimination Agenda

A new argument in the citizenship debate, combining this new European agenda with the strong criticism on French Republicanism initiated by ethnic minorities in France, has been voiced in France since 1997. The hypothesis that legal citizenship does not guarantee substantial equality and that discrimination must be addressed by corrective policy has gained a stronger legitimacy.

However, addressing discrimination is not an easy line for French legal doctrine. As Marie-Thérèse Lanquetin shows:

> The principle of equality is the ground of the French juridical system; the principle of discrimination is not. And yet equality and discrimination are not two sides of a the same coin. Actually, every

difference of treatment, every inequality, does not constitute discrimination. They become so only if they are illegitimate. Discrimination is an arbitrary, illegitimate and outlawed difference (Groupe d'Etude et de Lutte contre les Discrimination, 2000b, p. 12).

The aim of the 1996 Council of State's annual report was to agree on a definition of equality in connection with the issue of discrimination. The authors suggest it is necessary to favour equality in a differentialist perspective, called 'reverse discrimination' (*'discrimination justifiée'*). This new legitimacy regarding differentiated treatment in order to achieve equity breaks the logic of Article 1 of the 1958 Constitution, which professes 'equality in law for all citizens without any distinction based on origin, race, or religion'. In short:

Being the basis of the juridical order in a society, the principle of equality is threatened when new and serious inequalities expand in a society. ... When ties [between individuals and society] become fragile or even broken [because of discrimination], the equality of rights seems to be a mere formal petition. Hence, the credibility of the principle of equality is more at stake in regard to equal opportunities (Conseil d'Etat, 1997, p. 45).

This new line logically paves the way for re-conceiving the notion of integration. Citizenship is, therefore, profoundly redefined. The first step is to *de-legitimise* the radical republican notion of national integration. National belonging can no longer be a condition for equality. There is a trend to consider citizenship as something distinct from nationality, as well as from loyalty or allegiance to the French polity. The second step is to *re-legitimise* the notion of citizenship in providing a new niche for ethnic minorities in France. Ethnic minorities must have a place in the Republic.

However, strong controversy still holds back this revisited conception of citizenship. For example, in 1998, a polemic occurred among scholars about statistical tools for apprehending the reality of ethnic minorities in France. Proponents of such a perspective claimed that there was an urgent need for public knowledge on this issue. Opponents claimed that it was a counter-revolutionary way that contradicted the very principles of the Republic (Tripier, 1999).

6.10. New French Politics of Citizenship: 1997–2002

On the 21 of April 1997, President Jacques Chirac dissolved the National Assembly. General elections were won by a left-wing coalition and a new government was established, led by Lionel Jospin. Somehow, that opened the way for a renewal of the question of migrants' and minorities' citizenship-cum-integration.

After the populist wave of the 1980s, the debate on French citizenship has been considerably de-dramatized. In terms of nationality law, a 1998 reform re-enacted the automatic birth right to citizenship (former Article 44) and revoked the Manifestation of Will (Weil, 1997). Dual *ius soli* was also restored even if not to its full extent.

But more importantly, the focus of the French citizenship policy has sharply shifted. Integration has yielded ground to another central issue: the struggle against discrimination.

From these French dilemmas, a new policy of integration was launched by the Socialist government in 1998 after the dissolution of the National Assembly in 1997. The Ministry of Employment and Solidarity enjoyed considerable importance in the new cabinet. Its minister, Martine Aubry, took the initiative of transferring the new doctrine on equality into public policy.

On the 21 October 1998, she made a statement on 'the policy of integration' in cabinet. This was the first time such a statement on integration was given at this level of the state since 1991. The minister set up a threefold programme: improving the reception of newcomers and the atmosphere of tolerance towards them; fighting against discrimination on the basis of a renewed conception of equality and facilitating the acquisition of French nationality.

On the 11 May 1999, a round-table meeting was held at the Ministry for Employment and Solidarity, bringing together the minister, trade unions and employers' organizations. They endorsed a joint declaration on racial discrimination in employment.[4] Five orientations on a new policy against discrimination were discussed with social partners: compiling a national resource on discrimination in France in order to better tackle it; training public servants and corporations on the issue; developing youth sponsorships to help them find jobs; grounding anti-discriminatory policies in an urban policies framework and expanding the existing legislation on discrimination.

The setting-up of a new anti-discrimination policy framework followed an inquiry into whether a specific administrative authority should be introduced or if the existing framework should be used and extended to fight racial discrimination. In his report of 6 April 1999, Jean-Michel Belorgey (a member of the Council of State) recommended the creation of a new authority similar to the British Commission for Racial Equality (Belorgey, 1999). However, this recommendation was not implemented. Instead, a new apparatus was set up combining three different institutions and services and has been in operation since 2000.

A hotline (called 114): created by the Ministry for Employment (Direction of Population and Migration) in May 2000. Its task is to receive calls from discrimination victims. This service refers people case by case for further action. Calls are registered on a document that is transmitted to the *Commissions Départementales d'Accès à la Citoyenneté* (CODAC). The 114 hotline is also a means for identifying the places where discrimination occurs. The *Groupe d'Etude et de Lutte contre les Discriminations* (GELD) analyses the resulting data.

The GELD: created by the Ministry for Employment in October 1999. Its mission is to analyse the extent of discrimination and the groups it concerns (foreigners, French nationals of foreign origin, French over-seas citizens, and so on). The GELD advises the government on public policies. It has published three reports since 1999, namely on: discrimination on the basis of nationality in the labour market; the onus of proof in a case of discrimination; discrimination in housing (GELD, 2000a; 2000b; 2001).

CODACs: created by the Ministry of the Interior in February 1999. They exist in every French *département* (however, some may have more than one) and are chaired by the Préfet (local representative of the central administration) on a quarterly basis. They may encourage people who dialled the 114 hotline to pursue further court action against the perpetuators of discrimination.

Eventually, the French Parliament incorporated the European Council directive on anti-discrimination in employment (EU Directive, 2000/43/CE). In November 2001, the Parliament passed a new law expanding the scope of anti-discriminatory provisions. First, the onus of proof in discrimination cases is to be shared between employer and employee. Second, the scope of anti-discrimination provisions in the labour legislation (Article 122–45, *Code du Travail*) is extended. So far, discrimination is only actionable in cases of employment and redundancy. The new text extends it to wages, promotion, transfer and mobility, training, and so on. Third, new types of discrimination are incorporated:

discrimination based on phenotype, name and sexual orientation (Law of 16 November 2001).

6.11. Equality of Opportunity: a New Perspective on Integration

At the very beginning of the 1980s, the election of François Mitterrand as President of the Republic created a strong expectation for changes in the way migrants were perceived and treated. The promise of municipal suffrage for foreigners symbolized the hope of reconciliation between the interests of immigration, ethno-cultural diversity and the nation-state.

At the beginning of the 2000s, new hope seems warranted on the central concern of incorporating migration and multiculturalism into citizenhood. Compared to the situation 20 years ago, it is clear that the political opportunities are considerably more favourable. Emerging models of citizenship in the European Union provide strong precedents for reassessments of national citizenship. Policies have shifted their bases from nationality to citizenship in terms of equal rights, from integration to anti-discrimination, from strict national understandings to European perspectives.

How far may France's citizenship policies go beyond the radical Republicanism experienced in the last two decades? The question is unanswerable for there is no clear evidence that the new policy framework will definitely and swiftly get rid of the legacy of republicanesque citizenship. Strong resistance in the administrational and the constitutional apparatus remains a sharp obstacle for reaching a real multicultural citizenship in France.[5]

That said, a big first step has been clearly made. The notion of integration is not relevant anymore in the policy-making process. The Minister of Employment declared in October 2000 to French Deputies that:

> For migrants' children, the second or third generation, the problem is not a problem of integration anymore. Let us stop asking them to integrate; they are already culturally integrated. They even have invented the cultural trends of our youth. They share the values of our society. They accept the rules of life, but they do not succeed, or they do so with more difficulties than others, in integrating socially, economically ... It is true that some of them do not respect the duties of citizenship. If nothing does justify these attitudes, however, one must try to explain them. For all those [children], speaking about a policy of integration is obsolete, and, to be

honest, outside the problem. The genuine solution stands in the implementation of a policy guaranteeing to everyone an equal access to fundamental rights and implementing specific actions against discrimination (Assemblée Nationale, 2000, p. 6765).

This is of prime importance for the future of the citizenship debate. It may be a starting point for reversing the Republican logic and moving from nationality to citizenship. The new dichotomy used by policy-makers does not create a distinction between 'culturally legitimate citizens' and 'bogus nationals', but rather 'citizens discriminated against' versus 'fully-fledged citizens'. Citizenship is not an issue of ethnicity or national belonging. Similarly, it is not an issue of formal or legal equality, but rather a challenge for making equality substantial and concrete. The change in the public lexicography is essential even if this programme is still limited.

The second foreseeable step may be a consequence of this re-orientation of the notion of integration/equality. It may provide a new niche for the recognition of ethnic minorities as such. Because of the over-loaded legacy of French Republicanism, the issue of recognition is as important as policies of wealth distribution and Welfare. By the same token, at the end of the day, it is recognized that there are 'invisible' people in France for whom citizenship is not a given. As an associative leader interviewed by J.-M. Belorgey stressed: 'I prefer discrimination to integration! When I am discriminated against, at least, that means that one knows I exist' (Belorgey, 1999, p. 45).

Hence, beyond the ethnic ambiguity of French policy (de Rudder et al., 2000; Schain, 1999; Hargreaves, 1995), new narratives may now legitimize cultural pluralism and identities. This is a direct import from the European agenda into French policy.

Finally, a further step appears to be the most critical. It concerns the taboo about post-national membership. All the French paradigm of equality has been sustained by the belief that the nation was the epitomized democracy. The side effects of nationalist citizenship policies between the mid-1980s and the mid-1990s have had a dramatic impact on the credibility of this tenet. As a result, racial discrimination and national discrimination tend to merge as a single issue (illegitimate inequality) in the European context (for an analytical approach of this, see Bertossi, 2001). It is no accident that the first report of the GELD addressed the issue of discrimination on the basis of nationality in the labour market (GELD, 2000a).[6]

Where to go from there? The last presidential election has blurred the alternatives. On the 21 April 2002, Jean-Marie Le Pen acceded to the second round of this election. This has had deep consequences on the new agenda developed by the new right-wing government, namely the merging of integration and citizenship with security and public order issues. This success of the French far right fits in a wider context: Austria, the Netherlands, Switzerland, Denmark, Belgium and Italy have seen similar developments. The European context has consequently changed. That leads to a sharp contradiction between an emerging policy problematic regarding citizenship, promoted by EU institutions and subsequently implemented in the member states, and the very national policy agenda that considers diversity as a threat to cohesion. Myriam Feldblum locates the parallel rise of post-national and neo-national politics as two elements of the same reality (Feldblum, 1998).

However, the question is now whether this divide only concerns political struggle and change in power (including the influence of the far right on those issues), or if it will become a feature of European integration, opposing national and European levels. Despite this cause for concern, I would still argue that the question of citizenship has critically shifted in Europe, showing the politics of identity have not, in any case, the same scale of opportunity that they had in the 1980s. It may appear as a path dependency on which the future of EU citizenship will depend, especially while it is part of the *acquis communautaire* and will remain an issue of the enlargement of the Union.

6.12. Conclusion

I have shown how far the re-definition of equality through the pluralist challenge and the European agenda on citizenship has led to new public doctrine and citizenship policies in France.

One the one hand, citizenship is no longer reduced to a narrow legal or formal equality of rights. Rather, it is now assumed as a broader societal issue in which the notion of equality of opportunity is at centre stage. On the other hand, national identity is not assumed as the relevant resource for achieving equality of membership. Nationality has been de-emphasized and cannot be found on any new populist agenda anymore. The 1980s national drama on France's identity is over.

However, despite this profound shift in integration policies over the last decade, the transition to a pluralistic understanding of citizenship in France remains extremely fragile. Strong resistance to the new agenda on anti-discrimination and the recognition of ethnic minorities remains. Tolerance towards diversity is still weak, be it in the public sphere or in institutional apparatuses. Administrations show limited acceptance of the new views on equal opportunity. In France, there has been no consensus on citizenhood that could possibly ground an in-depth pluralistic society. The legacy of Jacobin ideology, even if deeply challenged by ethnic minorities and the European Union, continues to make sense to mainstream society.

Moreover, beyond the limits and the weakness of new French policies, uncertainties arise through a much more worrisome process. Opposed to the perspective of a plural citizenship, a counter-agenda is emerging in Europe that crystallizes citizenship around issues of cohesion and security. This trend appears as a 'revenge' of Republicanism on pluralistic forms of citizenship in Europe. Civic virtues, national cohesion, welfare and nationalism become broadly held values whereas immigration is re-assessed as *the* societal problem in Europe.

But for all that, anti-discrimination policies are likely to become a common denominator in Europe. As such, it may be the nexus of an emerging common citizenship framework in Europe, subsuming the so-called 'national models' of citizenship. Such negotiation of the meaning of citizenship is part of the European identity-defining process. This may represent what makes the French example so relevant, in the way such a shift has occurred during only the past ten years.

Notes

1   The principle of dual birthright supposes that children born in France of 'foreign' parents who were born in France themselves become French automatically.

2   According to the 1999 Census, 553,663 Portuguese nationals live in France (17 per cent of the foreign population), compared to 504,096 Moroccans (15.5 per cent), 477,482 Algerians (14.6 per cent) and 154,356 Tunisians nationals (4.7 per cent). The foreign population is 3,263,186 or 5.57 per cent of the whole population of France (data from the National Institute for Statistical and Economic Studies, 2001).

3   Namely on visas, asylum, immigration and other policies related to free movement of persons. The Presidency Conclusions of the Tampere European Council (1999) opened the way for new expectations regarding fair treatment of third-country nationals and the extension of their rights of citizenship.

4   This declaration is available on
     www.social.gouv.fr/htm/pointsur/discrimination/dec.htm.

5   Such constraints may be found for example in the government's attempt to ratify the 1992 *Charter on Minority and Regional Languages* of the Council of Europe or on the new Statute of Corsica, debated by the Constitutional Council in January 2002.

6   The GELD inventoried in 1999 the professions for which French nationality was a condition. Belorgey's (1999) unpublished report already insisted on the necessity to find new perspectives concerning public or semi-public jobs (that is for national enterprises or services such as national insurance). Some statute professions of the private sector still discriminate against non-nationals (for example: architects, news agents, solicitors and chartered surveyors). In 1991, the recruitment in public services has been liberalised for EU nationals, insofar as those jobs do not bear on national sovereignty. In April 2001, the Information and Support for Migrants Group (GISTI) launched a new campaign on the topic, emphasizing that nationality-based employment discrimination affected one third of the whole employment supply (about seven million jobs).

References

Assemblée Nationale, 'Débats parlementaires', *Journal Officiel de la République française* (13 October 2000).

Assemblée Nationale, 'Débats parlementaires', *Journal Officiel de la République française* (11 May 1993).

Belorgey, J-M., *Lutter contre les discriminations. Rapport à Madame la Ministre de l'Emploi et de la solidarité* (Paris: Ministère de l'Emploi et de la solidarité, 1999), available at www.social.gouv.fr.

Bertossi, C., *Les Frontières de la citoyenneté en Europe. Nationalité, résidence, appartenance* (Paris: L'Harmattan, Collection Logiques Politiques, 2001).

Bouamama, S., *L'ambiguité laïque. Vers une nouvelle citoyenneté. Crise de la pensée laïque* (Lille: Boite de Pandore, 1992).

Bruschi, C., 'Droit de la nationalité et égalité des droits de 1789 à la fin du XIX siècle', in S. Laacher (ed.), *Questions de nationalité. Histoire et enjeux d'un code* (Paris: CIEMI-L'Harmattan, 1987), pp. 12–59.

Césari, J., *Musulmans et républicains. Les jeunes, l'islam et la France* (Paris: Editions Complexe, 1998).

Césari, J., *Etre musulman en France. Associations, militants et mosquées* (Paris: Kartala-IREMAM, 1995).

Conseil d'Etat, *Rapport public 1996. Sur le principe d'égalité* (Paris: La Documentation française, 1997).

Costa-Lascoux, J., *De l'immigré au citoyen* (Paris: La Documentation française, 1989).

De Rudder, V., F. Vourch, C. Poiret, *L'inégalité raciste. L'universalité républicaine à l'épreuve* (Paris: PUF, 2000).

Etienne, B., *La France et l'islam* (Paris: Hachette, 1989).

Feldblum, M., *Reconstructing Citizenship. The Politics of Nationality Reform and Immigration in Contemporary France* (Albany: SUNY, 1999).

Feldblum, M., 'Reconfiguring Citizenship in Western Europe', in C. Joppke (ed.), *Challenge to the Nation-State. Immigration in Western Europe and the United States* (Oxford: Oxford University Press, 1998), pp. 149–78.

Groupe d'Etude et de Lutte contre les Discrimination (GELD), 'Une forme méconnue de discrimination: les emplois fermés aux étrangers', *Note du Conseil d'Orientation du GELD*, No. 1 (Paris, March 1999).

GELD, 'Le recours au droit dans la lutte contre les discriminations: la question de la preuve', *Note du Conseil d'Orientation du GELD*, No. 2 (October, 2000a).

GELD, 'Les discriminations raciales et ethniques dans l'accès au logement social', *Note du Conseil d'Orientation du GELD*, No. 3 (May, 2000b).

Hargreaves, A., *Immigration, 'Race' and Ethnicity in Contemporary France* (London: Routledge, 1995).

Haut Conseil à l'Intégration, *L'intégration a la française* (Paris: UGE, 1993).

Haut Conseil à l'Intégration, *Lutte contre les discriminations: faire respecter le principe d'égalité* (Paris: La Documentation française, 1998).

Hessel, S., G. Johanet, P. Schiettecatte, C. Hamon, *Immigrations, le devoir d'insertion: rapport du Groupe de travail Immigration* (Paris: Documentation française, collection: Plan, 1988).

Kepel, G., *Les banlieues de l'islam. La naissance d'une religion en France* (Paris: Albin Michel, 1991).

La Lettre de la Citoyenneté, September-October, No. 53 (2000).

La Médina, 'Croire et oeuvrer. Entretien avec Ali Rahni, travailleur social a Roubaix', No. 4 (February-March, 2000), pp. 40–4.

Leca, J., 'Individualism and citizenship', in J. Leca, P. Birnbaum (eds), *Individualism. Theory and Methods* (Oxford : Clarendon Press, 1990), pp. 141–89.

Long, M., *Etre Français aujourd'hui et demain* (Paris: La Documentation Française, 1988).

National Institute for Statistical and Economic Studies (INSEE), *Recensement de la population de 1999* (Paris: INSEE, 2001).

Ministère de l'Emploi et de la Solidarité, *Communication de Mme Martine Aubry, Ministre de l'Emploi et de la solidarité sur la politique d'intégration en Conseil des Ministres* (unpublished, 21 October 1998), available at www.social.gouv.fr.

Niessen, J., 'The Further Development of European Anti-Discrimination Policies', in I. Chopin, J. Niessen (eds), *The Starting Line and the Incorporation of the Racial Equality Directive into the National Laws of the EU Member States and Accession States* (Brussels, London: MGP/CRE, 2001), pp. 7–21.

Noiriel, G., *Le creuset français. Histoire de l'immigration XIX et XX siècles* (Paris: Seuil, 1988).

Ramadan, T., *Etre musulman européen. Etude des sources islamiques à la lumière du contexte européen* (Lyon: Tawhid, 1999).

Schain, M., 'Minorities and Immigrant Incorporation in France: The State and the Dynamics of Multiculturalism', in C. Joppke, S. Lukes, (eds), *Multicultural Questions* (Oxford: Oxford University Press, 1999), pp. 199–223.

Schnapper, D., *La France de l'intégration. Sociologie de la nation en 1990* (Paris: Gallimard, 1991).

Schnapper, D., *La Communauté des citoyens. Sur l'idée moderne de nation* (Paris: Gallimard, 1994).

Tribalat, M. (ed.), *Cent ans d'immigration, étrangers d'hier Français d'aujourd'hui* (Paris: INED, collection 'Travaux et Documents', 1991).

Tribalat, M., *Faire-France. Une enquête sur les immigrés et leurs enfants* (Paris: La Découverte, 1995).

Tripier, M., 'De l'usage de statistiques "ethniques"', *Hommes & Migrations*, No. 1219, (May-June, 1999), pp. 27–31.

UNCHR, 'Report by Mr. Maurice Glèlè-Ahanhanzo, Special Rapporteur on contemporary forms of racism, racial discrimination, xenophobia and related intolerance, submitted pursuant to Commission on Human Rights resolution 1993/20 and 1995/12', Document E/CN.4/1996/72/Add.3 (UNHCR and Social Council, 1996).

Weber, E., *Peasants into Frenchmen, the Modernization of Rural France, 1870–1914* (Stanford: Stanford University Press, 1976).

Weil, P., *La France et ses étrangers. L'aventure d'une politique de l'immigration de 1938 à nos jours* (Paris: Calmann-Levy, 1991).

Weil, P., *Mission d'étude des législations de la nationalité et de l'immigration : des conditions d'application du principe du droit du sol pour l'attribution de la nationalité française, pour une politique de l'immigration juste et efficace* (Paris: La Documentation française, 1997).

Weil, P., R. Hansen (eds), *Nationalité et citoyenneté en Europe* (Paris: La Découverte, 1999).

Wihtol de Wenden, C., *La citoyenneté et les changements de structures sociale et nationale de la population française* (Paris: Edilig, 1988).

Wihtol de Wenden, C., R. Leveau, *La beurgeoisie. Les trois âges de la vie associative issue de l'immigration* (Paris: CNRS, 2001).

Wihtol de Wenden, C., R. Leveau (eds), *Les associations créées dans les années 1980 par les jeunes militants issus de l'immigration. Bilan de leurs activités et de l'engagement de leurs promoteurs* (Paris: FAS/FNSP (CERI), 1996), unpublished.

7

The Revival of Ethnic Consciousness: the Case of Poland

Krystyna Iglicka

7.1. Introduction

This chapter is devoted to issues relating to established minorities and to new immigrant groups now forming in Poland. The aim here is not to provide a detailed description of the socio-demographic characteristics of all the minorities, but rather to address problems associated with the revival of the ethnic consciousness and multiculturalism in a Central European country — Poland — in the context of the enlargement of the EU.

This chapter examines the political and social situation of some 'old' minorities, namely Germans, Ukrainians, Jews and Armenians before and during the transition period. It also analyses the phenomenon of recent arrivals from Ukraine, Armenia and Vietnam.

Since 1945, virtually all highly-developed countries in the Western World have experienced relatively large-scale immigration. In comparing these countries, Castles and Miller (1993) found the following common characteristics: (i) a dynamic process of migration, which transforms the temporary entry of workers and refugees into permanent settlers who form distinct ethnic groups; (ii) economic and social marginalization of the immigrants; (iii) community formation among immigrants; (iv) increasing interaction between immigrant groups and the local population; and (v) the imperative for the state to react to immigration and ethnic diversity (Castles, 1995, p. 293). Of course these represent only the key structural similarities, but they made it possible to establish some common patterns despite differences in detail.

Although isolated from these phenomena for much of the post-World War II period, Central European countries are now experiencing the first stage of the inflow of foreigners. As yet, it is hard to draw any broad conclusions for this region regarding either the features of the immigration or the reactions of national and local governments and local communities to this phenomenon. I think, however, that the globalization of migration will soon involve Central and East European countries in ways that will soon exemplify Castles's model. The influx of foreigners into Poland takes all forms — illegal, temporary stay, marriages of convenience, setting up a business, and permanent settlement. This represents the beginning of processes of a 'new' ethnic diversity and also the creation of new ethnic consciousnesses. These issues are highly topical and should not be overlooked at this moment in time (Hamilton, Iglicka, 2000).

As far as the matter of ethnicity is concerned, one can observe two different trends in the broader, European perspective. Europe as a continent is becoming more and more involved in nationality and ethnic issues; however, forces are pulling in two opposite directions: first, there is the process of the integration of existing and future member nations into the EU structure. The second force is the disintegration of multinational (post-Communist) states. The social and political transformation initiated in the late 1980s have proven that ethnic issues in Central and Eastern Europe had not been permanently solved and that they were certainly not eliminated in the Communist era. On the contrary, they became doubly significant and erupted equally from suppressed xenophobia and from nationalism, as well as from delay in the development of civic societies in this part of Europe (Nolte, 1995; Kurcz, 1997, p. 8).

The ethnic minorities who have been living in Poland for generations are there for different reasons. The Jews came here of their own free will. Ukrainians, Lithuanians, Belarussians, and Armenians are relics of the multinational Polish republic from a bygone century. However, ethnic Germans maintain their idea of non-Polish origin in a different way: oftentimes they stress they remain in their own land, despite the borders having been changed (Kurcz, 1997).

The other important problem relating to population structure is that, since the beginning of the 1990s, Poland has transformed itself slowly from a being a longstanding country of migrant origin into a country of destination and transit for migrants, especially ones from East Europe and Asia. For example, diasporas of Vietnamese and Chinese, who are completely new and exotic for this region, are rapidly forming. The mass presence of foreigners (primarily foreigners from ex-Soviet countries) has created a dilemma and challenges for European and Polish migration policies in the contexts of NATO and EU expansions (Iglicka and Sword, 1999).

National differences occur not only in this part of Europe. Ethnic questions have always been a significant issue for Western democracies, meaning that the EU enlargement will result in the problematics of minorities and immigrants living in Poland becoming not only a local but rather a European question.

7.2. Policy towards Minorities before and during the Transition Period

After 1945 Poland ceased to be the ethnically pluralistic country it had been before the World War II. The profound changes in its ethnic structure resulted from many factors but mainly from: territorial changes, Nazi extermination of entire groups (particularly Jews and Gypsies) and forced 'repatriation' of populations (Germans, Ukrainians) during and after the war (Kersten, 1974; Piesowicz, 1987).

The processes of social and economic shifts since 1950 — mainly industrialization, urbanization and the development of mass culture in the Polish language — were also influential in achieving post-war ethnic homogenization of Polish society. Under these conditions, only education in mother-tongue languages and local cultural activities (mainly in the form of 'rural' folklore) became channels by which ethnic minorities could preserve their ethnic identity (Łodziński, 2000).

The first post-war population census held in 1946 included a question about ethnic origin. However, the data from this census are not credible as the census was conducted in unstable, political, social and demographic situations. Since other Polish censuses (held in 1950, 1960, 1978 and 1988) did not contain any direct questions about ethnicity or mother tongue, one has to resort to various estimations.

All but one ethnic group from Table 7.1 have lived on Polish soil for several, even very many generations. The exception is the Greek and Macedonian group, which is of immigrant origin from the 1949–54 period. Besides these two minority societies, there are also very small groups of Hungarians, French, Serbs, Bulgarians, Georgians, Palestinians and Kurds who constitute small communities numbering from the hundreds to up to 2000 persons. Thus, the total population of all ethnic minorities in Poland ranges between 1.0 to 1.5 million persons, or just 3–5 per cent of the total population. Therefore, it is still a relatively ethnically homogeneous country.

Table 7.1 Changes in the population of national minorities in Poland 1931–91 (in thousands)

Ethnic minority	1931 census	1931 estimate	1946 census	1946 estimate	1961 estimate	1988 census	1991 estimate
Belarussian, Local People'	990 707	1,955–1,965	–	220	148	300	200–230
Ukrainian and Lemko/Ruthenian	3,215 1,227	4,985–5,025	506	520–570	162	300	200–250
Lemko/Ruthenian[a]	In number of Ruthenian	120–130	–	120–130	–	80	50–60
German	741	780–785	2,300	3,200–3,500	200	600	350–400
Jewish	2,733	3,115–3,135	–	40–120	70	10–15	15
Lithuanian	83.1	186–200	–	10	9	30	20
Roma/Gypsy	–	30–50	–	10–15	12	30	25
Russian, including Old Believers	138.7	139–140 30–35	–	–	17	15	10–15 2.5–3
Slovak	–	0.8–0.9	–	–	19	25	20–23
Czech	38.1	39	–	–	2	–	2–3
Armenian	–	5.2	–	–	–	15	8
Tatar	–	5.5	–	–	–	4–5	3–4
Karaim	–	1.0–1.5	–	–	–	0.2	0.2
Greek and Macedonian	–	–	–	–	9	5	5
Total population	32,100		23,400		29,800	38,640	

[a] Included in the number for the Ukrainian minority — preceding category

Source: Olszewicz (1989, p. 112); Statistical Yearbooks, Central Statistical Office (various years); Kwilecki (1963, pp. 87–8); Tomaszewski (1991); Sakson (1991); Hołuszko (1993); afterwards Łodziński (2000, p. 37)

Issues surrounding minorities in Poland were treated in post-1945 policy in Poland as being difficult and 'sensitive'. There was no consistent policy between 1945 and 1989, and attitudes to particular ethnic minorities varied. Until the end of the 1940s, federal policy aimed at assimilation. In the 1950s and 1960s it underwent gradual liberalization and minorities gained new opportunities to learn their mother-tongues and create their own organizations. However, all ethnic associations and organizations were controlled and financed by the Ministry of Internal Affairs. The principle 'one minority — one organization' was adopted. Ostensibly these organizations were officially aimed at cultivating cultural traditions of the ethnic minorities but the reality was that they functioned as an instrument of control over minorities by the central state administration. Moreover, minorities had limited access to social, cultural and political activities. Certainly, representatives of ethnic minorities were present in both administrative and party structures (local and central) and in the Parliament; however, they were not there as the representatives of their own ethnic groups but as members of political parties (Łodziński, 2000).

After the 1989 collapse of communism, the issue of ethnic minorities became crucial for several reasons. Firstly, democratic changes after 1989 meant ethnic minorities were given an opportunity to involve themselves in local and national policy. Their activity rapidly increased. Initially, this was a great surprise both to the authorities and to most of the public who had previously regarded minorities as a remnant of Poland's multinational history or as a vestige of outdated, 'rural' tradition. Secondly, integration with West European structures required positive relations with neighbours and avoidance of ethnic conflict. Thirdly, the geopolitical structure and nature of Poland's international relations have changed. All Poland's neighbours have undergone change and are now keen to protect the interests of their ethnic kin in Poland; likewise, Poland has become interested in protecting the rights of Poles living in these countries (Łodziński, 2000).

Shortly after the first Solidarity government took power, minority affairs were transferred from the jurisdiction of the Interior Ministry to a new office in the Ministry of Culture. The state became a sponsor rather than a supervisor.

The *Sejm* (lower chamber of Parliament) Committee on National and Ethnic Minorities began work on the re-regulation of the legal status of national minorities at the beginning of the 1990s. The result of its work — included in the new Constitution (1997) — is an article (Article 35) dealing with the protection of national and ethnic minorities. This Article contains a positive commitment of the state to ensure minorities' rights to maintain and develop their own culture (language, traditions, customs). It also grants them the right to establish organizations of various characters. The Constitution restricts the protection of minority rights to persons possessing Polish citizenship, at the same time providing separate protection of the rights of foreigners (article 56). Such a 'citizen's clause' conforms to the standards of minority protection established within the European framework (Organization for Security and Co-operation in Europe (OSCE), the Council of Europe) (Łodziński, 2000).

Poland's obligations to protect the particular rights of minorities living in its territory were also set forth in bilateral treaties between Poland and all its neighbours and other Central and East European countries in the years 1990–94. By including appropriate minority clauses in these treaties, Poland has played a significant role in establishing principles for the protection of minority rights in Central Europe. Reference to international standards in formulating bilateral treaties was, to a certain degree, an innovation. Instead of attempts to find special ways of protecting particular minorities and ensuring their more favourable position, the solutions applied were based on the document adopted within the Commission on Security and Cooperation in Europe (CSCE) framework (Barcz, 1996; Łodziński, 2000).

Besides international commitments stemming from its bilateral treaties, Poland has undertaken numerous obligations resulting from ratified conventions dealing with the protection of human and minority rights elaborated within the frameworks of the UN and the Council of Europe. Poland is also active in the work of the CSCE (OSCE). It also signed (in April 1995) an Instrument of Central European Protection of Minority Rights within the framework of the Central European Initiative.

Generally, ethnic minorities' political, social and the legal positions have improved since 1989; however, they are far from ideal. The important thing is that the 'political context' of minority issues has been eliminated. Poland treats minorities as an equal part of its society and respects their rights to preserve their own ethnic and cultural identity, as well as their social and political aspirations. On the positive side, the authorities have taken several steps to improve the standing of ethnic minorities as far as their political, cultural and social activities are concerned. On the negative side, due to tight budgetary constraints, state funding for minorities are very low, which can exacerbate political tensions.

The change in state policy towards minorities was accompanied by appropriate changes in attitudes among the minorities themselves, who nowadays feel more secure and actively defend their interests. The nature of their contacts with authorities has also changed. At present, both sides refer to concrete problems and do not perceive each other as a threat.

In my opinion, the most urgent matter for legislative action is a guarantee for the protection of the rights of ethnic minority members who do not hold Polish citizenship. From the point of view of a revival of 'multiculturalism' and in the light of new diasporas of immigrants, the protection of their rights will become an important issue very soon (Michalska, 1997).

7.3. Ethnic Consciousness among Selected 'Old' Minorities and 'New' Immigrants' Groups

7.3.1. Germans

For centuries, German colonization and the changing German state hegemony over Polish lands affected relations among the populations in the region and explains why many German families' ancestries are traceable to what is now Polish territory. Events of the World War II also bear on the German minority in today's Poland. At that time, the German authorities introduced a German nationals' list (*Volksliste*) into which the people of Upper Silesia and Gdansk Pomerania (the Danzig Corridor) were forcibly entered; as well, the populations of other conquered territories were recruited with the promise of a better life. Several hundred thousand Germans from eastern and southern Europe were also resettled onto Polish territory in operation '*Heim ins Reich*' (Home in the Reich). These people (that is the *Volksdeutsche* German re-settlers and their descendants) but primarily a considerable part of the native population of Upper Silesia, Warmia and Masuria constitute the German minority in contemporary Poland (Kurcz, 2000).

The Germans who remained in Poland after the expulsions of 1946–50, when more than two million of them were expelled, experienced a relatively positive attitude of the Polish authorities (Ociepka, 1994; Kurcz, 1994). In 1950, schooling in the German language was inaugurated, Germans were empowered to pursue their own cultural activities and they were granted citizenship rights. It should also be noted that, throughout the entire post-war period,

German Protestants enjoyed freedom of worship, which was overseen by German clergy (Kurcz, 2000).

The years 1956–57 are known as the 'October thaw' because in October 1956 there were several attempts by the new, post-Stalinist authorities to democratize the system; for the German minority, this entailed the right to emigrate, leading to a wave of departures to both East and West Germany. 217,000 self-designated Germans emigrated to the West Germany and almost 38,000 to the East Germany — that is, almost all the Germans living in Poland. As a consequence, the cultural activities of German societies ceased (Kurcz, 2000).

The social reality proved to be yet more complicated since with the passage of time, permit applications to leave for the German Federal Republic came in their thousands, motivated by the wishes of families to reunite. 'The Notification by the Government of the Polish People's Republic (PRL)' announced on 18 November 1970, was the direct cause for a dramatic increase in the number of applicants for permanent emigration to West Germany. As of 31 December 1971, 131,823 such applications had been filled, an increase of more than 54,000 over 1970. At the same time, German statistics put the number of persons eligible for migration from Poland, both on grounds of family reunification and on self-affiliation with the German people, at 270,000. One should also remember that emigration (mainly illegal) to Germany in the 1980s (of ethnic Germans, their family members and those who simply made the most of West Germany's lenient policy towards *Aussiedler* status applicants) provided the opportunity to live better and people just simply grabbed it. Official statistics show that between 1980 and 1989 around 271,000 persons emigrated legally. However, the actual number for this period has been estimated at 1.1–1.3 million (most of whom to Germany) (Okólski, 1994). The outflow to Germany accelerated especially in 1989 and in 1990 when a more restrictive German immigration policy was expected (Iglicka, 2000a).

What made the numbers of claimants of German ethnicity grow so rapidly? The changes in national self-identity are particularly noticeable among the native population of Silesia (in South-West Poland); their ethnic malleability lies in the mixed ethnic structure of the region. According to some researchers (Kurcz, 1997; Rogalla, 1992), the native population of Silesia was formed through the centuries by both Poles and arrivals from Germany. The same researchers state that their long-term coexistence and interaction has created a distinctive culture and the emergence of a new community.

Undoubtedly, this community perceived Germanness as something very attractive (but such perception of German characteristics existed among native Poles as well) as it was associated with refinement and better living conditions. Against that, Poland, with its tragic history, economic backwardness and greater social inequalities, could not compete. Secondly, the tragic period during which communist authorities conducted 'ethnic verification', when many people who felt Polish were counted as Germans, was conducive to the perception of Germanness as something against the authorities. The third reason for pro-German self-identity of the native Silesian population lies in the alien character of the Polish population repatriated from the eastern territories of Poland (annexed after the war by the USSR) to this region. The extent of the differentness of the native population from the new arrivals manifested itself in everything: from culture to ill-will. Fourthly, the pro-German orientation of the native population was also shaped by the battlefront that steam-rolled ever westwards in 1945. The Silesian and Mazurian populations had not experience real war earlier as their territories lay beyond the reach of Allied aircraft from the west. The population of these areas came face to face with wartime horror only upon the arrival of the Polish and Soviet forces. That is why many older Silesians used to claim that '1945 was no liberation; only then did war visit us', something antithetical to the experiences of most Poles (Kurcz, 2000).

However, for some researchers the economic factor in shaping pro-German identity seems to be the most important. The German author, Thomas Urban (1993, p. 142), in his study of the German minority in Poland recalls the well-known Silesian saying 'the homeland is where the sausages hang!' The influence of economic factors on ethnic self-identification is also illustrated by the fact that interest in belonging to German minority organizations in Poland is waning. Another phenomenon is the return to Poland of thousands of people who once proclaimed German identity (Heffner, 1999). These return migrants include both representatives of the native population as well as others who had claimed to be German to gain material benefits from West German society (Heffner, 1999).

The German minority still numbers about 300,000, although this is a maximum estimate (Kurcz, 2000). In 1992, it was represented by almost 50 associations, totalling 299,580 members (Kurcz, 1997, p. 43).

What are the prospects for this minority? We know from our knowledge about this community that everything depends on the economic situation in Poland and also on the different forms of assistance that the Federal German authorities offer this group.

> If the gap between Polish and German living standards stops increasing, and the German authorities limit privileges for ethnic Germans living abroad, especially the right to work in Germany, it may be assumed that in a short period the German minority will shrink to a five-figure population. However, those who remain within the ranks of the minority will of course be people tied with German traditions, culture and language, and they will perceive their Germanness as intrinsically valuable. If, however, the differences in living standards between Poland and Germany continue to increase, and the German authorities in various ways continue to support those who declare themselves German, the number of people claiming to be German minority could even double (Kurcz, 2000, p. 86).

7.3.2. Jews

After their near extermination during the World War II, Jews — the biggest minority till 1939 — represented a negligible group in Poland. Estimates made right after the war of the number of Jewish survivors living within Poland's post-1945 borders ranged from 50,000 to 80,000. As part of the repatriation of Polish citizens from the USSR, some 240,000 Jews returned in 1944–46. So, the numbers of Jewish community increased until the beginning of the 1950s but would be diminished some years afterward.

Since before and during the war, the Polish Left, especially the Communists, fought anti-Semitism resolutely, the Jewish minority was the only one to be accepted by the new communist authorities in the second half of the 1940s. Thus, in a country where opposition groups and the Catholic Church regarded the Jews *a priori* and innately as the Communists' allies, and hence enemies, the Communists could thus count on Jewish support (Kersten, 1992).

Despite the political and social uncertainty, Jewish political and cultural life revived in the second half of the 1940s in almost all its pre-war aspects. There existed a broad spectrum of Jewish political parties operating legally, including a Zionist party (Adelson, 1993). However, when in 1948 the USSR withdrew its support for the nascent state of Israel, the open Polish state's policy towards Jewish parties changed radically. From that moment onwards, 'Zionist' became a term of abuse in party propaganda (Datner and Melchior, 2000).

The year 1948 was a watershed in Jewish social and political life, as it was for Polish society. Poland was entering the Stalinist phase, with the destruction of all vestiges of pluralism. For the Jewish community, that year represented the end of a relatively autonomous social, cultural and political existence. By 1949 all Jewish political parties had been dissolved, Hebrew and the religious schools had been abolished and most of the newspapers had been closed down. Hebrew- and Yiddish-language schools were nationalized. The activities of the Religious Congregation were completely marginalized. In 1950, one all-Jewish organization was called into being, The Socio-Cultural Society of Jews in Poland. Of a rich range of press publications, only two titles managed to survive, the Yiddish *'Folk Sztyme'* and the literary review *'Literarisze Bleter'* (Datner and Melchior, 2000).

The October thaw of 1956 revived anti-Semitic tendencies suppressed during the Stalinist era. The party's grass roots sought to settle scores with Stalinism with the help of catchphrases like 'Jewish-communists' (Machcewicz, 1993). Migratory trends among the Jewish community increased. They revived significantly when the last group of Polish citizens (which included Polish Jews) returned from the USSR. These of Jewish origin who arrived from the east to Poland re-emigrated almost immediately. In total, in the 1957–60 period, about 30,000 Jews emigrated (Kwilecki, 1963). At the beginning of the 1960s, the administrative offices registered about 30,000 Jews in Poland. However, contrary to their political life, which did not revive after Stalinism, Jewish culture did re-emerge to some extent during the thaw (Datner and Melchior, 2000).

Like elsewhere, students were in revolt in Poland during 1968. The government's propaganda campaign to derail or defuse student protest centred on public Jew-bashing, which brought tragic consequences for the remnants of Polish Jewry (Eisler, 1968). What happened then had all the hallmarks of expulsion: people were thrown out of work, birth certificates were checked for racial origins and the press wrote despicable nonsense. March '68 was the real end (at least that's what it seemed like at the time), of the Jewish community in Poland: in the 1968–71 period, about 20,000 people of Jewish origin, many of whom were completely assimilated, left Poland. Jewish institutions in the 1970s were desolate places and in fact did not function. In practice, Jewish public institutional life ceased to exist (Datner and Melchior, 2000).

The Solidarity period of 1980–81, a time of social hope, broke the silence about the Jews, and publications — on the topic of the presence of Jews in Polish history and culture, Polish-Jewish relations and wartime experiences — began to appear in ever-increasing numbers.

The 1989 transformation, which brought freedom, caused fundamental transformations in the Jewish community. First of all, Jewish institutions such as the Ronald Lauder Foundation offices in Poland, the Children of the Holocaust Association, the Union of Jewish Religious Communes and the Shalom Polish-American-Jewish Foundation (to mention only the most numerous ones) started to flourish. Apart from the creation of official structures, there has also been an observable process of the discovery of Jewish origins by very young and young people. This self-awareness is treated as something important and relevant. Interestingly enough, the language (hitherto almost forgotten) and a Jewish culture seem to play a certain role in the self-identification of younger generation Jews. This culture is in practice unknown to these young people yet, significantly, some of them are learning Yiddish (though more are learning Hebrew) (Rosenson, 1995).

The rediscovery of Jewish roots has many positive aspects (Rosenson, 1995). At the bottom of today's rediscovered identity with Jewry lies the conviction that 'I want to, but don't have to, be a Jew'; there are also motives such as: curiosity, interest in otherness and regard for the multi-faceted nature of the world. In effect, it may be asserted that the once seemingly extinct Jewish community in Poland is reviving itself. As a result of the process of disassimilation, its numbers are increasing and the middle-aged and older generations are affirming their Jewishness with ever-increasing fervour. For the last few years one can observe another phenomenon unseen in Poland for many decades: a return to Jewishness through religion. This surprisingly concerns young people, usually from totally assimilated families, and frequently from mixed marriages.

7.3.3. 'Old' Ukrainians

It may be surprising that it is not the Polish-German but the Polish-Ukrainian relationship that is most burdened with mutual resentments and stereotypes reaching as far back as the nineteenth century (Jedlicki, 1999, p. 228). The most tragic story began in 1943 when the Ukrainian national guerrilla movement (UPA) started ethnic cleansing in Volhynia and eastern Galicia. Reciprocal slaughters and the razing of whole villages were perpetrated (Jedlicki, 1999). The final chapter of Polish-Ukrainian strife happened in 1947. At that time, Polish security forces, unable to destroy the UPA, displaced approximately 150,000 Ukrainians and Lemkos from south-eastern Poland (an area which was ethnically Ukrainian) to the northern and western territories (formerly part of Germany) in what was named *Akcja Wisła*. The events of the World War II and the period of forced migration after the war have had a significant impact on the Ukrainian minority in Poland during the past 50 years (Babiński, 2000).

Ukrainians' demographics in post-war Poland show that the majority lived in the countryside and worked in agriculture. There were upper-middle class and lower-middle class Ukrainians (though they were proportionately fewer than Poles') as well as working class Ukrainians. The social structure had been effected by political emigration after the war, which was relatively greater among the higher echelons of society (Babiński, 2000).

The Ukrainians who were forcibly resettled in *Akcja Wisła* (1947) were virtually all relocated to agricultural areas, both to vacant individual farms and to large state farms. Over the next decade, they found themselves under individual house arrest without any rights either to return to their homeland or to travel outside the area in which they lived. This meant they were unable to get an education, a better job or improve their social status.

Between 1945 and 1947, literally all forms of organized life among the Ukrainians in Poland were wiped out. This concerned not only formal institutions and organizations such as their Church, political parties, military organizations and cultural groups but even informal neighbourhood societies and circles as well as individual and collective forms of ownership. Only after 1956 (Pudło, 1993) was it possible for them to create cultural and educational organizations. Government policies tended to be restrictive (with certain fluctuations) and all forms of organized ethnic activity and culture were strictly controlled (Babiński, 2000).

The Ukrainians obtained the same rights as Poles only after 1956, and though there were many hurdles to be overcome, they did get permission to return to their homeland (Ukraine). They could also move about, relatively freely, both spatially and socially.

The main changes in Ukrainians' social and political situation occurred after 1989. Firstly, their institutions flourished. The Ukrainian Socio-Cultural Society founded in 1956 and, until 1990, the only recognized Ukrainian organization in Poland was dissolved and replaced by the Union of Ukrainians in Poland (ZUP) (Czarnecki, 1991). Within the structure of the ZUP, the following organizations are currently active: the Ukrainian Union, the

Ukrainian Society of Teachers in Poland, the Ukrainian Society of Doctors, the Lawyers Club, the Association of Businessmen and the Piast Ukrainian Youth Organization. There are also independent organizations such as: the Union of Ukrainians in Podlasie and the Independent Union of Ukrainian Youth.

After 1989 the legal status of the Greek Catholic Church went through very profound changes. Some churches and other church properties taken over by the Roman Catholic Church after the World War II started to return to the Orthodox or Greek Catholic Churches. Irrespective of some local conflicts and resentments, there is no doubt that there has been a real renaissance of Greek Catholic Church in Poland (Babiński, 2000).

One can also observe a revival of Ukrainian schooling in the 1990s. The number of pupils in Ukrainian schools, which had steadily declined through the 1970s and 1980s, has increased in numbers of both schools and pupils during the last five years (Pudło, 1993).

Ethnic Poles and Ukrainians live together and are generally mixed both spatially and socially without any serious conflicts or tension. This is evident, above all, in the number of mixed ethnic marriages. However, deep under the surface, the events of 1939–47 are still indelibly imprinted in reciprocal attitudes. Generally it can be said that the majority of Ukrainians in Poland feel that the Poles are waiting for them to become assimilated. It is indeed the former's opinion that, even in the best of cases, Ukrainian culture is merely tolerated since it is perceived by the dominant group as being incomplete, quaint and backwardish.

Luckily, the mutual resentments present no direct political threat today. Their potential is limited to noisy battles for and against symbolic values, since there exists mutual political will to co-operate (Jedlicki, 1999, p. 29).

7.3.4. 'New' Ukrainians

The fall of the communist system has given rise to the new spatial mobility of people of the former Soviet bloc countries. In 1989, fewer than three million citizens of the former USSR entered Poland. Their number more than doubled the next year and continued until peaking at more than 14 million in 1997. After Russians, Ukrainians constituted the second largest citizenship group.

Citizens of the former Soviet Union come to Poland to search for economic opportunities. Hundreds of thousands of them have been involved in petty cross-border trading, profiting from the difference in prices and exchange rates. They also work in Poland, often illegally, engaging in agriculture, construction and in services. Shuttle mobility helps people solve their vital material problems and has become an important component in the survival strategy of many households in the Western Ukraine (Iglicka, 1999; Iglicka, 2001). According to surveys, regular trips abroad to earn a living have become the revenue source for 5 per cent of the economically-active population in Ukraine, that is for more than one million people. A further 20 per cent of working-age people resort to such trips occasionally to supplement their income (Khomra, 1994, p. 13).

The massive flux of arrivals from the former Soviet Union caused many positive phenomena such as development of some sectors of the Polish economy, competition on the labour market, and so on. However, one of the negative aspects of this flow is particularly visible: crime. Ukrainians are particularly associated with it. Statistics depicting crime committed by foreigners do not indicate a large-scale phenomenon but they do indicate a rising trend in the most serious crimes (including armed robbery and homicides) committed especially by Ukrainians (Iglicka, 2000b).

After a decade of penetration of Polish trade and labour markets by petty-traders and seasonal workers, some of them, and especially those with a pre-established network and connections in Poland, having come to terms with restrictions in West European policy towards mobility from the 'East', are considering long-term or permanent emigration to Poland. This is particularly true for Ukrainians.

This phenomenon is confirmed by both research findings and official statistics. In the second half of the 1990s, ephemeral and typical for a transitional period primitive mobility of petty-traders changed into typical migration in the Central European buffer zone (Iglicka, 2001).

Official statistical data indicate an increasing tendency of people from the former USSR to apply for work permits and permanent residence permits (PRP). Although it is not possible to prove that these are just the people who started arriving in Poland as petty-traders, the mass character of shuttle mobility inclines me to the assumption that many of them are. As far as visas with work permits granted from the beginning of the 1990s until 1996, Ukrainians ranked first, from 1996 until this chapter was written (mid-1999) they were at the second position.

Table 7.2 Visas with work permits granted in 1994–48, most numerous nationalities (%)

Country of origin	1994	1995	1996	1997	1998
Ukraine	13.0	14.0	15.8	15.2	13.1
Vietnam	11.0	13.0	14.6	17.8	15.1
Russia	8.5	7.5	7.6	6.5	5.6
USA	7.0	7.0	6.0	5.3	4.1
China	7.8	7.0	7.8	6.5	6.7
Great Britain	7.0	7.0	6.0	5.0	5.0
Belarus	5.0	3.5	3.0	3.3	4.0
Germany	4.6	5.0	6.0	6.0	5.5
Total (absolute numbers)	8,690	9,057	7,019	8,978	10,505

Source: Office for Migration and Refugees (1999)

If we look at the citizenship of foreigners who were granted a permanent residence permit (PRP), we see that the most numerous nationality is undoubtedly Ukrainian.

Table 7.3 Foreigners granted permanent residence permits (PRPs) in Poland, most numerous nationalities, 1993–98 (%)

Country of citizenship	1993	1994	1995	1996	1997	1998
Ukraine	15	21	19	22	23	24
Russia	11	12	11	10	8	7
Belarus	7	6	7	7	8	7
Germany	5	5	6	5	4	4
Vietnam	4	4	7	9	8	10
Kazakhstan	1	2	8	8	15	10
Lithuania	3	3	2	3	2	2
Armenia	1	2	2	2	2	5
Total (absolute numbers)	1,964	2,457	3,051	2,844	3,973	1,567

Source: Office for Migration and Refugees (1999)

In a study on the spatial distribution of Ukrainians, who were the most numerous foreign-born population in Poland in 1991, (understood as resident foreigners with a PRP), it was noticed that they were registered in four types of locations: 1) large urban areas, 2) towns were Soviet garrisons had been located, 3) areas along the eastern border (ethnically Ukrainian) and 4) former German territories in the north and west of Poland (Jerczyński, 1999). It was these latter territories where Ukrainians and Lemkos were resettled in 1947. Jerczyński (1999) also noticed that a map of the territorial distribution of Orthodox and Greek Catholic churches coincides with where 'new' Ukrainians live. It proves that networks between 'old' and 'new' group play an important role in the spatial formation of the latter.

Mixed marriages are another interesting phenomenon as far as 'new' Ukrainians are concerned. It is not possible to state what percentage of these marriages are shams (if any), but a sudden growing trend may suggest that there are other factors (beyond the customary ones) behind Ukrainians' hasty willingness to marry Poles.

Table 7.4 Mixed marriages; 1990–96 (selected years)

Country of origin of a foreign wife	1990	1995	1996	Country of origin of a foreign husband	1990	1995	1996
Ukraine	–	331	340	Ukraine	–	89	108
Russia	–	119	151	Russia	–	–	–
Belarus	–	95	104	Belarus	–	–	–
Lithuania	–	41	40	Lithuania	–	–	–
Armenia	–	27	28	Armenia	–	–	64
Latvia	–	6	10	Latvia	–	–	–
Kazakhstan	–	13	11	Kazakhstan	–	–	–
USSR	255	–	–	USSR	210	–	–
Germany	370	61	63	Germany	1,494	748	698
Vietnam	–	15	42	Vietnam	–	44	64
USA	88	46	33	USA	263	185	138
United Kingdom	14	–	–	United Kingdom	44	–	–
Canada	–	17	15	Canada	–	46	43
Others[a]	184	149	140	Others[a]	1,318	1,164	1,062
Total	911	920	977	Total	3,329	2,320	2,177

[a] Mainly western European countries
Source: Statistical Yearbooks, Central Statistical Office (various years)

So far, there have not been any in-depth anthropological studies on the 'new' Ukrainians community. The partial information that exists portrays dynamic, very young and young people, people who are rather not (so far) interested in maintaining their ethnicity while trying to settle in Poland. 'Survival strategy' seems to be most important for them. Furthermore, the 'new' Ukrainian group is not homogenous and there are many strategies and variants of them. It is possible, however, to distinguish some types. Firstly, those who are in Poland illegally as seasonal workers or petty-traders with the aim to earn quick money and return home will engage in shuttle mobility as long as it is profitable and provided the visa-free movement will be possible. Here, I predict a decrease in the numbers of petty-traders and an increase of seasonal workers. Secondly, those who want to settle legally will try to integrate with the majority group. They perceive Poland as a country of opportunities and do not want to be negatively stereotyped as being *Ruski* (a common, derogative term in Polish for all people from the former Soviet Union). With the further development of formal and informal networks and institutions, the numbers of Ukrainians granted visas with work permit and PRPs will grow. There is, however, an element in this group that treats Poland only as a transit stop on their way to the West. Therefore, we may assume that a third strategy, that is to obtain Polish citizenship (through application or marriage) in order to subsequently emigrate to the West, exists.

As yet, it is hard to draw any broad conclusions for this group regarding either the formative process of their new community or their future in the context of the reactions of government and local communities to their appearance. The process has only just begun.

7.3.5. *'Old' and 'new' Armenians*

There were two migratory waves of Armenians into Poland. First, when Armenians settled in Poland's eastern marshlands in the late Middle Ages and the second occurred after the World War II, when about 99 per cent of those from the Polish eastern territories annexed by the USSR were repatriated. Armenians' existence in Poland frequently comes as a surprise to foreign academics. Repatriated or forcibly resettled from their old places in Ukraine and dispersed throughout Poland after the World War II, they scattered and settled in groups of a dozen families (and sometimes much fewer) in one place. Now they are almost totally assimilated. Religion (and sometimes merely denomination) is currently the only factor distinguishing Poles from Armenians, since they represent the remnants of close historical links with Oriental Europe and Central Asia; some of them are also Unites (Marciniak, 2000).

The traditional, long-settled Armenian community descended from the ancient Armenians, which is of about 15,000 strong, began to be strengthened in the 1990s by new immigrants, whose growing numbers may now equal half of the original community. There are some common features between these two groups but the differences are greater.

'Old' Polish Armenians abandoned their own language in the sixteenth century without creating any dialect or pidgin language and adopted the languages of the dominant groups. Similarly, the third wave of Armenians in Poland is learning Polish rapidly (Kęsicka, 1996).

'Old' Armenians are religious whereas the new immigrants, if they show any ties at all with a Church, they are only incidentally so. The third wave seems to be displaying the post-Soviet indifference in matters of faith.

'Old' Armenians and their direct descendants stopped cultivating many of their customs, including cuisine. Contrary to this, the expansion of the 'new' Armenian ethnicity is strongly noticeable in the gastronomy sector. Specifically Armenian restaurants are increasing, in some others Armenian dishes are served. The activities of the Armenian Cultural Society are aimed at reviving Armenian native traditions (Marciniak, 2000).

Who are the 'new' Armenians in Poland? First of all, their arrival is a result of the drama in the Caucasus. Contrary to other asylum seekers in Poland, Armenians do not treat Poland mainly as a country of transit to the West. As far as asylum applications are concerned, Armenians are the only nationality present for each year of the whole 1992–98 period. Other nations (with the exception of the former Yugoslavia) exemplify mainly some trends in the popularity of Poland as a gateway to Western Europe. According to the Border Guard statistics, Armenians were also the last among the seven most numerous nationalities who were stopped for crimes (illegal border crossing, false documents, and so on) at the frontiers (Central Statistical Office, 1999; Border Guard, 1996).

For some, the road to Polish residence seems to be through application for a permanent residence permit (see Table 7.3), for others through marriage with Polish citizens (see Table 7.4). The majority of them seem to prefer irregular status (for example extended visas), treating their multiple-year stay in Poland as still temporary. Some of them reside in the country illegally.

Trade, for many centuries, has been an Armenian domain and motivated the first migratory wave of this ethnic group. The activities of the third wave in this field are notably true to type (Kęsicka, 1996). Such activity may collide with the law, especially when it is conducted without legal permits. The third Armenian wave is commonly but exaggeratedly associated mainly with illegal street market trade and crime due to their depiction in the mass media (Marciniak, 2000).

'New' Armenians have created their own micro-communities in northern and eastern Poland. They seem to choose small towns, allowing them to set up communes (characterized by solidarity) (Cieślińska, 1997; Łukowski, 1997). Besides those involved in trading at local markets, their number includes teachers, academics and doctors. The new arrivals are mostly educated people who rarely find employment commensurate with their knowledge and skills (Marciniak, 2000).

This group's intra-community activities are smaller in comparison to the activities of other ethnic minorities. Strengthened by new arrivals, the Armenian Cultural Society in Cracow's bulletin has appeared on average twice a year since 1993. In turn, the Armenian Culture Circle, which is attached to the Polish Ethnographic Society, has concentrated its activities on putting out compact publications. The latest issues in this series of over 28 publications to date concentrate on history and tradition (Marciniak, 2000). All of them are published in Polish. They seek to revive ethnic consciousness among members of the 'old' group.

7.3.6. Vietnamese

Until the early the 1990s, immigration to Poland was not statistically significant. However, one of the existing and quite visible inflows was movement of students from African and Asian countries — particularly from Vietnam — who arrived in Poland under intergovernmental programs for 'socialist cooperation' and academic exchange. After graduation, most of them returned to their home countries where their European diplomas placed them high up in the social hierarchy.

Until the end of 1980s, Poland and Vietnam belong to the so-called brotherhood of socialist states, but found themselves in under different political systems after 1989. Though remaining a communist country, Vietnam invigorated its migration policy, causing inflows to Poland. This time, the influx comprised not only students (from privileged families), but also people who were looking for a place to work and to live.

Since the end of 1993, the number of Vietnamese citizens applying for work-permit visas in Poland has seen a sharp increase, and there has been a corresponding rise in the number of Vietnamese legally coming to Poland. While until 1996 Vietnamese were the second largest group (after Ukrainians) in terms of the number of visas with work permit granted, since 1997 they have ranked first (see Table 7.2). Moreover, the growing presence of the Vietnamese is also due to an illegal flow. Some of these illegals have attempted to legalize their stay through an application for permanent residence permit or through marriage with a Polish resident (see Table 7.3 and 7.4). At the end of 1995, the Vietnamese were the third largest group of immigrants receiving residence permits. By 1996, they were the second, and this tendency continued through the century's end (see Table 7.3). There are an estimated 30,000 or so Vietnamese living in Poland (Halik, 2000).

The Vietnamese have become one of the main groups of foreigners involved in small trade. It is a group that is well-organized socially and, contrary to Armenians and Ukrainians, has not been involved much in crime. They try to assimilate with traditional Polish norms; they send their children to Polish schools, try to learn the Polish language, read Polish papers and watch Polish TV. They also establish contacts with Polish families. This is the natural behavior of people who intend to live in Poland for a longer period of time, maybe forever (Halik, 2000).

One should, however, remember that 'the Vietnamese form a fairly close-knit society which externally adopt and adapt themselves to dominant culture, "internally" however, they still maintain their own individuality in the ethnic and cultural sense and as far as language is concerned'. And, what is more, they cultivate this distinctness (Condominas and Pottier, 1983; Khoa, 1983).

There is much to indicate that they feel 'at home' in Poland. They carry on a vigorous economic activity that extends beyond small trade and gastronomy. The Association of Vietnamese Businessmen in Warsaw has been legally registered. Vietnamese trading firms and enterprises are present in more than half of the voivodeships of the country. The Vietnamese themselves declare a feeling of 'well-being' within the Polish cultural sphere and they stress the tolerance and the possibility of being able to have an 'economic existence' within it. The Socio-Cultural Association of Vietnamese publishes its own periodical, holds meetings for its members and associates, and organizes the cultural life of the Vietnamese in many cities (Halik, 2000).

Through an analysis of official data on Vietnamese society and an examination of research on the cultural self-awareness of the Vietnamese in Poland (Halik, 1995), four scenarios for the future development of Vietnamese community can be proposed. First, if the bulk of immigrants are young, poorly educated men who are in Poland illegally only to earn money, they will probably decide to return to Vietnam or try to migrate on to the West after achieving their financial goals. Such a scenario would mean that, in the foreseeable future, there will either be fewer Vietnamese immigrants in Poland or the number living there will remain at the present level. Secondly, Vietnamese who are in Poland legally, especially those who have permanent residence as well as network of connections with their countrymen in Germany or France, will probably treat their stay in Poland as a 'stop-over'. Thus in a 'friendly environment' and in 'an atmosphere of tolerance', they can save up money and wait for Polish citizenship to facilitate onward migration to a western European country. Thirdly, there is also a possibility of stabilization or even a small increase in the number of Vietnamese permanently residing in Poland and a coincident tendency to become isolated from Polish society. In this scenario, one may assume that the language barrier (Polish is considered to be one of the most difficult languages) will effectively prevent them from appreciating elements of Polish culture. This would strengthen immigrants' inner social life leading to social isolation. A decline of inter-ethnic marriages is also foreseeable in this scenario. Finally, another possibility is that the Vietnamese could become gradually assimilated into Polish society. The number of Vietnamese children born or brought up in Poland could be large enough to fulfil the role of an intermediary between their parents and the Polish environment. The lives of the younger Vietnamese-Polish generation would be closely bound to Poland and, assuming the spread of Polish language, internal ties within the Vietnamese community would become less binding. These are only some of the possible variants and may not necessarily follow a uniform course. Most probably the future will bring a mixed model (Halik, 2000).

7.4. Conclusions

After the World War II, Poland ceased to be a multiethnic country; today, ethnic minorities comprise between 3–5 per cent of the total population. State policy after 1945 was not conducive towards maintaining an ethnic consciousness among those who survived holocaust, expulsion or resettlement. However, two factors gave rise to a sudden revival of ethnic consciousness after the collapse of the system: first, ethnic groups' political, social and legal situation substantially improved after 1989. Second, minorities themselves started actively defend their interests. The revival of ethnic consciousness is particularly visible among Jews and Ukrainian-Poles. As far as the German minority is concerned, we observe a slow decline in interest in membership in this group. Return migration to Poland by those who once claimed German ethnicity has already began.

One other interesting phenomenon is the revival of ethnic consciousness among Armenians, who used to represent small and almost totally assimilated group. It is occurring under the influence of new immigrants from Armenia who, being political refugees, try to keep up their own ethnic identity.

That is not the case for another group from the former Soviet Union — Ukrainians — who do not seem so 'ethnically oriented'. It may be due to Soviet propaganda's greater success in Ukraine than Armenia or it may be the fact that, contrary to Armenians, Ukrainians come to Poland on their own free will. A dynamic migratory process is transforming their typically temporary coming and going into settlement.

The other interesting case is the Vietnamese, who are maintaining their own individuality in the ethnic and cultural sense. All three groups aim at integration with Polish society.

As yet, it is hard to draw any broad conclusions for prospects of ethnic groups since all are in the process of formation or change in Poland. Will they encounter economic and social marginalization? Will there be tension between them and the local population requiring the state to react to growing ethnic diversity? It is not yet possible to answer these and other questions stemming from the model proposed by Castles (1995). This is only the beginning of the process.

References

Adelson, J., 'W Polsce zwanej Ludową', in J. Tomaszewski (ed.), *Najnowsze dzieje Żydów w Polsce* (Warsaw: PWN, 1993), pp. 87–132.

Babiński, G., 'The Ukrainians in Poland after the Second World War', in F.E.I. Hamilton, K. Iglicka (eds), 'From Homogeneity to Multiculturalism. Minorities Old and New in Poland', *SSEES Occasional Papers*, No. 45 (London: School of Slavonic and East European Studies, University of London, 2000), pp. 114–36.

Barcz, J., 'Klauzule dotyczące ochrony mniejszości narodowych w nowych dwustronnych traktatach Polski z państwami sąsiedzkimi', *Przegląd Zachodni*, No. 2 (1996), pp. 36–48.

Castles S., M. J. Miller, *The Age of Migration: International Population Movements in the Modern World* (London: Macmillan, 1993).

Castles, S., 'How nation-states respond to immigration and ethnic diversity', *New Community*, Vol. 21, No. 3 (1995), pp. 293–308.

Central Statistical Office, *Poland-Statistical Data on Migration* (Warsaw: Central Statistical Office, 1999).

Central Statistical Office, *Polish Statistical Yearbooks* (Warsaw: Central Statistical Office, various years).

Cieślińska, B., 'Ormianie w Białymstoku', paper presented to the conference on ethnic minorities at the Jagiellonian University (Cracow, March 1997).

Condominas G., R. Pottier, 'Les refugies originares de l'Asia du Sud-Est', Rapport au President de la Republique (Paris: La Documentation française, 1983).

Czarnecki, R., 'Polska lat 1990-tych wobec mniejszości narodowych', Głos, No. 67/69 (1991), pp. 21–7.

Datner H., M. Melchior, 'Absence and return: Jews in Contemporary Poland', in F. E. I. Hamilton, K. Iglicka (eds), 'From Homogeneity to Multiculturalism. Minorities Old and New in Poland', SSEES Occasional Papers, No. 45 (London: School of Slavonic and East European Studies, University of London, 2000), pp. 90–113.

Eisler, J., Marzec 1968. Geneza, przebieg, konsekwencje (Warsaw: PWN, 1991).

Halik, T., 'The Vietnamese in Poland. Images/Scenes from the Past, Present and Future', in F. E. I. Hamilton, K. Iglicka (eds), 'From Homogeneity to Multiculturalism. Minorities Old and New in Poland', SSEES Occasional Papers, No. 45 (London: School of Slavonic and East European Studies, University of London, 2000), pp. 225–39.

Halik, T., 'Wyniki badań ankietowych prowadzonych w środowisku imigrantów wietnamskich' (Warsaw: Institute for Social Studies, Warsaw University, 1995), unpublished.

Hamilton, F. E. I., K. Iglicka (eds), 'From Homogeneity to Multiculturalism. Minorities Old and New in Poland', SSEES Occasional Papers, No. 45 (London: School of Slavonic and East European Studies, University of London, 2000).

Heffner, K., 'The Return of Emigrants from Germany to Upper Silesia: Reality and Prospects', in K. Iglicka, K. Sword (eds), The Challenge of East-West Migration for Poland (London: Macmillan, 1999), pp. 168–206.

Holuszko, M., 'Mniejszości narodowe i etniczne w Polsce', Społeczeństwo Otwarte, No. 2 (1993), pp. 5–21.

Iglicka, K., 'Immigrants in Poland — Patterns of Flow', in F. E. I. Hamilton, K. Iglicka (eds), 'From Homogeneity to Multiculturalism. Minorities Old and New in Poland', SSEES Occasional Papers, No. 45 (London: School of Slavonic and East European Studies, University of London, 2000), pp. 167–85.

Iglicka, K., 'Mechanisms of Migration from Poland Before and During the Transition Period', Journal of Ethnic and Migration Studies, Vol. 26, No. 1 (2000), pp. 61–75.

Iglicka, K., 'Shuttling from the former Soviet Union into Poland: from "primitive mobility" to migration', Journal of Ethnic and Migration Studies, Vol. 27, No. 3 (2001), pp. 505–18.

Iglicka, K., 'The Economics of Petty-trade on the Polish Eastern Border', in K. Iglicka, K. Sword (eds), The Challenge of East-West Migration for Poland (London: Macmillan, 1999), pp. 120–45.

Iglicka, K., E. Jaźwinska, E. Kępińska, P. Koryś, 'Imigranci w Polsce w świetle badania sondażowego', ISS Working Papers, Migration Series, No. 10 (Warsaw: Institute for Social Studies, Warsaw University, 1997).

Iglicka, K., K. Sword (eds), The Challenge of East-West Migration for Poland (London: Macmillan, 1999).

Jedlicki, J., 'Historical memory as a source of conflicts in Eastern Europe', Communist and Post Communist Studies, Vol. 32, No. 3 (1999), pp. 225–32.

Jerczyński, M., 'Patterns of Spatial Mobility of Citizens of the Former Soviet Union', in K. Iglicka, K. Sword (eds), The Challenge of East-West Migration for Poland (London: Macmillan, 1999), pp. 105–19.

Kersten, K., Polacy, Żydzi, komunizm. Anatomia półprawd 1939–1968 (Warsaw: Nowa, 1992).

Kersten, K., Repatriacja ludności polskiej po II wojnie światowej. Studium historyczne (Warsaw: Ossolineum, 1974).

Kęsicka, K., 'Holding Stadion', *Gazeta Wyborcza* (23–24 November 1996).

Khoa, L. H., 'Les Vietnamiens en France: la dialectique insertion — identité. Le processus d'immigration depuis colonisation jusqu'à l'implantation des réfugies', MA Thesis (Nice, 1983).

Khomra, A., 'Torgova migratsya ukrainskogo naselenyea w Polshu', NISS Report (Kiev: NISS, 1994).

Kubiak H. (ed.), *Mniejszości polskie i Polonia w ZSRR* (Wrocław: Wrocław University, 1992).

Kurcz, Z. (ed.), *Mniejszości narodowe w Polsce* (Wrocław: Wydawnictwo Uniwersytetu Wrocławskiego, 1997).

Kurcz, Z., 'The German Minority in Poland after 1945', in F. E. I. Hamilton, K. Iglicka (eds), 'From Homogeneity to Multiculturalism. Minorities Old and New in Poland', *SSEES Occasional Papers*, No. 45 (London: School of Slavonic and East European Studies, University of London, 2000), pp. 69–89.

Kwilecki, A., 'Mniejszości narodowe w Polsce Ludowej', *Kultura i Społeczeństwo*, Vol. 3, No. 4 (1963), pp. 87–104.

Łodziński, S., 'National Minorities and the "Conservative" Politics of Multiculturalism in Poland after 1989', in F. E. I. Hamilton, K. Iglicka (eds), 'From Homogeneity to Multiculturalism. Minorities Old and New in Poland', *SSEES Occasional Papers*, No. 45 (London: School of Slavonic and East European Studies, University of London, 2000), pp. 34–66.

Łukowski, W., 'Społeczeństwo wędrujące. Wyniki badań jakościowych', paper presented at the seminar of Institute for Social Studies, Warsaw University and Ministry of Labour (Warsaw: Institute for Social Studies, Warsaw University, 19 April 1997), unpublished.

Machcewicz, P., *Polski rok 1956* (Warsaw: Oficyna Wydawnicza Mówią Wieki, 1993).

Marciniak, T., 'Armenians in Poland after 1989', in F. E. I. Hamilton, K. Iglicka (eds), 'From Homogeneity to Multiculturalism. Minorities Old and New in Poland', *SSEES Occasional Papers*, No. 45 (London: School of Slavonic and East European Studies, University of London, 2000), pp. 135–48.

Michalska, A., 'Pracownicy-migranci jako nowa "mniejszość narodowa"', *Sprawy Narodowościowe. Seria Nowa*, Vol. 2, No. 1 (1997), pp. 15–28.

Nolte, H.H., '"Spóźnione" narody w Europie Środkowej i Wschodniej', *Przegląd Zachodni*, No. 1 (1995), pp. 31–6.

Ociepka, B., *Niemcy na Dolnym Śląsku w latach 1945–1970* (Wrocław: Wydawnictwo Uniwersytetu Wrocławskiego, 1994).

Office for Migration and Refugees, *Statistical Data on Migration, 1994–1998* (Warsaw: Office for Migration and Refugees, 1999).

Okólski, M., 'Migracje zagraniczne w Polsce w latach 1980–1989. Zarys problematyki badawczej', *Studia Demograficzne*, Vol. 17, No. 3 (1994), pp. 3–59.

Olszewicz, B., *Obraz Polski dzisiejszej. Fakty, cyfry i tablice* (Warszawa, 1989).

Piesowicz, K., 'Demograficzne skutki II wojny światowej', *Studia Demograficzne*, Vol. 87, No. 1 (1987), pp. 103–36.

Polish Border Guard, *Polish Border Guard Statistics* (Warsaw: Polish Border Guards, 1996).

Pudło, K., *Polityka państwa polskiego wobec ludności ukraińskiej (1944–1991)* (Bialystok, 1993).

Rogalla, J., 'W poszukiwaniu tożsamości: Mazurzy i Warmiacy w XIX i XX wieku. Dyskusja', *Borussia*, No. 1 (Olsztyn, 1992).

Rosenson, C., 'Jewish Identity Construction in Contemporary Poland: Influences and Alternatives in Ethnic Renewal', PhD Thesis (Ann Arbor: University of Michigan, 1997).

Sakson, A., 'Mniejszości narodowe w Polsce ze szczególnym uwzględnieniem mniejszości niemieckiej', *Kultura i Społeczeństwo*, No. 4 (1991), pp. 4–28.

Tomaszewski, J., *Mniejszości narodowe w Polsce XX wieku* (Warszawa: Editions Spotkania, 1991).

Urban, T., *Deutsche in Polen. Geschichte und Gegenwart einer Minderheit* (Munich, 1993).

Part III

Migration Policies at Different Stage of Development: between National and European

8
Migration Policy and Politics in Poland

Ewa Kępińska, Dariusz Stola

8.1. Introduction

In the contemporary Western understanding of the term, an *immigration* policy has only recently emerged in Poland. Before 1990, international migration was certainly a political issue and a topic attracting public attention, but the focus was exclusively on outmigration; the words 'immigration' and 'immigrant' appeared only with reference to other countries and the key issue was the exit policy of the Communist regime. Moreover, Poland had had a rich history of outmigration while immigration, in the modern era, had been a marginal phenomenon. This was by no means unique in Central and Eastern Europe, which had been traditionally (except for Bohemia and Silesia) a migration sending area.

Consequently, Poland had had very little experience in dealing with international migration and no public debate about immigration. When migrants began to move in and through Poland in the early 1990s, the country lacked not only resources but also a proper legal and institutional framework to deal with the arriving foreigners.[1] Today, such framework evidently exists, some of its sections being quite sophisticated. The 1990s brought a gradual development of regulations and policies, institutions and political discourse that could match the new migratory phenomena. Poland has clearly made substantial progress in building institutions and a legal framework for immigration while gradually clarifying its policy objectives, all of which were practically non-existent at the beginning of the decade.

Since settled immigrant groups in Poland have been relatively small and recent whereas international mobility quickly reached a large scale,[2] the emergent issues centred around the mass movements of people and the questions related to the early stages

159

of foreigners' settlement processes rather than matters pertaining to their extended residence, such as societal integration, the problems of second generations, and so on The key terms for describing migrations in Poland have been flow rather than stock and mobility rather than residence. Despite such a nature of the main migrations to (and from) Poland, one may note a tendency in legislation, policies and administrative practice to focus on less fluid and more manageable forms of migration.

A key feature of the emergence of the new Polish immigration regime was its reactive character. Developments in migration were usually ahead of developments in migration policy, which emerged in response to more or less unexpected phenomena. Besides the developments in migration itself, the policies reacted to the ongoing process of Poland's (re)integration with the West. This included ratification of certain international conventions and new bilateral agreements, adopting EU/Schengen border control standards, responding to the advice or demands of friendly and powerful countries, including calls to crack down on illegal transit, and copying/adopting various solutions from abroad that Polish officials believed appropriate.

Another key feature of Polish immigration policy has been the very limited reflection on what its aims and guiding principles should be and, even more generally, on the national interest in migration matters. Polish policy makers, legislators and media did not seriously consider the question 'do we really want or need immigrants, and why?'. Recently, immigration has been discussed more frequently. Government officials admit that Poland lacks a coherent and well-thought-out migration policy. They have begun to invite non-governmental organizations and academics dealing with migration issues to share their opinions and discuss the topic.

This paper is to present how the relevant institutions and legislation concerning immigration to Poland has evolved in the course of 1990s and what have been the major directions and causes of their changes. Also, selected issues in Polish immigration policy on the eve of Poland's accession to the EU will be discussed.

8.2. Institutional Actors

Just a few months after the end of communist rule, the new Polish government had to face problems resulting from the 'victory of freedom', that is from the disappearance of the highly restrictive regime for international mobility and emergence of new forms of migration, especially migration to Poland. To cope with them, the government appointed the Commissioner for Migration and Refugee Affairs. This was the beginning of the emergence of a special government agency to deal with migration. The Commissioner's Bureau — a small body intended as temporary — grew and became a permanent Department of Migration and Refugees within the Ministry of Interior and Administration. The Department continued to grow and expand its functions. In 2001, a separate Office for Repatriation and Aliens (ORA) was established, which is the main institution responsible for migration matters today. Among its major tasks are granting refugee or asylum status, handling appeals on visas and residence permits, and dealing with so-called repatriation, that is the immigration of ethnic Poles. Supplementary to ORA is the Council on Refugees, serving as an appeal body for ORA's decisions on refugee status. The Council was established in 1999 and consists of 12 members appointed by the Council of Ministers for a five-year period.

While formally just a law-enforcing agency, the Border Guard plays an important role in shaping migrations. It was established in 1990 to replace the communist-period Border Protection Troops with a Western-style police force and to respond to fast-growing border traffic and crime. Thanks to increased government allocations and foreign grants for the modernization of equipment, new infrastructure and training, the Border Guard's capacity and efficiency have grown significantly. The Border Guard has secured growing resources as well as growing powers. In particular, since 2001, it can operate throughout Poland, whereas previously it had operated only in the border zone. Accession to the EU, making Poland's eastern border the external border of the Union, favours the further strengthening the Border Guard.

The Ministry of Foreign Affairs governs activities of Polish consulates abroad, which are responsible for issuing visas to foreigners. The implementation of the new visa regime required by the EU is costly and consulates need to be better staffed and equipped to deal with high numbers of visa applications. In particular, the efficiency of Polish consulates in Belarus, Russia and Ukraine, countries that started to be party to a visa regime with Poland in 2003, has been quite often called into question.

Decisions on visa extensions, on temporary and permanent residence permits and registration of the invitations for foreigners are issued by regional (voivodship) administrations. They are also responsible (with the help of the police and Border Guard) for raiding sites where illegally-employed foreigners are suspected. Regional Labour Offices take part in issuing work permits. These regional authorities have a substantial amount of discretionary powers within the framework of relevant regulations. Moreover, the regulations have changed quite often, the quality of regional bureaucracies has raised doubts, and there are areas of Polish immigration policy without clearly-articulated principles. Consequently, the practice of migration policy has differed from one regional office to another. As one official of the ORA noted, Poland had as many migration policies as it had regional offices (49 until the administrative reform in 1999, 16 at present).

Because immigration has not been a big political issue, it did not attract much political or parliamentary attention. Legislation of migration-related acts did not have high priority nor did it spark major controversies. Most of the relevant bills were tabled by the cabinet.

The role of non-governmental organizations is worth mentioning. They were recognized as a partner in shaping the relevant legislation during the debate on the 1997 Alien Act and proved to be efficient and competent. In particular, the Helsinki Foundation for Human Rights and its legal experts have contributed to many provisions on foreigners (mainly refugees), especially from the human-rights perspective. Polish NGOs and quasi-NGOs contributed also to the development of special policies and regulations on 'repatriates'. This has been a highly emotional question of solidarity with ethnic Poles in the former Soviet Union, especially Polish communities in Central Asia, where they were deported by the Soviets in the 1930s and 1940s.

Another actor worth noting in refugee matters is the UNHCR, which in 1992 opened a branch office in Warsaw.[3] Since then, it has watched the refugee-status determination procedure and its accordance with the Geneva Convention as well as shared expert knowledge with Polish administration and legislators.

As mentioned above, various actions of the Polish government were consequences of the priority that migration problems were given by other governments. This applies in particular to the influence of the German government and of the European Commission. In the early 1990s, German fears of mass influx of illegal migrants coming through Poland from third countries initiated a series of readmission agreements that has had its own inherent dynamics. Having signed a readmission agreement with Germany, Poland had to reach such agreements with other countries in order not to become a 'dumping ground' or a trap for illegal third-country migrants readmitted from Germany. Since 1993, Poland has signed a series of more than 20 readmission agreements with countries of such migrants' possible transit or origin. It is worth mentioning here that Poland has never managed to sign such agreements with Belarus and Russia, which share a 600 km border with Poland.

The European Commission has been vital in urging Poland's adoption of Schengen standards. Since the transfer of asylum and immigration matters to a European Commission pillar at Amsterdam in 1998, the annual reports on Poland's progress towards accession to the EU to a great extent have focused on the need to improve border controls. Non-returnable aid from the EU that Poland has been receiving since 1990 (since 2000, in particular)[4] as part of the Phare Fund played a crucial role in this matter.

8.3. Legal Framework

Poland has developed an increasingly complex set of laws that regulate immigration matters. Relevant provisions have been, for the most part, introduced or fundamentally amended since the 1989 transformation. The paramount ones are the Constitution of 1997 and the international agreements that Poland has ratified. In particular, the Constitution introduced the principle that foreigners should enjoy equal rights with nationals and any restrictions to this rule must be justifiable and specified by law. The adoption of the new Constitution, substantially delayed by lengthy discord and protracted negotiations, came after Poland had undertaken most of its international commitments on migration.

Among these international obligations are treaties on free-visa tourist movement, including those made before 1989. In particular, the agreements on visa-free entry signed in the 1970s with countries of that era's 'socialist community', including the Soviet Union and applying also to its post-1990 successor states, have greatly influenced mass short-term migrations to Poland.[5] The accession to the European Union made Poland withdraw from these agreements in 2003, which essentially changes the conditions for the largest inflow of migrant labour.

Poland's entry to the Council of Europe in 1991 also had implications for the treatment of foreigners in Poland. Similar effects followed Polish delegates' admission to European Commission committees on migration. One result of this was Poland's 1993 ratification of the European Convention on the Protection of Human

Rights and Fundamental Freedoms of 1950,[6] which includes references to foreigners. In 1997, Poland ratified the European Social Charter,[7] including its Articles 18 and 19 that refer to foreigners.[8]

As far as domestic law is concerned, at the beginning of the 1990s the key act dealing with migration was the Aliens Act of 1963. It was clearly inadequate for the migratory situation that emerged after the opening of the borders. The first amendment to this Act followed Poland's ratification of the Geneva Convention and New York Protocol in 1991,[9] introducing to the Polish legal system the institution of a refugee, as well as providing for the possibility of granting asylum.[10] Work on a new act on aliens started as early as 1992 but took five years to complete.

The Aliens Act of September 1997[11] was to enable the free movement of persons while preventing unwanted foreigners from arriving and staying in Poland (Łodziński, 2001). Therefore, it focused mostly on the conditions for entry, stay and transit through Poland. In particular, it introduced provisions required by the Schengen Treaty, with detailed regulations on expulsion of unwanted foreigners, the principle of carrier's liability for bringing into Poland aliens lacking proper documents and various kinds of records of foreigners, especially with regard to undesirable ones. To the pre-existing settlement permit (permanent residence permit), the Act added the temporary residence permit, thus completing the catalogue of documents on which foreigners may reside in Poland.

In the field of asylum and protection of refugees, the Act introduced satisfactory procedural standards, including the right for asylum seekers to be informed in a language they understand, the right to personal interview and the right to contact with the UNHCR Office. An appeal procedure covering decisions on refugee status has been established as well.

Although the Aliens Act appeared consistent with European standards when it was passed in 1997, it quickly became just a step in the accession process. This process has continued at a varied pace, depending on the changing political climates in Poland, but has not ended. Adopting EU *acquis* turned out to be similar to following a moving target. Already in March 1998, when the Polish government adopted a National Programme of Preparation for Membership in the European Union, it was clear that much was to be done in the fields of Justice and Home Affairs, which encompasses issues of asylum law and practices as well as such aspects of immigration policy as the control of external borders of the Union/Schengenland, a common visa policy and combating illegal migration.

Consequently, in April 2001, the Polish Parliament passed comprehensive amendments to the Aliens Act.[12] The range of changes it introduced was significant and included the establishment of the first separate government agency to deal with migration issues and to co-ordinate efforts of other segments of administration — the above-mentioned Office for Repatriation and Aliens. It also defined a new, accelerated procedure to avert the initiation of asylum procedure for migrants from 'safe countries' and 'manifestly unfounded' claims, the obligation of *non-refoulement* to an unsafe country as well as the concept of the temporary protection status. Moreover, the concept of family reunion was introduced.

In January 2001, a separate Repatriation Act came into force.[13] Although the first principles of 'repatriation' policy occurred in 1996 and a special 'repatriation visa' was introduced in 1997, the 2000 Repatriation Act represented the first comprehensive document regulating resettlement of people of 'Polish ethnicity or descent' living in the Asian part of the former USSR to Poland. It offers special, favourable conditions for acquiring Polish citizenship and provides for public assistance to the 'repatriates' (including occupational reorientation, housing, and language courses).

Most recently, January 2003 saw news of new bills on foreigners reaching the media. The legislation is going to bring further changes to Poland's migration regime. What will be completely new in Polish legislation, according to the drafts, is a division between asylum and other immigration matters. Consequently, the Aliens Act will cover issues on principles and conditions of entry, residence and transit through Poland by citizens of non-EU countries (*extracomunitari*). The future Act on Protections of Aliens will include principles and conditions for extending various forms of protection to foreigners,[14] including a new concept of 'tolerated status'. The condition of entry and stay of EU citizens and their family members was adopted in July 2002 to come into force with Poland's formal accession.[15]

Therefore, three main acts will rule the situation and statuses of foreigners in Poland according to distinctions among those seeking protection, 'repatriates' of Polish origin and other foreigners (that is other *extracommunitari*). Among the latter there is one more important category, namely foreign workers. The Act on Employment and a number of decrees, mostly by the Ministers of Internal Affairs and of Labour, provide detailed guidelines on the hiring and employment of foreigners.

Besides the above laws, several acts regulate the conditions for public assistance to foreign residents and their access to education.

The 1996 Act on Social Relief includes provisions on access of refugees and permanent residents to welfare and makes regional administrations responsible for assisting the integration of refugees. The Act on National Education allowed foreigners with refugee status or settlement permits to send their children to public schools. This right has been recently extended to all foreigners (even those of irregular status).

8.4. Selected Issues of Immigration Policy

The following part of this article is to illustrate the development of migration policies and practices and implementation of legislation over the last decade in selected areas. Our selection of issues to present was discretionary, just like many decisions concerning foreigners in Poland are, but the problems we intend to cover seem to be the basic ones. Firstly, we will pay attention to the admission, residence and labour market policies as they pertain to aliens. Then, we focus on two privileged categories of migrants: refugees and 'repatriates'. Lastly, we take a closer look at irregular migration. By 'foreigner', we mean the legal definition of foreigner, that is a person without Polish citizenship.

8.4.1. Admission, residence and labour market

Looking at the development of immigration policies during the 1990s, it seems that more rigid conditions were imposed for foreigners' entry, ability to enter the labour market and right to permanently reside in Poland.

Aliens entering Poland, including those intending to stay for over six months or permanently, need to prove their sufficient financial standing while in Poland. This does not apply to those who enter with a formal invitation from a Polish national, as the inviting person is responsible for covering all expenses of the guest during the visit, including the costs of expulsion should the guest violate a law and be ordered to go. Lack of means may be a reason for not allowing entry into Poland, refusing a temporary or permanent residence permit, or issuing a decision on expulsion.

Looking at the 1997 Alien Act and its 2001 amendments, one notes that the periods a foreigner needs to reside in Poland in order to climb the hierarchy of legal statuses became more demanding. Before 1998, a foreigner could relatively easy acquire permanent resident status, as she or he could apply for the status immediately after his/her arrival. Since 1998, an applicant needed to have had a temporary residence permit for a minimum of three years to become eligible for a settlement permit. In 2001, this requirement was extended to five years. Bearing in mind that temporary residence permits usually do not include the right to work, such a requirement may have ambiguous consequences, especially with regard to the labour market, forcing those legally staying in Poland to take up jobs without proper work permits, that is illegally.

The right to take up employment is also rationed in the case of the family members of foreign residents. The right for family reunion, developed in 2001 in line with EU recommendations, applies to foreign residents capable of meeting the above-mentioned financial requirements, that is those able to prove possession of sufficient financial resources, social security insurance and health insurance. 'Temporary' residents and refugees have the right to have their family members join them after three years of legal residence in Poland. Nevertheless, those family members are entitled only to a temporary residence permit without formal access to the labour market, until they become eligible to apply for their own settlement permit in three years time. This means that during these three years[16] they are entirely dependent on the person they came to join.

Interestingly, a foreign spouse of a Polish citizen may apply for the settlement permit only after five years of living in Poland and having the temporary residence permit. Moreover, since 2001 such immigrants are also under special scrutiny, to make sure the marriage is not fraudulent or one of convenience. Thus, it seems that foreign families are treated much better by Polish law than mixed families.[17]

The five-year period (or three-year in case of family reunion) is not the only condition foreigners need to fulfil in order to apply for a settlement permit, which gives them most of the rights Polish citizens have (apart from voting ones). An applicant needs to prove his/her strong family and/or economic ties with Poland, prove he/she has a place to live and sufficient means for his/her living expenses. As of December 2001, more than 27 thousands foreigners were living in Poland on the basis of the settlement permit (Kępińska and Okólski, 2002). However only 2344 of them were granted it in 1998–2001. It seems that since 1998 (that is with the introduction of the 1997 Alien Act), the above-mentioned requirements have made it quite difficult for a foreigner to present a sufficiently justified application for settlement permit, especially bearing in mind that the 'sufficient means' may not have as its source legal work in Poland.

Polish law restricts access to the labour market. There is nothing exceptional either in such restrictions or in their official rationale (preventing the unemployment of natives) and the restrictions are similar to ones elsewhere in Europe. Foreigners generally are not allowed to take up employment or to be involved in any income-generating activities unless they have been granted a settlement permit or refugee status. In all other cases, a Polish employer needs to apply to local administration for a permit to employ a specific worker in a specific job, meaning that a foreigner cannot seek work in Poland on his or her own initiative. Before granting such permit, the authorities (local labour offices) are supposed to 'test the labour market' in order to protect job opportunities for native workers. In addition, the foreigner needs to apply for a visa or temporary residence permit. The procedure is time-consuming, costly (a fee equalling the official minimum monthly salary must be paid by the employer) and decisions are quite often arbitrary. All this contributes to the expansion of the irregular labour market for low-skilled foreign workers. During the 1990s, the number of work permits issued never exceeded 20 thousand annually and only a small fraction of them have been issued to low-skilled workers. At the same time, according to various estimations, hundreds of thousands of migrants were taking irregular jobs, mainly in construction and agriculture but also in domestic service (Okólski, 1997; Stola, 1997). The protectionist policy towards the labour market is thus inadequate (as the large irregular labour migration shows) and inflexible. For example, contrary to West European countries, Poland still has no programmes for selective recruitment that would attract specially-designated categories of foreign workers.

8.4.2. Refugees and repatriates

Refugees and repatriates are different categories of migrants but they share a privileged position among immigrants to Poland. What makes their situation similar is the obligation-based attitude of Polish authorities, which has, however, dissimilar roots. The development of the Polish asylum regime has been shaped by adoption of international standards on Poland's path to the European Union. The recent history of repatriation results from a perceived moral obligation of Poland to assist and admit ethnic Poles living in the former Soviet Union.

By ratifying the Geneva Convention and the New York Protocol on refugees and asylum seekers in 1991, Poland joined the international refugee regime. Further development of asylum policies and practices followed the general trend of tightening asylum policy in the European Union. The readmission agreements with Schengen countries also contributed to this trend.[18] Since 1993, the number of asylum claims has grown quickly but most applicants evidently treated Poland as a transit zone.[19] Nevertheless, with only slightly over 30,000 applications in 1992–2002, Poland is not a country with a major refugee problem. In this period, only some 1700 asylum seekers obtained refugee status[20] and most of them evidently left Poland as soon as possible, heading for West European countries.

The present standards for the treatment of asylum seekers in Poland seem similar to those in the EU as are the problems, the key one being a backlog of unprocessed applications. Although the period within which a decision should be made was extended to six months (from three months) in 2001, the Polish administration quite often fails to meet it. The Polish Border Guard and ORA lack also qualified translators, especially in exotic languages (Phuong, 2002). As well, there is an urgent need to fill a gap between those granted refugee status and those refused it, that is the problem of those whom the authorities refused refugee status but cannot deport. If they do not get a temporary residence permit (which is very rare), they find themselves in limbo, as neither legal nor evidently illegal residents. Hopefully, some sort of tolerated status that the planned changes to the asylum law intend will remedy this situation.

In the frenzy to seal frontiers and tighten asylum policy, securing due procedures and protection for refugees became increasingly difficult, especially as the abuse of asylum procedures by economic migrants became widespread. Applicants for refugee status benefit from (limited) public assistance and, more importantly, cannot be deported until a decision is made. For many migrants apprehended during attempts at illegal border crossing or in illegal transit across Poland, this is the easiest way to avoid deportation, albeit temporarily. For several years, the processing of many asylum claims was discontinued due to applicants' disappearance. It is likely that they succeeded in reaching a country further west. Thus, the fact that recognition rate is lower than five per cent per annum has resulted from both increasing scrutiny and the erosion of the group of applicants. Even the introduction of the so-called accelerated procedure in 2001 to exclude an asylum procedure in 'safe country' cases and for manifestly unfounded claims has not yet changed the general, quite suspicious, attitude of Polish authorities towards asylum seekers.

The resettlement of ethnic Poles from the former Soviet Union has attracted attention since the beginning of the 1990s. The issue was raised quite often in the Parliament and media. Relevant debates seem to have reflected some essential problems of Polish identity, including what makes a person Polish. Eventually, the 'repatriates', as they are misleadingly called (in fact most of them originate from lands now part of ex-Soviet republics which were Polish territory historically, prior to World War II or earlier), were given privileged immigration rights, similar to the *Aussiedler* status in Germany (Iglicka, 1998; Łodziński, 1998). In particular, upon entry in Poland with the 'repatriation visa' they automatically acquire Polish citizenship. They are also entitled to public assistance in housing and finding employment.

The target group of the repatriation policy has been primarily Poles in Central Asia, whom Stalin deported from Ukraine, Belarus and Lithuania in the 1930s and 1940s and who could not resettle under the great population transfers after the World War II. Some of these people are actually elderly ex-deportees, who with great determination preserved their Polish identity and culture. Others are descendants of the deportees, often Russian-speaking and living in mixed families. Thus, the rationale for the 'repatriation' policy is similar to the German *Aussiedler* policy. Nevertheless, the repatriation programme sparked interest not only in Asiatic ex-Soviet republics but also in post-Soviet European countries, such as Ukraine and Belarus, where substantial groups of ethnic Poles have lived for centuries. Between September 1996 and December 2001, 1335 families (3995 persons) arrived in Poland under the repatriation program. Most of them were citizens of Kazakhstan but a considerable number originated from Ukraine, Belarus and Russia (Kępińska and Okólski, 2002).

The repatriation started to attract the interest of EU countries fearing larger inflow of ex-USSR citizens to Poland. Some of them perceived the repatriation as a 'gate' in the wall of immigration restrictions that may become difficult to control. They are afraid that, especially while differentials in wage and living standards between Poland and Western Europe continue, the 'repatriates' will settle in Poland only temporarily and then move further West (Weinar, 2003).

The 2000 Repatriation Act tightened the conditions for granting 'repatriate' status. The criteria for recognizing who is 'of Polish origin' became narrower and the programme was explicitly restricted to citizens of post-Soviet countries of Asia. The key novelty of the amendments was to transfer the cost of public assistance to the 'repatriates' to local governments. Now, before coming to Poland, a repatriate needs to have an invitation from a local government, which must commit adequate resources for assistance. Local governments may receive some help from the central budget and employers willing to hire the repatriates are offered tax discounts. This measure shows that the national government is not ready to finance the resettlement of all those eligible.

It is impossible to estimate how many of those applying desire to live in their ancestral homeland and how many are motivated mainly by economic reasons. Given the poor living conditions in the former USSR, it is reasonable to conclude that both of those factors play a role. For some applicants (especially those whose Polish identity was questionable), repatriation had clearly been a relatively easy channel for leaving Kazakhstan (where economic hardships and growing Kazakh nationalism make the life of the Russian-speaking population difficult) and immigration to a 'Western country', as Poland is perceived. Indeed, compared to other opportunities to immigrate to Poland, repatriation is relatively quick, leads straight to naturalization and gives some material benefits, albeit limited.

8.4.3. Irregular migration

Over the last few years, Poland has been under considerable pressure from the EU and West European national governments to adopt effective measures against illegal migration. Tighter visa policies and border control systems are the major ones. Thanks to substantial budget allocations and EU grants, the Polish Border Guard grew in size and significantly expanded and modernized its infrastructure at the eastern border, which will become the EU external border. As per its visa policy, Poland has gradually reduced the list of countries with visa-free entry to Poland. Nationals of Poland's three eastern neighbours — Russia, Belarus and Ukraine — need visas for any entry since October 2003. There was wide public debate on this, in which arguments of close historical, cultural and economic ties with these countries, of ethnic Polish communities living there and of the need to maintain good diplomatic relations, especially with Ukraine, were used to counter EU demands. It seems that some of the Polish arguments eventually reached our Western partners and may help develop special provisions for visitors from the East.

As a matter of fact, irregular migration to Poland is large and illegal migrants come mostly form Poland's eastern neighbours, but their illegality does not result from illegal border crossing or visa overstaying but from mass illegal employment. Both data on foreigners apprehended during illegal entry and interviews with Border Guard officers confirm that the eastern border is increasingly well protected (Kępińska and Okólski, 2002). At the same time, reasonable estimates of annual flows of unregistered labour from the East reach into the hundreds of thousands (Okólski, 1997; Stola, 2001). Thanks to bilateral agreements signed in the Communist period, Ukrainians (mainly) as well as Belarussians and Russians enter Poland visa-free and may legally remain up to 90 days, which greatly facilitates their short-term, sometimes pendulum, labour migration.

The Polish administration tried to crack down on this phenomenon. Since 1998, visa-free visitors need to produce upon arrival either a notarized invitation from a Pole or a sufficient amount of money to cover their needs while in Poland. The latter is more popular — Border Guard officers talk about visitors who proudly show off 100-dollar bills sealed in a plastic wrap, which they use at consecutive entries. Several thousand visitors from Eastern Europe are refused entry each year due to having insufficient funds or being reasonably suspected of coming to work rather than tourism. This represents, however, a tiny fraction of the inflow. The border, the place where migration policy enforcement is the easiest, is therefore not used to enforce any consistent policy on labour migration. There have been periods of greater and lesser scrutiny of border controls, sometimes following more demanding guidelines from Warsaw, yet it is difficult to detect any consistent, long-term policy in these efforts. Variations in border control scrutiny in different periods or at different checkpoints seem to depend more on the whims of local officers rather than on any general policy.

The presence of huge numbers of irregular workers from the East evidently moots the doctrine of protecting the Polish labour market. Although recent changes in immigration law gave adequate instruments to the Border Guard, police, labour inspectors and local governments to fight illegal work and residence, they do not seem to be frequently used. There were several major operations against illegal migrants, but they targeted overstaying Romanian Roma (Gypsies), foreign prostitutes and westward transit migrants. The authorities seem largely passive towards the main stream of migrants, consisting of illegally employed visitors from the ex-USSR.

There are also other aspects of illegality that should not be omitted. It applies to foreigners who have lived in Poland for many years but due to various reasons, such as the expiration of their passports, their stay is illegal, that is they do not have valid, legal documents (Rutkiewicz and Rzeplińska, 2000). Polish law does not give any possibility for legalizing the status of illegal migrants and for many years there has not been any regularization programme or even a need to introduce one. However, in the new draft of the aliens law, the opportunity to legalize the status of foreigners that have been living in Poland for many years without proper documents has been discussed.[21] Last but not least, no special programmes for rejected asylum seekers exist. For over 90 per cent of those whose refugee applications have been refused, their residence and employment in Poland becomes, by definition, illegal. However, they may continue to work without proper documents or try to cross the green border into the West.

8.5. Conclusions

Immigration is not regarded as one of the Poland's fundamental problems during its building of a new political and economic order. Nor has it been a big issue in political debates or in the media. The usual agents of anti-immigrant backlash, such as nationalist right-wing parties and nativist trade unions, do not seem much interested either. Thus, with the exception of responding to the growth in crimes committed by foreigners and the aspects of migration important to Poland's foreign partners (of which combating illegal transit was the key one), defining a migration policy has not been a high priority. The emerging migratory regime has lacked clear objectives; migration policies have been reactive and lack long-term goals and guidelines.

In general, the development of relevant legislation may be divided into two periods: pre- and post-1998. Up until the introduction of the 1997 Aliens Act, Poland was chiefly responding to an unexpected influx of short-term migrants, an inflow of asylum seekers and illegal migrants heading westward, as well as obligations resulting from new international agreements. The introduction of the Aliens Act marked the beginning of a new stage in Polish migration policy. At this stage, policy development has reflected mainly Poland's efforts for EU accession and related negotiations. This resulted in a tendency towards greater control over and restriction of inflow from the East, as well as further strengthening of migration-control institutions and the growing complexity of the relevant regulatory framework. Also, a legal basis has been laid for the post-accession equal treatment of citizens of other EU countries.

The privileged groups of incoming foreigners are repatriates and refugees, and this will continue as long as their numbers are small. However, even for these groups, Poland's hospitality is limited.

Asylum seekers do not have a right to work; the proportion of approved claims is low and public assistance for the integration of recognized refugees is modest. Repatriates need to meet increasingly narrow criteria and find a local government sponsor.

Other foreigners allowed to reside in Poland are, or at least should be, self-sufficient. They are tolerated as long as they can live self-sufficiently (that is brought resources with them or managed to get a work permit) but they are not encouraged to settle, as proven by the long and difficult process preceding the granting of a settlement permit. Alongside this rather restrictive migration regime is large-scale irregular labour migration. Tolerance of the latter, be it due to the state's inability to counteract it, its low priority or a conscious decision not to oppose it, is a stable part of domestic migration policy/practice. The termination of visa-free entry for visitors from the East is a major change in this area.

Notes

1   This article does not aim at presenting the recent migration trends in contemporary Poland. For this, please see for example Kępińska and Okólski (2002).
2   The number of entries of foreign nationals to Poland rose from 6.2 million in 1988 to 36.8 million in 1991, and then to 88.6 million in 1998.
3   Before that, UNHCR had been invited to Poland for short-term missions. The first such mission arrived in Poland in March 1990 after Sweden had returned a large group of asylum seekers, and UNHCR was asked by the Polish Government to assist in determining the status of aliens seeking international protection.
4   In 1990–99 Poland was granted over two billion Euro. In 2000, it received a record sum of 484 million Euro, and in 2001 — 468.5 million Euro. Continuing financial aid is planned till 2006. 70 per cent of the resources is foreseen for investment projects and 30 per cent for projects concerning institutional development (www.europa.delpol.pl).
5   Most visa-free agreements had been already terminated as former Soviet republics and other former Communist states are on the EU 'black list', meaning that Poland needs to introduce a visa regime with them before accession. For the remaining countries of Belarus, Ukraine and Russia, this is planned for autumn 2003.
6   *Dziennik Ustaw (Journal of Law)*, No. 61, Item 284 and 285 (1993); No. 36, Item 175, 176 and 177 (1995); No. 147, Item 962 (1998).
7   *Dziennik Ustaw (Journal of Law)*, No. 8, Item 67 (1999).
8   It is worth noting that Poland did not accept the European Convention on Migrant Workers of 1977 (Łodziński, 2001).
9   *Dziennik Ustaw (Journal of Law)*, No. 119, Item 515, 516, 517, 518 (1991).
10 *Dziennik Ustaw (Journal of Law)*, No. 7, Item 30 and No. 25, Item 112 (1992).

11   *Dziennik Ustaw (Journal of Law)*, No. 125, Item 128 (1997). The 1997 Aliens Act came into force on 27 December 1997. The new stage of immigration policy in Poland started though in 1998.
12   *Dziennik Ustaw (Journal of Law)*, No. 42, Item 475 (2001). It followed EU recommendations (including decisions of the Tampere summit) as of the end of 1999 (Łodziński, 2001). It came into force on 1 July 2001.
13   *Dziennik Ustaw (Journal of Law)*, No. 106, Item 1118 (2000). It came into force on 1 January 2001.
14   According to one of its articles, a foreigner who applies for refugee status without a valid visa or stays in Poland illegally may be placed in a guarded or deportation centre. This is based on the Australian model and, in reality, is considered as one of the most restrictive systems in Europe.
15   *Dziennik Ustaw (Journal of Law)*, No. 141, Item 1180 (2002).
16   The three-year period applies only to foreigners coming to Poland under family reunion. Other foreigners may apply for permission for settlement, which gives them unrestricted access to the labour market, only after five years of legal residence in Poland.
17   Fortunately, in the draft of a new Aliens Act, foreign spouses of foreigners and Poles will be treated equally, not having access to the labour market for three years.
18   The first wave of asylum seekers was received before Poland became a party to the Geneva Convention. Nearly 600 persons were sent back by Sweden while trying to cross the border illegally and almost all of them claimed asylum in Poland (Lavanex, 1999).
19   Poland was encouraged to sign the readmission agreement with Germany in exchange for 120 million DM of assistance for the development of border control and asylum systems (Stola, 1998).
20   Additionally, in 1992 a group of Bosnian women and children and in 1999 a group of Kosovo Albanians (1000 persons each) were offered temporary protection.
21   Those foreigners who have continuously stayed in Poland for at least six years (since 1 January 1997), have a place to live and proper financial means to cover necessary expenses (or work promise from an employer) are allowed to apply for a temporary residence permit.

References

Głąbicka K., M. Okólski, D. Stola, 'Polityka migracyjna Polski', *ISS Working Papers, Migration Series*, No. 18 (Warsaw: Institute for Social Studies, Warsaw University, 1998), available also at www.iss.uw.edu.pl/osrodki/cmr/wpapers/pdf/018.pdf.

Iglicka K., 'Are they fellow-countrymen or not? Migration of Ethnic Poles from Kazakhstan to Poland', *International Migration Review*, Vol. 32, No. 4 (1998), pp. 995–1014.

Kępińska E., M. Okólski, 'Recent trends in international migration. Poland 2002', *ISS Working Papers, Migration Series*, No. 48 (Warsaw: Institute for Social Studies, Warsaw University, 2002), available also at www.iss.uw.edu.pl/osrodki/cmr/wpapers/pdf/048.pdf.

Kozłowski T. K., 'Migration flows in the 1990s: Challenges for entry, asylum and integration policy in Poland', in K. Iglicka, K. Sword (eds), *The Challenge of East-West Migration for Poland* (London: Macmillan, 1999), pp. 45–65.

Lavanex, S., *Safe Third Countries. Extending the EU Asylum and Immigration Policies to Central and Eastern Europe* (Budapest: Central European University Press, 1999).

Łodziński S., 'Guarded welcome. A review of new legislation and institutions dealing with migration and foreigners', in K. Iglicka, K. Sword (eds), *The Challenge of East-West Migration for Poland* (London: Macmillan, 1999), pp. 66–89.

Łodziński S., 'Papierowa kurtyna wiz. Wybrane problemy polityki migracyjnej Polski a porozumienie z Schengen', in P. Jaworski (ed.), *Polska droga do Schengen. Opinie ekspertów* (Warszawa: Institute for Public Affairs, 2001), pp. 169-200.

Łodziński S., 'Repatriacja osób narodowości lub pochodzenia polskiego w latach 1989–1997. Problemy prawne i instytucjonalne', *Information*, No. 586 (Warsaw: Bureau of Research of Chancellery of the Sejm, 1998), http://biurose.sejm.gov.pl/teksty/i-586.htm.

Łodziński S., 'Wybrane problemy prawne polityki migracyjnej Polski a członkostwo w Unii Europejskiej', in P. Korcelli (ed.), *Przemiany w zakresie migracji ludności jako konsekwencja przystąpienia Polski do Unii Europejskiej* (Warsaw: KPZK PAN, Wydawnictwo Naukowe PWN SA, 1998), pp. 79–121.

Okólski M., 'Migrant trafficking in Poland. Actors, mechanisms, combating', *ISS Working Papers, Migration Series*, No. 24 (Warsaw: Institute for Social Studies, Warsaw University, 1999).

Okólski M., 'Najnowszy ruch wędrówkowy z Ukrainy do Polski', *ISS Working Papers, Migration Series*, No. 14 (Warsaw: Institute for Social Studies, Warsaw University, 1997).

Phuong C., 'Controlling asylum migration to the enlarged EU: the impact of EU accession on asylum and immigration policies in Central and Eastern Europe', paper presented at the conference on Poverty, International Migration and Asylum (Helsinki, 27–28 September 2002).

Rutkiewicz A., I. Rzeplińska, 'The rights of migrants on the border line of law', in K. Hakola (ed.), *Migration Management on the Eastern Border of the EU* (Jyväskylä: Jyväskylä University, 2000), pp. 44–77.

Stola D., 'Mechanizmy i uwarunkowania migracji zarobkowych do Polski', *ISS Working Papers, Migration Series*, No. 11 (Warsaw: Institute for Social Studies, Warsaw University, 1997), available also at www.iss.uw.edu.pl/osrodki/cmr/wpapers/pdf/011.pdf.

Stola D., 'Poland', in C. Wallace, D. Stola (eds), *Patterns of Migration in Central Europe* (Houndmills, New York: Palgrave Macmillan, 2001), pp. 175–202.

Stola D., 'The Social and Political Context of Migrations between Central Europe and the EU', in E. Guild (ed.), *The Legal Framework and Social Consequences of Free Movement of Persons in the European Union* (Hague, London, Boston: Kluwer, 1998), pp. 128–39.

Wallace C., D. Stola (eds), *Patterns of Migration in Central Europe* (Houndmills, New York: Palgrave Macmillan, 2001).

Weinar A., 'Tak daleko stąd, tak blisko — europeizacja a integracja legalnych imigrantów, uchodźców i repatriantów w RP', in K. Iglicka (ed.), *Integracja czy dyskryminacja? Polskie wyzwania i dylematy u progu wielokulturowości* (Warsaw: Institute for Public Affairs, 2003), pp. 122–83.

9

When Domestic Labour is not Native Labour: the Interaction of Immigration Policy and the Welfare Regime in Italy

Giuseppe Sciortino

Immigration is currently a controversial issue in most Western European public forums. The present and future functioning of European welfare states is another issue that triggers controversy and conflict. Not surprisingly, the links between the two phenomena are a matter of serious concern. According to the 2000 Eurobarometer survey, 52 per cent of European citizens think that migrants abuse the welfare system. Such opinion is particularly widespread in France and Belgium (66 per cent) and least shared in Italy (42 per cent) and Spain (42 per cent) (Thalhammer, Zucha, Enzenhofer, Salfinger, and Ogris, 2000). There are few doubts that a better knowledge of the relationship between immigration and welfare is needed.

The difficulties in empirically investigating such relationships are great. There is a lack of adequate data on immigration and welfare practices and realities for comparative research. The available country-level information is grounded in very different structural contexts and their legal and empirical meanings are often difficult to code reasonably for comparative work. The rate of immigrants' welfare dependency, moreover, is highly correlated with states' regulations of foreigners' statuses, with refugees being the most remarkable example. Not surprisingly, the available research does not seem to identify any straightforward trend for the reciprocal impacts of immigration and welfare in Europe, with the possible exception of some very specific areas.[1]

It may be argued, however, that such investigations suffer also from a theoretical shortcoming. As a consequence of a low differentiation between scientific research and public opinion concerns, many researchers seem to have unduly correlated the relationship between immigration and a welfare system with the separate issue of immigrants' welfare dependency. Most efforts have been directed at deciding if and why settled foreigners do use welfare resources more than natives or at determining whether generous welfare provisions draw unwanted immigrants (Brucker et al., 2001). The migrants, in other words, are nearly always seen as consumers of welfare provisions.[2] There is, however, no need to restrict the topic to such issues; indeed, those two focuses have blinded many commentators to wider aspects of immigration, the labour market and the welfare system. To understand the relationships between welfare states and migration flows, it is necessary to ask ourselves also the following questions.

- What are the relationships between different welfare regimes and the demand for foreign labour? *Do specific welfare regimes produce a need for foreign labour and, if so, why?*
- How does immigration policy affect the migrants' welfare entitlements?

In the following pages, such a broad focus on the multiple relationships between immigration and the welfare state will be developed in reference to Italy. Such investigation requires, first, a description of the Italian case and its comparison to other welfare systems in Western Europe (Chapter 9.1). This chapter's second section will highlight some ways the structure of the Italian welfare system interacts with the dynamics of the migratory system Italy is part of. It will be argued that different welfare regimes do indeed produce different demands for foreign labour (Chapter 9.2). The analysis will then switch to what kind of welfare provisions immigrants have access to. It will be argued that the scope and impact of welfare programs — those which are usually clustered under the label of 'integration policy' — are, in fact, contingent upon the specifics of the countries' migration regimes (Chapter 9.3).

9.1. The Italian Welfare State: a Comparative View

The comparative study of welfare states is now a major academic industry. The search for an adequate framework for the analysis of welfare states (and an explanation of their evolution) has informed some of the most significant social science studies of the previous two decades (Castles, 1993; Esping-Andersen, 1990). This research has identified significant differences in the structure of European welfare states. It has also triggered a lively debate on the 'types' of existing welfare arrangements and on the items that should be selected to classify them.

Table 9.1 Public social expenditure as a per cent of GDP (1998)

Type of public social expenditure	Italy	Germany	France	Sweden	UK
Old age cash benefits	12.84	10.46	10.59	7.46	9.77
Disability cash benefits	0.99	1.05	0.87	2.10	2.64
Occupational injury and disease	0.45	0.34	0.24	0.32	0.32
Sickness benefits	0.71	0.32	0.51	1.13	0.14
Services for the elderly and disabled	0.17	0.75	0.66	3.71	0.81
Survivor benefits	2.60	0.49	1.59	0.69	1.01
Family cash benefits	0.58	1.93	1.46	1.63	1.73
Family services	0.30	0.80	1.23	1.68	0.49
Active labour market services	0.67	1.26	1.30	1.96	0.31
Unemployment	0.71	1.32	1.32	1.93	0.32
Health	5.51	7.80	7.27	6.64	5.62
Housing benefits	0.01	0.18	0.92	0.81	1.61
Other contingencies	0.00	0.61	0.40	0.93	0.21
All Social Expenditure	25.54	27.31	28.36	30.99	24.98

Source: OECD, Social Expenditure Database (2001)

If we look at welfare as strictly defined (as a set of entitlements and provision provided by the state or guaranteed by it), it is possible to identify some features of the Italian system that stand out in international comparison. The Italian social expenditure as a percentage of GDP is lower than the EU average.[3] The main difference, however, is in the structure of such expenditure: Italy has a much larger expenditure for pensions (both old age and survivor). A second important feature is the very limited use of means-tested benefits. The percentage of benefits that are payable only after means-testing in Italy is less half the European average (Table 9.2).

Table 9.2 Social benefits: eligibility and eligibility conditions (1998)

Country	Means-tested in cash	Means-tested in kind	Non-means-tested in cash	Non-means-tested in kind
Italy	2.3	2.0	75.1	20.6
Germany	4.9	4.9	64.8	25.4
France	6.4	5.1	59.9	28.6
Sweden	3.0	2.6	56.2	38.1
United Kingdom	8.4	8.6	56.5	26.6
EU-15	5.6	4.8	63.3	26.3

Source: Eurostat (2001)

As matter of fact, the Italian welfare state may be described as a combination of:

- very generous programs of retirement benefits for the aged and for (presumably aged) survivors,

- absence of income-support for the young and never-employed or little employed,
- absence of income-support for the long-term unemployed;
- generous allowances, albeit varying with economic sector and firm size, for unemployment linked to economic contingencies and market downturns (that is the so-called *cassa integrazione guadagni*),
- fairly generous unemployment benefits for seasonal workers in the agricultural sector,
- comparatively low income-support for single parents (less than 50 per cent the CE average),
- a second circuit of disability pensions and subsidies, often distributed through patronage networks (Ferrera, 1996),
- universal, full health coverage through a national health system (though sometimes partly means-tested),
- residual and means-tested programs in the area of housing, child care and student benefits.

Other Mediterranean EU states feature similar traits in their labour law and welfare and social programmes. It has then been claimed that there is a 'Mediterranean' cluster of welfare states with a specific and distinctive identity (Ferrera, 1996; Leibfried, 1991).[4] Such Mediterranean clustering highlights some important features shared by most Southern European welfare states. For the task at hand, such clustering has the disadvantages of being focused mainly on similarities among welfare programs and explaining differences nearly exclusively with the structure of national labour markets. The evidence for such clustering, furthermore, is far from definitive (Esping-Andersen, 1999). An alternative option is the classification of welfare regimes according to their structural logic (liberal, social-democratic or conservative) proposed by Esping-Andersen in 1990, and subsequently revised in 1999 (Esping-Andersen, 1990; 1999). Esping-Andersen's work brings to light the important similarities that Mediterranean welfare systems have with some other traditionalist-type systems of other Western European welfare states. Mediterranean welfare systems appear as variations of a much larger cluster, including Germany, Austria and — with significant differences in the familism score — France and Belgium. As matter of fact, Italy shares with the four other countries the following features:

- provisions are arranged mainly through compulsory social insurance programs (with a widespread presence of status segmentation and corporatist traits),

- families are entrusted with the ultimate responsibility for the welfare of their members (including legal responsibilities for their adult offspring and for their elderly members) as well as being seen as the best potential care-givers,
- the approach to employment management is passive, but it is matched by strong labour market regulations targeted to protect already-employed (usually adult male) householders and to guarantee incomes sufficient to maintain a family,
- welfare programs are based more on monetary transfers to households rather than the provision of services.

Esping-Andersen's approach has the theoretical advantage of seeing welfare structures as embedded in a matrix of structural relationships among households, the state and the economy. It is precisely within this framework that the relationships between welfare structures and migratory processes may be investigated in full.

The Italian welfare regime is clearly characterized by the key role mandated to families for most welfare matters. Families' responsibilities for their members are not only legally proscribed (both in reference to parents and progeny) but most of the procedures are actually centred on the expectation that this will happen. Families are also the main buffer institution. It is within families that the resources available to labour-market insiders (the employed, the self-employed, the retired and those on leave) are shared with the outsiders and the semi-insiders: the pensions of the aged may finance unemployed adult children or sustain the study of non-working nephews, the tenure of the husband may shelter the fragmented or shadow career of his wife from many risks, the level of protections guaranteed to survivors makes the lack of retirements benefits in the shadow economy less frightening. The centrality of the *male breadwinner* model in the structure of employment protection is derived largely from a vision of the centrality of the family and of the wider responsibilities the primary breadwinner assumes 'on behalf' of his household.

Such a relationship between the welfare system and households may be seen clearly in the channels used by the welfare state. In general, conservative welfare regimes are centred on compulsory social insurance and are therefore service-lean and transfer-centred (Eurostat, 2000). Not surprisingly, Italy has a larger percentage of non-means tested cash provisions (75 per cent of the social benefits delivered, against a EU average of 63 per cent) and a corresponding very low percentage of social benefits delivered in-kind (23 per cent against an European average of 31 per cent). The few areas (such as housing and family services) where there is a larger proportion of provisions in kind are also the areas where Italian public expenditure is more limited and residual. Italian households have a fairly high likelihood of being recipients of some kind of public monetary transfer and they enjoy strong labour market protection for at least one member.

Table 9.3 Children in formal day care and elderly in institutions

Country	% children (aged 0–3) in daycare institutions	% aged 65 or more in institutions
Austria	4	4.9
Belgium	30	6.4
Denmark	64	7
Finland	22	5.3 to 7.6
France	29	6.5
Germany	8	6.8
Ireland	38	5
Italy	6	3.9
Netherlands	6	8.8
Norway	40	6.6
Portugal	3 to 5	–
Spain	5	2.9
Sweden	48	8.7
United Kingdom	34	5.1

Source: OECD (2001b), www.oecd.org

At the same time — with the exception of health care — transfer and protections are embedded in a context where few services are available on a generalized basis. Italian households must, indeed, provide a very large share of personal services to their members (Table 9.3). Many Italian households actually operate as 'general contractors', that is as integrators of a large share of personal services, partly self-produced, partly acquired through public bodies and partly bought on the market.

9.2. Demand for Immigrant Labour Attributable to the Presence of a Welfare Regime

The above description has stressed how the Italian welfare regime works in transferring, directly and indirectly, monies and guarantees to the (usually male) head of household, who will subsequently select the most appropriate channel (a kind of *make or buy* alternative) for the provision of essentials to household members and to the household as a whole. Such a solution has some advantages, as the limited number of jobless households and the limited number of people in institutions demonstrate.[5] But such a solution also, has its own problems. The main of such problem is that purchasing personal and household services is not easy. As early as the 1960s, it was observed that productivity gains in service industries lag behind those of manufacturing: most personal services cannot raise productivity much (Baumol, 1967; Baumol et al., 1985). This has a very serious implication for their development, known in the literature as *Baumol's cost disease*: the provision of personal services oscillates between the risk of a sharp reduction in their supply (if the wages in the sector follow its relative productivity) and the risk of a sharp reduction in the demand for them (if their wages follow the trend established by the most-productive sectors and services, labour costs will price personal services out of the market). The latter is precisely the case of Western Europe, including Italy, where the relative cost of labour-intensive services is high.

In some welfare states, the service productivity differentials are absorbed by the state through the direct provision of the services. Where it is not, as in Italy, such productivity differentials will operate as a strong incentive for households to self-produce them. As such self-production is mostly considered women's work, the implication is the structurally-low female participation rate in the labour market. Another, more indirect, consequence is delayed and low fertility, as the opportunity cost of having children becomes higher. Both are very well-known features of the Italian context.[6]

Self-production, however, is an increasingly difficult strategy for the growing number of both dual-career households and aging couples. As a result, there is in Italy, as in the other Mediterranean countries, a large demand for personal services. Most of such work activity is undocumented and under-reported, thus making official statistics largely unreliable. Such shortcomings notwithstanding, the comparative data summarized in Table 9.4 show that the personal services market is larger in the Mediterranean countries. Even more interestingly, the size of household and personal services is larger in all the transfer-based welfare states (Table 9.4). The extent of such a market, moreover, is quickly growing under the pressure of the rising female participation rate and of the aging of the population.

In a closed system, the demand for personal services would quickly encounter Baumol's cost disease. Wages would outpace productivity, thereby pricing the services out of the market. Such an outcome, in turn, would severely strain the relationship between the male breadwinner model, embedded in the welfare regime, and the reality of increasing female participation to the labour market. Such tension may be managed only if a way were found to maintain a comparatively cheap and flexible provision of household services.

Table 9.4 Employment in selected service sectors as a per cent of working age population (1997)

Country	Health and social work	Personal and household	Total social services
Sweden	13.6	0.5	26.0
Denmark	13.0	0.8	27.3
Belgium	6.2	0.9	19.5
Netherlands	9.5	1.0	22.3
Greece	2.5	1.2	12.5
United Kingdom	7.8	1.3	21.4
Germany	5.7	1.4	17.8
Ireland	3.0	1.7	15.2
Italy	3.0	1.7	13.5
Spain	2.7	1.8	11.8
France	6.3	2.0	20.4
Portugal	3.1	3.2	16.9
EU-15	5.7	1.5	21.4

Source: US Bureau of Labour Statistic and Community Labour Force Survey; on the basis of (EC, 1998)

This is precisely where immigration comes in. Historically, the Italian structural demand for personal services has been always managed through some kind of migratory system. Traditionally, the system has consisted of rural-urban migration and, subsequently, migration from the South and the North-East to the more developed cities of the industrial triangle and the bureaucratic conurbation of Rome. For most of the 1900s, generic domestic service — as well as a variety of more specialized jobs like cook, laundry-maker and nanny — was the Italian female equivalent of the assembly line.[7] Contracts ranged from full-day, in-house servant (with as little as half a day free time in a week) to hourly-paid specialized work, sometimes done for a pool of different employers. The significance of such a sector was such that Italy is one of the few countries where, in the immediate post-war period, there were sustained attempts to collectively organize domestic workers (Andall, 2000). Domestic work was considered a suitable occupation for women (for its symbolic links with family values), whose honourable reputation during migration was protected precisely by their being 'entrusted' to the middle-class households they were working in.[8] It was, moreover, one of the very few job opportunities open to Italian women, thus guaranteeing a steady supply of potential workers.

The mid-1970s marked the beginning of a substantial shift. From one side, the demand for domestic labour was strengthened by the growing number of middle-class women entering the labour force as well as from rising quality-of-life standards. If servants had been traditionally a key element of middle-class status, their presence was now also functional to other women's labour market participation. At the same time, however, the pool of domestic workers shrank as women had new opportunities for unskilled work opened in industry. Simultaneously, stronger working class households started to withdraw their female members from the unskilled labour market. Such changes shifted the balance of bargaining power: the remaining domestic workers opted more and more for hourly jobs rather than for the traditional live-in variety. Such a change, accompanied by the introduction of a national contract in 1969, contributed to make Italian women less cheap and flexible as resources for households' needs.

The end of the 1960s and the 1970s witnessed several attempts to reform the Italian welfare system in a more social-democratic direction, including the expansion of public social services. Such attempts, however, have largely failed (Ferrera, 1984). As the welfare state did not absorb the productivity differentials, the setting was characterized by both a sharp increase in the demand for personal services and a sharp decrease of their supply. The result was a powerful pull factor for the recruitment of foreign domestic workers. Since the early 1960s, many women — mostly from the former Italian colonies in the horn of Africa and from the Catholic strongholds of Philippines, Cape Verde and from Latin America — migrated to Italy to work as live-in maids (Andall, 1998; Salazar and Parrenas, 2001). Their presence was openly recognized in the Italian press, much earlier than many other immigration flows starting at the time (Colombo and Sciortino, 2003). In the first half of the 1970s, the number of resident foreigners increased by 26 per cent whereas the number of permits for domestic workers nearly doubled. Such active recruitment — managed mostly by the Catholic Church through its mission network — is actually one of the structural roots of the current Italian migratory system, an early sign of the transition of Italy from sending to receiving country.[9]

Not by chance, women were the majority of the foreign residents in the genesis years between 1970 and 1980; domestic workers' countries of origin played (the significant undercounting produced by endemic irregularity notwithstanding) a significant role in the structuring of the non-European flows (Table 9.5). The increase in foreign domestic work was both demand-induced and policy-constructed. In 1972, apparently with the intention to protect native domestic workers, the Ministry of Labour restricted foreign domestic work to live-in contracts, thus denying foreign women the more appealing option of hourly-paid work. The same administrative order, moreover, locked in employment and residence. Foreign workers were put in a very vulnerable position: a change of employer would have entailed returning to the sending country for at least three years (Andall, 1998). Such regulations, valid until 1986, were one of the factors producing the widespread undocumented structure of earlier flows. They contributed, however, also to a high flexibility of the labour of foreign domestic workers, thus making it an attractive substitute for other sources of personal services.

Table 9.5 Foreign immigrants in Italy — selected nationalities (1970–90)

Country	1970	1975	1980	1985	1990	% women (1990)
EU-15	43.8	44.5	39.7	37.7	20.9	–
Albania	0.1	0.1	0.2	0.2	0.2	14
Former — Yugoslavia	4.4	4.0	4.1	3.3	3.8	37
Poland	1.0	0.9	1.1	1.9	2.2	56
Egypt	0.6	0.6	1.1	1.6	2.5	14
Morocco	0.1	0.2	0.3	0.6	10.0	10
Tunisia	0.2	0.3	0.5	1.0	5.3	9
Cape Verde	–	–	0.8	0.8	0.6	86
Nigeria	0.1	0.1	0.6	0.9	0.9	43
Senegal	0.0	0.0	0.0	0.1	3.2	3
Ethiopia	0.3	1.3	1.7	1.7	1.5	66
Mauritius	0.0	0.0	0.1	0.1	0.7	47
Somalia	0.3	0.4	0.4	0.4	1.2	61
People's Republic of China	0.1	0.1	0.2	0.4	2.4	40
Philippines	0.2	0.4	1.4	1.8	4.4	67
Bangladesh	0.0	0.0	0.0	0.0	0.6	3
India	0.7	0.9	1.1	1.3	1.4	43
Iran	1.2	1.2	3.1	3.1	1.9	35
Sri Lanka	0.1	0.1	0.3	0.6	1.6	31
Lebanon	0.5	0.5	0.7	0.9	0.7	24
Turkey	0.6	0.6	0.6	0.6	0.6	32
Argentina	1.4	1.3	1.2	1.2	1.6	52
Brazil	1.0	0.9	0.9	1.1	1.8	68
Chile	0.2	0.2	0.5	0.6	0.5	54
Columbia	0.4	0.4	0.4	0.5	0.7	71
Peru	0.3	0.3	0.3	0.3	0.7	64
Others	42.5	40.9	38.7	37.1	27.8	–
Total	146,989	185,715	272,163	422,904	781,158	40

Source: Own elaboration on the basis of Prof. A. Birindelli, and Prof. P. Farina Archives

Foreign domestic workers have become in more recent years one of many differentiated flows with Italy as a destination (Ambrosini, 2001). Moreover, foreign labour continues to support the Italian welfare regime. Foreign workers account for 46 per cent of all registered domestic workers in Italy. Such statistics, however, are far from covering the whole segment of domestic work, which is mostly undocumented or underreported. A more accurate picture is provided by the Fondazione ISMU Lombardy Survey, which covered both documented and undocumented foreign residents (Blangiardo, 2002).[10] The Fondazione ISMU survey data further document the structural relevance of foreign labour in personal and household services. While the distribution of foreign workers by sector is similar to those of natives, migrants are highly over-represented in the sub-sector of personal services. Currently, 22 per cent of foreigners work within a household. Not surprisingly, the personal services sector is also — with construction — one with the most undocumented migrants (Table 9.6).

Table 9.6 Employment by economic sector of natives and foreigners in Lombardy

Economic sector	Overall labour force (%)	Foreign workers (%)	*of whom irregular* (%)
Agriculture	2.1	1.2	17.1
Manufacturing	32.6	30.8	10.5
Construction	7.9	11.2	35.2
Services	57.5	56.8	–
of whom:			
Services to production	13.0	9.4	29.7
Distributive services	19.4	10.1	23.4
Social Services	17.1	3.3	5.6
Personal services	7.9	33.5	34.2

Source: ISTAT, Labour Force survey (2001) and Fondazione ISMU, Lombardy survey (2001)

The role of foreign domestic work in the maintenance of the Italian welfare regime is duly acknowledged even in Italian political debate. Throughout the 1990s, nearly half of the scarce legal admissions of foreign workers were granted to domestic workers. They also enjoyed a fair degree of tolerance in most of the amnesty programmes that marked the decade. And it is worth noting that the right-wing government in power since May 2001 has accompanied the enactment of a new repressive immigration bill with a new amnesty targeted only at domestic and personal care workers. Although the parliament subsequently extended the proposed amnesty to all kinds of wage-earning workers, the domestic sector has accounted for 341,121 applications out of 702,156.[11]

Should the large demand for foreign domestic work be considered an Italian peculiarity? Comparative data are not reliable enough to allow a definitive answer. The available data, however, do show that foreign workers are over-represented in the personal service sector in several European countries, in a way that apparently reflects the structure of their welfare regimes (Table 9.7). We may conclude that immigration is indeed connected with the activities of a welfare state. Such connection, however, is not only a matter of welfare expenditure *for* and *on* migrants. *It is above all a matter of the kind of labour demand welfare regimes produce, and of the segment of such demand that can be satisfied with foreign labour.*

Table 9.7 Employment of foreigners by service sector, 1999–2000 average[a]

Country	Health and community services	Households
Austria	11.3	**0.8**
Belgium	12.4	**0.8**
Denmark	**26.8**	–
France	8.7	**7.1**
Germany	12.3	**0.6**
Greece	4.2	**19.6**
Italy	6.7	**10.9**
Netherlands	12.4	0.2
Portugal	**10.3**	**6.8**
Spain	8.1	**18.0**
Sweden	23.1	–
United Kingdom	**20.2**	1.6

[a] The numbers in bold indicate that foreigners are over-represented
Source: OECD (2001c)

9.3. Rights and Eligibility: Regularity of Residence as a Filter for the Access to Integration Policies

The previous section has argued that each of the various types of welfare regimes has significantly different impacts on the structures of immigration systems. Traditionalist-type welfare states require the availability of a large pool of household services. Immigration is a way to diminish or prevent Baumol's cost disease, embedded in the differentials between wages and productivity in such sectors. Immigration, in other words, is a functional alternative to the direct provision of services by the state. Immigration should be considered not only as a welfare burden but also as a structural resource for the functioning of certain welfare regimes.

Such a viewpoint has some interesting implications for the analysis of the integration policies enacted by Western democratic states. In most cases, the study of integration policies is focused on how receiving states manage the inclusion of migrants into their welfare programs. In many cases, 'integration policy' is identified with the study of the basket of welfare services provided to immigrants. Not enough attention, however, is paid to the structural pre-conditions that regulate *ex-ante* access to the welfare system.

Comparative works show that an important feature of the contemporary Western European migratory context is resident foreigners' ability to access key welfare provisions. In most European countries, legally-resident foreigners actually enjoy access to welfare programs nearly exactly on the same terms as citizens.[12] An equally important element is the principle of equal pay for equal work, regardless of nationality. Such a principle is embedded in all ramifications of immigration policies of Western European states. It is such elements that sharply differentiate the Western European migratory situation from those of Gulf countries or of the newly industrialized countries of South-East Asia (Sciortino, 2000).

Such a liberal vision is in a state of constant strain with the economic mechanisms triggering the large-scale migration of foreign service workers. What the welfare regimes need from foreign migrants is different from what the welfare states say should be given to them. If migration is a way to manage the tensions between wages and productivity in the service sector, the integration of migrants would cause a constant renewal of Baumol's cost disease. After a while, foreign workers start moving to sectors where wages are higher and conditions of work more appealing. Legal domestic workers tend to move from live-in domestic work to hourly-paid work for a pool of employers (Salazar and Parrenas, 2001; Andall, 2000). Within the medium term, they may end up leaving the household service sector altogether. Without further immigration, the domestic services sector will again totter between lack of supply and skyrocketing costs.

The movement of workers out of the domestic service sector, however, is contingent on the availability of a legal title for residence since legal residence status is a prerequisite for leaving the service sector or for climbing up its ladder. Given such contexts, irregular migration may well have a buffer function. Undocumented workers, after all, have a strong incentive to be domestic workers: households are often able to provide accommodation and they are much less likely to be raided by labour inspectors. All over Europe, since 1973 the enactment of restrictive legislation on new entrants has created a sizable segment of irregular resident foreigners, available for work but excluded from welfare programs and from the protection under the principle of equal pay for equal work. It is no surprise that many of them are employed in households and the personal service sector for lengthy periods.

Such processes, however, do not operate in reference only to undocumented workers. Some restrictive filtering may be observed also within the legally resident population. Such filtering reduces migrants' access to welfare services and affects their work strategy. Integration policies act through the granting of rights. The enjoyment of such rights, however, depends on a legal residence status consistent with the categories recognized by the receiving states. At one extreme, as for refugees in most Western European countries, welfare dependency is an almost automatic consequence of their status as foreigners unentitled to work. At the other end, a fairly generous granting of rights to legally resident foreigners may easily coexist with a restrictive management of the legal statuses available to the foreigners working in a country's territory. The latter describes with a certain accuracy the Italian situation as well as the situation of many other countries with traditionalist-type welfare regimes.

Italy started developing an immigration policy virtually from scratch in the early 1980s; the first National Immigration Act was passed in 1986. Starting from scratch, however, does not imply having a free hand. In designing its immigration policy, Italy was constrained by a variety of international conventions (Sciortino, 1999). The result was an early and straightforward introduction of the principle of equal treatment and equal access to welfare measures for citizens and resident foreigners alike. The subsequent legislative evolution has introduced remarkable restrictive changes in the Italian control policy, but it has also shown a remarkable continuity as far as equal treatment is concerned. One example will suffice: the right-wing government that has ruled the country since May 2001 rushed to introduce several restrictive changes in the Italian immigration control policy. At the same time, however, it has been fairly careful in avoiding dramatic changes in existing integration policies. The section of the immigration code related to integration measures has in fact survived basically unaltered, although its implementation has considerably slowed down.[13]

Such early inclusion of foreigners in the welfare programs, however, does not imply their large presence within the system. Legal migrants' use of the welfare programs in Italy is actually more limited and uncertain than the increase in the overall foreign population would lead us to expect (High Commissioner for Immigrants Integration Policies, 2001). Such a phenomenon is surely connected with their stage on the life cycle, as most immigrants are currently young and working. It is, however, also connected to a very sharp selection and delay processes, operated indirectly through the filtering of legal statuses. The structure of the immigration regime categorizes migrants into a variety of residential statuses, with very different levels of rights and entitlements. Furthermore, there is evidence that the overall structure of such a migratory regime keeps migrants as long as possible in the categories where fewer rights are enshrined and where the protection of such rights is less stable.

The most-excluded group is that of *undocumented migrants*. As in most Western European countries, this group is entitled only to emergency medical care and to a limited degree of education for their children. A second group consists of *asylum seekers, refugees and temporarily protected persons*. The members of this group, whose size is quite limited, are entitled to special assistance programs of very limited duration and amount. As matter of fact, social assistance for the group is basically left to NGOs and to a handful of local authorities. A third, and by far the largest, group consists of *immigrants with a residence permit*. This group is entitled to access all the employment-related insurance programs at the same conditions of natives, as well — when and if employed — as to most services provided in kind. Given the frequency of their irregular employment, either as a consequence of their being in the shadow economy or as a strategy to avoid taxation, their access to employment-related programs is often illusory. A forth group is constituted by *immigrants with a residence card*. Such title, introduced only in 1998, is granted after five years of regular sojourn with an income sufficient to sustain both the immigrant and his/her dependents. Residence card holders are fully included in the welfare system and are eligible for non-contributory cash benefits and income-support programs.

The long-term pattern of Italian immigration policy — and a similar argument could be made about other Mediterranean states — may be identified with a restrictive filtering, targeted to keep migrants in the least guaranteed statuses for as long as possible. At the most basic level, the failure to develop an adequate active immigration policy — even in the presence of a strong demand for foreign labour — entails a constant reproduction of irregular situations at the bottom of the hierarchy. Since its beginning, immigration to Italy has mostly taken place through the back doors of overstaying and of illegal entry (Colombo and Sciortino, 2003).

In the last 15 years, amnesties have been used frequently to manage the transition from irregular statuses to legal presence. As matter of fact, most legally-resident foreigners in Italy acquired their residence permit through an amnesty (Carfagna, 2003). The frequency with which amnesties are enacted is often quoted as evidence for a relative tolerance of undocumented immigrants by Italian authorities. Less attention, however, is paid to the dark side of such tolerance: the high discretion granted to administrative authorities in the handling of regular migrants. Residence permits must be renewed at regular times. Even long-term residents must frequently undergo a general check, since the permits granted are usually valid for one or two years. Changes in the necessary requirements, given to police officers' discretionary power and immigration offices' organization guarantee that such renewal is far from being a simple process. As a matter of fact, most immigrants' regular status is often contingent upon the willingness of police authorities and administrative staff to handle their situations in a way that keeps unbroken their legal permanence (and the rights potentially associated to such length of residence).[14] The result is a rather perverse mechanism, whereby precarity of residence and low access to social services favour employment in the shadow economy, particularly in households. Such employment conditions, in turn, make the transition to stable legal status even more fragile.

The instability in the holding of valid residence permits represents a by-product of a more general and wide-ranging desire for discretionality in the management of immigration (Sciortino, 1997). While the presence of foreign residents is by and large accepted, the idea that such category should be protected by clear-cut legislation and homogeneous procedures is empirically resisted. Most of the administrative decrees and memos that usually follow the enactment of new immigration laws have interpreted it in ways that would allow or restore room for local discretionality, often to very large extent. Such instability has deep impacts on the possibility to get access to welfare measures in a systematic way.

A similar preference for discretionality over automatic entitlement is observable in the filtering process associated with the passage from the *residence permit* to the *residence card*. When the residence card was introduced by the centre-left government in 1998, it was clearly targeted to the creation of stable denizen status[15] for long-term residents. In the bill, the requirements for the granting of such card were quite straightforward: five years of lawful residence, no criminal record and evidence of being lawfully employed. When the immigration bill was passed, around 65 per cent of the regular foreign residents had been living in Italy for more than the required five years. The residence-card holders were expected to number in the hundreds of thousands. This, however, has not happened. From one side, the whole process received a very low administrative priority, with territorially contiguous offices adopting different procedures and requesting different — and additional — paperwork (Fondazione ISMU, 2000). At the state level, the Home Ministry released an administrative interpretation of the norm that allowed only a tiny percentage of the foreign residents to apply for the card. Although such a restrictive administrative interpretation was overturned in the summer of 2002, the number of residence-card holder is currently little more than 20,000, out of a resident foreign population of a million and a half.

Such restrictive management of migrants' statuses is even more evident in naturalization laws. In 1992, the houses reformed the citizenship law in a way that severely restricted the eligibility for naturalization on the grounds of prolonged residence. Such reform, approved by a large parliamentary majority without visible opposition, may be taken as a proof of a strong, though not outwardly very visible, exclusionary view in the Italian polity. Before the 1992 citizenship law, the Italian state allowed foreign residents to apply for naturalization after five years and, in certain circumstances, after three. The reformed 1992 law requires ten years of uninterrupted residence before an application for Italian citizenship can be made. The law, moreover, makes explicit the introduction of an ethno-cultural principle in the definition of the boundaries of the Italian polity. According to the new law, the most remote descendants of Italian emigrants are embraced within such polity, while the naturalization of individuals of no Italian ancestry is heavily discouraged. The emphasis on *ius sanguinis* is increased enormously: the right to citizenship is extended to any grandson or granddaughter of an Italian citizen (provided they have lived in Italy three years), whereas *ius soli* is applied only to children born in Italy from unknown parents. The strategy seems to have been quite successful. Since the 1992 law, the number of newly-naturalized foreigners is quite limited (Pastore, 2003). The analysis of the Italian migratory regime reveals an embedded preference for discretionality, as well as a systematic filtering designed to keep migrants within the less protected statutes for as long as possible. There is no evidence that such filtering is directly aimed at restricting foreigners' access to welfare state services. There is even less evidence that such filtering is targeted to keep a large number of them in labour pool of domestic workers. It sometimes happens that the room for interpretation left open by legislation to local immigration decision-makers is sometimes used in an inclusive way (depending on times and contexts) (Zincone, 1999). Such discretionality should be considered as the product of a generalized preference for a regulative structure where migrants' claims are to be evaluated locally and case by case. At the same time, it would be difficult to deny that such generalized preference has, as a by-product, two important consequences: it severely reduces migrants' access to the welfare system and it provides a structural incentive for them to work in personal and household services. The actual configuration of the migration regime, in other words, does produce a context whereby the demand for foreign labour originated by the welfare regime can be met.

9.4. Conclusions

The chapter has presented an introductory exploration of the ways in which welfare regimes interact with migration regimes. Using Italy as its main reference point, it has been argued that such interaction cannot be understood by looking only to the welfare provisions immigrants may expect to enjoy. The alleged 'welfare overuse' by migrants is an issue of great concern that deserves to be investigated in full. However, this chapter has tried to argue that an equally important aspect is the specific demand for foreign labour produced by different kinds of welfare regimes. Welfare states, indeed, can turn out to be 'migration magnets'. Welfare states' drawing power, however, is not only a matter of the kind of welfare provisions immigrants may expect to enjoy. Migration is also a resource for managing the relationships between households, labour markets and the state. In this vein, the chapter has shown that the Italian migratory system can hardly be understood without taking into account the structural tension between a welfare system largely designed according to a male breadwinner logic and Italian women's rising labour participation. It has been argued that such tension is likely to be present in most other traditionalist-type welfare states.

A second, and related, argument has been developed in reference to the basis of integration policies in Western European states. This chapter has contended that an adequate analysis of the integration policies enacted by those states cannot be performed using undifferentiated notions of either welfare or immigrants. It is known that different programs within a welfare system may have widely different access rates according to their intrinsic logic. An equally important point, however, is that each program has its own conditions of eligibility. Such eligibility, however, is contingent on the kind of legal statuses available to the resident foreigner. The impact of immigration on the welfare system may be restrained, even when access has been liberally defined by a discretionary and restrictive regulation of the granting of such statuses. In reference to the Italian case, it has been shown how comparatively liberal welfare legislation can coexist with a restrictive regulation of legal presence, thus sharply reducing foreigners' chances of accessing many welfare programs and escape the domestic labour force.

Notes

1   The best reviews of the available literature I know are Baldwin-Edwards (2002) and Brücker et al. (2001).
2   A notable exception, from a gender perspective, is Kofman et al. (2000).
3   If calculated per head of population in purchasing power parity, the difference is –4 per cent (Eurostat, 2000).
4   According to such a perspective, such similar features would derive — or at least be interconnected to — a sharply polarised labour structure: a large section of the population (public employees, employees in medium and large firms, some sectors of agricultural work) are supposedly sheltered from any short- or medium-term risk while enjoying generous incomes, whereas other sections (employees of small firms, the long-term unemployed, the young and never employed and the employed in the shadow economy) are basically excluded from protection or only marginally included through political patronage.
5   Beside the high percentage of people aged 65 or more residing outside institutions, it is worth noting that, in 1999, in Italy there were 4.3 disabled institutionalised for every 10,000 individuals (National Institute of Statistics, 2002).
6   Although the female participation rate in the Italian labour market is rising, the increase is unable to match the more sustained growth of Western Europe as a whole. While the Italian female participation rate was eight percentage points below the EU-15 average in the 1960s, it is today nearly 13 percentage points behind (Eurostat, 2000).
7   For a history of the Italian domestic service sector, see Sarti (2003).
8   Such a familistic vision did in fact help in keeping the availability of domestic workers highly flexible: a law enacted in 1958 still failed to limit the length of the working day and to remove the traditional exemption of domestic work from a whole range of protective employment norms.
9   The early history of the Italian migratory system is poorly documented and little researched. Certainly, the flow of domestic workers is only one, albeit major, flow. Migration from China had been recorded as early as the 1930s, while local migratory systems had never stopped to link Sicily with North

Africa and the Italian Northeast with the territories of the former Yugoslav federation. A further link was established by Africans and Asians moving to Italy in the aftermath of the immigration restrictions of the early 1970s. Much later, the collapse of the Soviet bloc re-opened Italy to migratory systems rooted in Eastern Europe and the Balkans (Colombo, Sciortino, 2003).

10   Lombardy, besides being one of Italy's economic engines, has a large metropolitan reality (Milan) and a very high female labour participation rate. In short, it is a region where the identified structural tension should be felt with particular intensity.

11   Home Ministry data, 16 December 2002.

12   For an attempt to identify the impact of such a situation on the meaning of citizenship in the contemporary political arena, see Soysal (1994).

13   For an analysis of the main changes introduced by the right-wing government in the Italian immigration policy, see Fondazione ISMU (2003). The principle of equal treatment seems also to be popular (or at least not so unpopular) among the Italian population. Opinion surveys document how the Italian public opinion's fairly negative vision of immigration goes hand in hand with a fairly liberal attitude toward the rights of legal foreign residents (Diamanti 2001; ISPO, 2000).

14   There is a good deal of evidence, as documented also by quite frequent judicial reviews, that a residence permit does not provides in itself security and stability. Many immigrants have difficulties in documenting at renewal an acceptable amount of work activities while a variety of minor infractions of immigration rules may turn out to be fatal for the holding of such status. Furthermore, there is evidence of an astonishing degree of difference in the ways in which even territorially-close offices apply the procedures and interpret the norms.

15   On the notion of denizens, see Hammar (1990).

References

Ambrosini, M., *La Fatica Di Integrarsi. Immigrati e Lavoro in Italia* (Bologna: Il Mulino, 2001).

Andall, J., 'Catholic and State Construction of Domestic Workers: the Case of Cape Verdeans Women in Rome in the 1970s', in K. Koser, H. Lutz (eds), *The New Migration in Europe* (London: Palgrave, 1998), pp. 124–41.

Andall, J., *Gender, Migration and Domestic Service. The Politics of Black Women in Italy* (Aldershot: Ashgate, 1998).

Baldwin-Edwards, M., 'Immigration and the Welfare State: a European Challenge to American Mythology' (Barcelona, 2002), unpublished.

Baumol, W. J., 'The Macroeconomics of Unbalanced Growth: The Anatomy of Urban Crisis', *American Economic Review*, Vol. 57, No. 3 (1967), pp. 415–26.

Baumol, W. J., S. A. B. Blackman, E. N. Wolff, 'Unbalanced Growth Revisited: Asymptotic Stagnancy and New Evidence', *American Economic Review*, Vol. 75, No. 4 (1985), pp. 806–17.

Blangiardo, G., *L'Immigrazione straniera in Lombardia. La prima indagine regionale* (Milan: Fondazione ISMU, 2002).

Brücker, H., G. Epstein, B. McCormick, G. Saint-Paul, A. Venturini, K. Zimmerman, 'Managing Migration in the European Welfare State' (Rodolfo Debenedetti Foundation, 2001), www.fdb.it.

Carfagna, M., 'I sommersi e i sanati. Le regolarizzazioni degli immigrati in Italia', in A. Colombo, G. Sciortino (eds), *Assimilati ed esclusi* (Bologna: Il Mulino, 2002), pp. 53–90.

Castles, F. G. (ed.), *Families of Nations. Pattern of Public Policy in Western Democracies* (Avebury: Adelshot, 1993).

Colombo, A., G. Sciortino, 'Italy's Many Immigrations', *Journal of Modern Italian Studies* (2004), forthcoming.

Diamanti, I., *Immigrazione e Cittadinanza in Europa* (Venice: Quaderni Fondazione Nord-Est, 2001).

EC, *Employment rates report 1998*, www.europa.int.

Esping-Andersen, G., *Social Foundations of Postindustrial Economies* (Oxford: Oxford University Press, 1999).

Esping-Andersen, G., *The Three Worlds of Western Capitalism* (Cambridge: Polity Press, 1990).

Eurostat, *European Social Statistics. Social Protection 1980–1998* (Brussells: Eurostat, 2000).

Faist, T., 'Boundaries of Welfare States: Immigrants and Social Rights on the National and Supranational Level', in R. Miles, D. Thranhardt (eds), *Migration and European Integration: the Dynamics of Inclusions and Exclusions* (London: Pinter, 1995), pp. 177–95.

Ferrera, A., *Il Welfare State in Italia* (Bologna: Il Mulino, 1984).

Ferrera, M., 'Il Modello Sud-Europeo Di Welfare State', *Rivista Italiana Di Scienza Politica*, Vol. 26, No. 1 (1996), pp. 67–101.

Fondazione ISMU, *Ottavo Rapporto sulle Migrazioni 2002* (Milan: FrancoAngeli, 2003).

Fondazione ISMU, *Sesto Rapporto Sulle Migrazioni 2000* (Milan: FrancoAngeli, 2000).

Freeman, G., 'Migration and the Political Economy of the Welfare State', *Annals of the American Academy of Political and Social Sciences*, No. 485 (1986), pp. 51–63.

Hammar, T., *Democracy and the Nation-State: Aliens, Denizens and Citizens in a World of Intenational Migrations* (Avebury: Adelshot, 1990).

ISPO, *L'Atteggiamento Degli Italiani Nei Confronti Degli Immigrati* (Roma: High Commission for Immigrants Integration Policies, 2000).

Kofman, E., A. Phizacklea, P. Raghuram, R. Sales, *Gender and International Migration in Europe. Employment, Welfare and Politics* (London: Routledge, 2000).

Leibfried, S., 'Towards a European Welfare State?', in G. Room (ed.), *OECD European Development in Social Policy* (Bristol: Bristol University Press, 1991).

National Institute of Statistics, *La Situazione Del Paese Nel 2001* (Roma: National Institute of Statistics, 2002).

OECD, 'Balancing Work and Family Life: Helping Parents into Paid Employment', *OECD Employment Outlook* (Paris: OECD, 2001a), pp. 130–65.

OECD, 'Employment in the Service Economy: a Reassessment', *OECD Employment Outlook* (Paris: OECD, 2000), pp. 79–128.

OECD, *Society at Glance. OECD Social Indicators* (Paris: OECD, 2001b).

OECD, *Trends in International Migration 2001* (Paris: OECD, 2001c).

Parrenas, R. S., *Servants of Globalization: Women, Migration and Domestic Work* (Stanford: Stanford University Press, 2001).

Pastore, F., 'La comunità sbilanciata: Diritto alla cittadinanza e politiche migratorie dell'Italia post-unitaria', *CESPI papers*, No. 7 (Roma: CESPI, 2003).

Sarti, R., 'Quali diritti per 'la donna'?', in M. Palazzi, S. Soldani (eds), *Lavoratrici e cittadine* (Turin: Rosenberg & Sellier, 2004), forthcoming.

Sciortino, G., 'Planning in the Dark: the Evolution of Italian Immigration Control', in G. Brochmann, T. Hammar (eds), Mechanisms of Immigration Controls (Oxford: Berg, 1999), pp. 233–60.

Sciortino, G., 'Troppo Buoni? La Politica Migratoria Tra Controlli Alle Frontiere e Gestione Del Mercato Del Lavoro', *Sociologia Del Lavoro*, No. 46 (1997), pp. 50–84.

Soysal, J., *Limits of Citizenship. Migrants and Postnational Membership in Europe* (Chicago: University of Chicago Press, 1994).

Thalhammer, E., V. Zucha, E. Enzenhofer, B. Salfinger, G. Ogris, *Attitudes Towards Minority Groups in the European Union. A Special Analysis of the Eurobarometer Year 2000 Survey* (Vienna: European Monitoring Center on Racism and Xenophobia, 2000).

Wenzen, U., M. Bos, 'Immigration and the Modern Welfare State: the Case of USA and Germany', *New Community*, Vol. 23, No. 4 (1997), pp. 537–48.

Zincone, G. (ed.), *Secondo Rapporto Sull'Integrazione Degli Immigrati in Italia* (Bologna: Il Mulino, 2001).

Zincone, G., 'Illegality, Enlightment and Ambiguity: a Hot Italian Recipe', in M. Baldwin-Edwards, J. Arango (eds), *Immigrants and the Informal Economy in Southern Europe* (London: Frank Cass, 1999), pp. 43–82.

10

Bosnian Refugees in Britain: a Question of Community

Lynnette Kelly

10.1. Introduction

The war in Bosnia-Herzegovina, which began in 1992, produced the largest flow of refugees into the countries of Europe since the World War II. As the numbers seeking asylum increased, many countries sought to curtail the flow, and in Britain visa restrictions were introduced. These restrictions made it extremely difficult for Bosnian asylum seekers to enter Britain. After the discovery of concentration camps in Bosnia, the UNHCR called on the governments of the world to consider providing a refuge for the ex-detainees. Many countries offered places, and Britain agreed to accept 1000 plus their dependants and established a programme for their arrival and reception. This became known as the Bosnia Project. As a result of publicity surrounding the conditions in Sarajevo's besieged hospital, Operation Irma and subsequent medical evacuees were included in this programme.

Those brought to Britain as part of the programme were housed initially in reception centres, then moved into longer-term housing in one of the cluster areas chosen for the project. A range of support services were provided for them by the workers of the Bosnia Project, mainly focusing on access to housing and welfare benefits. Later, there were a number of Community Development workers appointed by the Bosnia Project, and Refugee Action's staff also became involved in work establishing and maintaining Community Associations in each cluster area.

The agencies involved in the Bosnia Project strongly encouraged the formation of community associations. The premises that the agencies adopted were, firstly, that the refugees, once housed in an area, would form a community and, secondly, that the best way for the needs of this community to be met was through the creation of a formal community association to empower the community's members. However, despite considerable support from a variety of organizations and individuals Bosnian community associations are either not functioning or are beset by problems in many parts of Britain. This experience is not unique to Bosnians as other refugee groups too have faced problems. As part of my work towards a PhD on the settlement of refugees from Bosnia in Britain, I have researched Bosnian community associations; the results of that research form the basis of this chapter.

10.2. Community Associations in Britain

The way in which migrants are incorporated and integrated into a society varies according to society under examination. The British model, and that of some other countries, is loosely based on notions of multiculturalism (Favell, 1998). Combined with the British traditions of volunteering and self-help, these translate into a group-based approach to countering social disadvantage, with a heavy reliance on the voluntary sector (Joly, 1996a). Many minority ethnic groups have formed community associations in order to protect and enhance the position of their community members, and British social policy has encouraged the formation of these associations. Immigrants and members of ethnic minorities are seen as being different from the majority population, and these differences are cultural and religious. A way of incorporating these groups into the rest of society is through their community. Groups of migrants are considered to constitute a community and it is believed that through community leaders the needs of the group can be conveyed to others (Favell, 1998; Shaw, 1988).

As the numbers of refugees arriving in Britain began to become significant — and in the absence of a formal policy of central Government on the integration of refugees — these same policies of encouraging the formation of community associations have been used with groups of refugees. The idea that refugees seek and need the company of others from the same group informs current legislation as the government seeks to disperse asylum seekers throughout the country while taking into account where others from the same group have been settled already. The Government funds a number of voluntary organizations in order to develop welfare services or community self-help structures. The integration of refugees has been considered an issue for non-governmental bodies, in line with a prevailing ethos in British society that places emphasis on the roles that can and should be played in society by charities, volunteering and active citizenship (ECRE, 1998). The Voluntary Services Unit at the Home Office is the only central government body with a specific remit to fund endeavours with or for refugees; similarly, it funds agencies such as the Refugee Council and Refugee Action. Its community-oriented approach can therefore be considered to be manifested via its funding relationship with those agencies.

Many local authorities also contribute to the community orientation of work with or for refugees. Political representation or influence at a local level can often be obtained in or through some community relations councils and religious councils functioning in areas of minorities' and/or newcomers' residence. However, this route is only open to formally-constituted groups. Local authorities often make grants of funds or services to established community groups, including refugee groups, and so play an important role in the creation and maintenance of formal associations.

The role of associations in the settlement of immigrants and the incorporation of ethnic minorities has been examined by many authors and found to have many positive aspects. Rex (Rex, Joly et al., 1987) found that community associations have four main functions: overcoming isolation, providing material help to community members, defending the interests of the community, and promoting the community's culture. In addition, it has been suggested that through networking and information sharing, associations can play an important role in assisting the adaptation of the community members to the host society (Joly, 1996b).

As with immigrants and minority ethnic groups, the formation of a refugee community association can perform many useful functions. They can help to rebuild and reinforce a sense of belonging for people whose lives have been disrupted by exile and they can play an important role in empowering the members of the community (Salinas, Pritchard et al., 1987). The benefits of community association formation are well-known to the various agencies involved in work with refugees and organizations such as Refugee Action devote a considerable proportion of their time to community building.

The focus on association formation by various refugee agencies reflects an agreement with Rex's assessment of the functions of associations, but fails to take into account the idea that, rather than being a 'natural' process, it may be a reflection more of British society than of immigrant inclinations. Some suggest that the basis for group formation may lie in the way British institutions create spaces for the recognition of groups rather than of individuals (Joly, 1996b). In Britain, individuals need to form themselves into an association in order to enter into dialogue with the state (Favell, 1998). There is also a failure to consider whether the needs of the group are best met by a formal association, or indeed whether there actually is a community.

10.3. The Community

A community association can be defined as a formal organization representing and defending the interests of a particular community. However, the term 'community' is widely and variously used. 'Community' is used without being defined by both civic authorities and minority groups, and has become an important feature and rationale for ethnic mobilization (Vertovec and Peach, 1997). The discourse around 'community' implies a warmth and inter-connectedness between members of the group, but also implicitly assumes that all the members will share some values and goals (Alund and Schierup, 1992; Vertovec and Peach, 1997). The idea that groups of refugees will form a community has rarely been challenged. Research on refugees often looks at one or more refugee 'communities', and more recently groups of refugees have been considered as transnational communities (Al-Ali, 1999) or as diasporas, that is scattered communities (Wahlbeck, 1999). I suggest that before taking this step, consideration should first be made as to whether a particular group of refugees can be described as a 'community'.

The usage of 'community' within social policy, particularly social policy concerning minority groups, refers to an ethnic community, and this ethnic community is assumed to be a bounded and easily-identifiable entity (Inglis, 1994).

Community has been defined as a form of relationship 'characterized by a high degree of personal intimacy, emotional depth, moral commitment, social cohesion and continuity in time' (Nisbet, 1967, p. 47). Other definitions of community are possible, but an important feature of definitions of community is the notion of the community as a form of collective; any definition of community must acknowledge the sharing of a cohesive element that provides a link among members of the community. This commonality may be real or imagined (Jenkins, 1996). Because of the feeling of interdependence and mutual interest, communities are able to act in unison in order to defend the rights of the group. The origin, for those in the community, lies within the community itself. 'People construct community symbolically, making it a resource and repository of meaning, and a referent of their identity' (Cohen, 1985, p. 118). For Cohen, the individual members of a community do not consciously create that community; instead, the notions of community and interconnectedness are instilled through that group's culture. The group conceives of itself as a community when its culture or contrasts with the culture of another group. The evidence of difference then strengthens the notion of community.

For an ethnic community, the sense of belonging together comes from a belief in a shared ethnicity. In this respect, an ethnic community is similar to Barth's (1969) ethnic group, which he defined as having four characteristics: being largely self-perpetuating, sharing certain fundamental cultural values, an identifiable field of communication and interaction, and, finally, the group's self-definition as being a distinct group and being considered by those outside the group as distinct.

10.4. Problems of Refugee Community Association Formation

When considering the associations formed by refugees, it must be remembered that there are important differences among individual refugees and/or members of ethnic minorities and that these differences may adversely affect the nature and functioning of those associations.

One of the differences between refugees and minority ethnic groups, who in the British context were initially labour migrants, is that labour migrants often follow a pattern of chain migration. Such a migration exists when new arrivals follow in the steps of earlier arrivals and receive support and advice from their predecessors. This has been described by Shaw in a study of Pakistani immigrants in Britain (Shaw, 1988). The immigration of Pakistanis to Britain began with the arrival of relatively few single men or men who came without their families. The primary motive was economic. Those that came were predominantly from a few particular areas of Pakistan. These early arrivals sent back remittances to assist those remaining behind, but also to enable others to come to Britain. Those later arrivals would in turn support the migration of someone else, a relative or someone from the same village. The earlier arrivals would assist those that came later to find work and somewhere to live. Because of this chain of migration, there often exists a kinship link between Pakistanis living in the same area in Britain. These kinship or personal links were also influential in determining the initial pattern of chain migration from villages in Pakistan. These pre-existing links have meant that community formation has not been difficult, since the affiliation between the members of the group has already been established.

Chain migration is not evident among those that come to Britain as refugees. Refugees tend to arrive in Britain as a result of a sudden upheaval in their country of origin. They frequently arrive without knowing anyone in the country and kinship links with other members of the group are often absent. The formation of an association can be very difficult for those who arrive *en masse* as opposed to groups who arrive through chain migration (Gold, 1992). This is an important difference between refugee groups and other minority groups, as chain migration is far more common among labour migrants than refugees.

Not all refugee community associations will be the same. Joly (1996a) has suggested that the nature of association that is established depends largely on the orientation of the refugees to their homeland. Two broad types of refugee settlement can be distinguished: refugees who once nurtured a collective project in their countries of origin and take this project with them into the country of exile and, secondly, those who either did not have a collective project in their countries of origin or who have given up that project. Patterns of group formation and interaction with the society of settlement differ between the two broad types. Those who hold a strong collective project in the society of origin and have maintained their orientation towards the homeland, for example Chilean refugees, are likely to reproduce this in the associations they form. Associations formed by Chilean refugees tend to be highly politicized and aimed to perpetuate the homeland-orientation of Chilean refugees in Britain. In contrast, Vietnamese refugees have little or no collective project and do not seek to orient themselves towards their homeland. Instead, their associations aim to improve the settlement of Vietnamese in Britain and do not undertake campaigning work aimed at Vietnam. In addition, those who never had a collective project in the country of origin are less likely to have the organizational skills necessary to form a formal organization and are therefore prone to marginalization.

A factor influencing the formation of associations among refugees is the availability of support services. Generally, when refugee organizations are formed, the organizations are established to meet a specific need of the community (Salinas, Pritchard et al., 1987). The very existence of support services can be a disincentive to the formation of an association since the provision of services takes away one of the main motives for forming an association (Gold, 1992). An example of the effect of support services is given by Wahlbeck (1999) in his study of Kurdish refugees in Britain and Finland. He found that associations were formed in Britain in order to overcome problems associated with the lack of support services available to them, whereas Kurds in Finland, where there was a range of practical support available, formed associations with an orientation more towards social and cultural activities.

Among refugee groups there is often little group-wide organization and a typical feature is factionalism and segmentation (Gold, 1992). There are often divisions within refugee groups based upon differences in class, politics, religion, and so forth (Salinas, Pritchard et al., 1987). This factionalism can inhibit attempts to create a formal association or, where and when an association is formed, the organization may turn out to be unrepresentative.

10.5. Problems Facing Bosnian Associations

The work of Wahlbeck (1999), Salinas et al. (1987) and Gold (1992) suggests that it is unrealistic to expect any formal associations to have much more than a social role when other support mechanisms exist. Yet this is precisely what was expected of Bosnian associations: associations were expected not to identify the needs of their community and find ways of meeting those needs, but to take over tasks that outside agencies had decided were important.

The majority of people who came on the programme had little or no experience of voluntary work or community associations. Partly this is because they came from a socialist state with few opportunities for voluntary organizations to operate. For most people, the concept of voluntary work was alien. Their experience was that work meant paid employment; Bosnians often questioned the motives of those who undertook work without pay.

The nature of the programme meant that many Bosnians were separated from their relatives. Although spouses and children under 18 were allowed to join principles in Britain, there was no agreement to permit the entry of siblings or extended family members. For many Bosnians, this has meant that their family has been scattered among several countries and that they have few close relatives nearby. There are, therefore, few kinship links among the group members.

There was a presumption on the part of the refugee support agencies and some local authorities that Muslim refugees from Bosnia would be supported individually and collectively by their co-religionists in Britain due to their shared religious beliefs; however, this support was not always forthcoming. For Bosnian Muslims to be able to identify with British Muslims, they need to have a pan-national concept of Islam as a factor that binds them to Muslims throughout the world. Bringa (1995) found that this concept was present among only a small number of Bosnian Muslims who were part of a small, urban-oriented economic and religious elite. This suggests that the assumption that Bosnian Muslim refugees would automatically look to the wider Muslim community for support was misplaced.

Islam in Bosnia was practised qualitatively differently than in some other parts of the world, particularly than in South Asia, from where the majority of British Muslims originate. Many in Bosnia were Muslim in name only and did not practice their religion. Even for those who were practising, there were major differences (Bringa, 1995) and these at times led British Muslims to accuse Bosnian Muslims of not being 'proper' Muslims, which in the context of the war in Bosnia was hurtful. Since their persecution and the death of their relatives had been predicated on their Muslimness, how could they then be questioned as to whether they were really Muslim? This lack of understanding between the two groups meant that the support of Britain's Muslim community could not always be depended on and, furthermore, that in seeking to create a community and association other resources had to be sought.

Joly (1996b) suggests that refugees who were in a minority group in their country of origin or who had a clear political project are more prone to develop a notion of community. However, if the group was not a minority and had little or no understanding of itself as a group, the community-building process and the creation of a formal association will be delayed or may never happen at all. Refugees from Bosnia mostly did not have a political project in Bosnia and their involvement in the war was very much forced upon them by circumstances rather than the result of, say, Bosnian Muslim political ambition. There is little history of formal organization of Bosnian Muslims within Bosnia except in the area of organized religion. The immediate history of Yugoslavia as a socialist state provided little opportunity for organizations along ethnic lines. Indeed, the conflict in Yugoslavia, though often portrayed in the media as the inevitable result of ethnic or national antagonism, can be seen as having a variety of causes other than the articulation of ethnicity (Janjic, 1995). The conflict was connected with the economic situation in Yugoslavia. Indeed, the ethnicization of politics in Yugoslavia has been described as the result of the country's economic history and the way socialism was implemented (Janjic, 1995) rather than the articulation of centuries of ethnic hatred (Bennett, 1995). If the ethnicization of politics in Bosnia and Herzegovina is recent, then the notion of a distinct Muslim Bosnian identity and hence a Bosnian Muslim community may also be relatively recent. Unlike the majority of refugees from Vietnam, those from Bosnia do not have a definite project in Britain, that is, they are unclear as to whether their future lies in Britain or in Bosnia. This means that their community associations are likely to be unclear as to their orientation, leading to difficulties in defining a role.

Among the Bosnian refugee population, the majority are Muslim but there is a minority who are Catholic or Orthodox, and the question of who should be considered to be part of a Bosnian community can be a source of conflict. The Bosnian government on the whole articulates a notion of Bosnia as secular, but with a majority Muslim component accepting of people claiming Serb, Croat and other identities. For the refugees themselves, there is sometimes a difficulty in accepting this notion. Whilst many profess to bear no grudges against whole peoples, there are some who distrust and resent all Serbs or Croats. This in itself is problematic, since Bosnia was almost like Orwell's 1984: the war had three protagonists and allegiances changed during the course of the war. Muslims in the north of the country were imprisoned by Serbs and many Croats in the region were treated as badly as Muslims. In the south and Herzegovina, Muslims were persecuted by Croats, and some owe their lives to Serb neighbours.

These, then, are some of the difficulties encountered in the formation of a formal association for Bosnian refugees. But the most basic difficulty is that the foundations for an association are largely absent. For Bosnian refugees, the notion that they comprise a discrete ethnic community is problematic and there needs to be some consideration of whether there actually is a Bosnian community.

10.6. A Question of Community

My experience and interviews with Bosnians suggest that, besides the problems already described, there is another issue affecting the formation and functioning of community associations. This is the

question of whether there actually is a Bosnian community and
I suggest that, in the sense described above, the community does
not exist. There are people from the same country with the same
language, broadly similar culture, and mostly affiliated with one
religion; however, the emotional links between the individuals
and the sense of mutual obligation that one expects to find in
a community are absent.

Many of the Bosnians in Britain arrived here without their
extended family and some found that there was no one in Britain
whom they knew from before the war. Many of the people I have
spoken to have talked of the lack of trust that exists among Bosnians.
Partly, this stems from experiences in the war. One man described
how, while in a concentration camp, survival was often a result of
someone else's death. If you could divert the attention of the guards
away from yourself and towards someone else, then you increased
your chances of surviving another day. He now feels that he cannot
trust other Bosnians because he has seen them betray each other.
Others find that, although when they first arrived in Britain they got
to know all of the Bosnians in their locality, with time they have
drifted apart and now they have a much smaller social circle.

'I keep away from most Bosnian peoples [sic]. I see Sejo, and
Ismet, and sometimes Mersid, but the others not really. They always
are jealous, always asking what have you got, why have you got
better house than me' (Mehmet, 19 October 1999).

'I don't see many people now, just five or six houses, close friends,
and visiting each other. Others if I see them in town just say hello
and that's it' (Sevla, 27 January 2000).

Despite being from the same land, the fact that Bosnia is such
a new country meant that there was no strong Bosnian identity.
Difficulties in deciding who is entitled to be considered for
membership in the community association are indicative of this lack
of a clear identity. Yet identity is a vital part of community since
there must be some agreement within the community as to their
group identity. In addition, there are many internal divisions, making
the notion of a cohesive group harder to maintain. Some assert that
people from a different town or district are really peasants. One
woman explained to me how people from Kljuc were more interested
in farming than education and many of them left school early. She
could never be very friendly with people from there because they
are 'so primitive'. Another explained that people from Herzegovina
looked down on people from Bosnia, and she couldn't be friends

with anyone who thought they were better than she. Yet another, who was from Herzegovina, said that most people from villages in Bosnia were illiterate, primitive people.

Some said that they felt Bosnian people should help each other and that at first they had tried to help their compatriots. However, they soon found that this was often a thankless task. A common complaint was that they were expected to do everything, for example to always be available to interpret. As long as they continued to do all they were asked, the relationship was friendly. But if they said they were too busy, or if they once let the other person down, then it was as if they had never done anything at all. The person they had been helping before would be angry and resentful, sometimes blaming the interpreter when, for example, benefit decisions went the wrong way. So, many people who at first tried to help others gradually withdrew their services.

'We are from different towns. ... Some people with poor education, they never travelled outside their village, they don't respect you' (Edin, 8 December 1999).

'I don't want to work with our club. I know what is like. Nobody say thank you. They want you to do everything for nothing. Then one day you can't come and they hate you for that. Even if before you did everything right, they change' (Mirsada, 17 July 1997).

As time has passed, and some Bosnians have now been in Britain for over ten years, the idea that there should be mutual support and assistance among Bosnian refugees has grown weaker. Many of those who felt they had a duty to support each other when they first arrived have grown disillusioned

One association used to run English classes for those who wished to learn, a Bosnian school on Sundays, a gardening project and a mental health project, made possible by a 1997 National Lottery three-year operating grant. Despite all the activities that the association undertook, the worker claimed that there still had been criticism from some Bosnians in the area.

Always some people are against what you are doing. I don't know if it is all peoples or just Bosnian peoples. If it is all people then I think Bosnian people are the worst. Some people always find some criticism in it. They will never turn into community but will criticize what you do (Jasmina, 6 January 2000).

10.7. If not Community, then What?

Perhaps the question of why the community associations are facing difficulties needs to be turned around. Perhaps one should ask instead, why is it that these associations continue to exist, despite all the problems that they face and despite the lack of any community feeling. The answer to this question lies partly in the origins of the associations.

When asked the origins of their association, one interviewee said:

> They told us to start one. The Bosnia Project said the project would close, and many groups here have community associations. We saw the Vietnamese group in Leeds. We were kind of pushed into it. We thought it was a great idea, but not our idea. They told us what we can do and what we can have (Eldina, 19 July 1997).

Another described being guided through the process of establishing a formal association by a woman from the local voluntary services council. Though it was not Bosnians who came up with the idea of forming an association, it was clear that there would be no assistance for Bosnians from any other quarter. The availability of funding from organizations such as the National Lottery has meant that there have been funds available to employ workers in some associations.

The contingent nature of the associations becomes evident at times of crisis. Some associations have found that when their chairman decides he has had enough, they are unable to find anyone else willing to take over. At other times arguments over who should take over became so fierce that a substantial part of the group withdrew from the association. This has meant that, in several areas, Bosnian associations have been started, folded, and restarted.

The paradox of Bosnian refugee groups is that while there exist formal community associations, there does not seen to be a community behind the association. If what exists cannot be termed a community, then what is it? To describe this, I use the term 'contingent community'. For me, a contingent community is a group of people who will to some extent conform to the expectations of the host society in order to gain the advantages of a formal community association, but whose private face remains unconstituted as a community. Unity is apparent rather than actual and among the members of the group there is no strongly-held belief that they are interlinked and interdependent. This, I suggest, is the situation with

Bosnian community associations. As long as there are benefits to be gained from constituting themselves as a formal community, Bosnians will strive to appear as such. But there is little to suggest that the members of the associations actually feel any obligation to each other. There are some kinship networks that assist each other and some individuals who try to establish group cohesion but on the whole people have retreated from each other. For many people, there are few contacts with compatriots they did not know before the war or to whom they are not related. What is viewed from the outside as a community is in fact an external construction.

10.8. Conclusion

Problematization 'develops the conditions in which possible responses can be given [and] defines the elements that will constitute what the different solutions attempt to respond to' (Rabinow, 1984), so understanding the way a solution is posed throws light upon the way the problem was initially constructed. The problematization of refugees from Bosnia has been constructed, it seems to me, as a problem of a community, and the solution has therefore been to foster the 'community'. The question of whether there really exists a community in the sense of a cohesive group with common aims and interests has not been considered. This fixation with community disempowers, since it is imposing a construct on a group, rather than allowing them the space to build, or indeed not build, their own idea of community.

References

Al-Ali, N., *Trans- or a-national? Bosnian refugees in the UK and Netherlands* (Brighton: Sussex Centre for Migration Research, 1999).

Alund, A., C. Schierup, *Paradoxes of multiculturalism: essays on Swedish society* (Aldershot: Avebury, 1992).

Barth, F., *Ethnic groups and boundaries* (Boston: Little Brown, 1969).

Bennett, C., *Yugoslavia's bloody collapse: causes, course and consequences* (London: Hurst & Co., 1995).

Bringa, T., *Being Muslim the Bosnian way* (Princeton, US: Princeton University Press, 1995).

Cohen, A. P., *The symbolic construction of community* (London: Routledge, 1985).

ECRE, *The state of refugee integration in the European Union* (Antwerp: ECRE, 1998).

Favell, A., *Philosophies of integration: immigration and the idea of citizenship in France and Britain* (Basingstoke: Macmillan, 1998).

Gold, S. J., *Refugee communities: a comparative field study* (London: Sage, 1992).

Inglis, C., 'Race and ethnic relations in Australia: theory, methods and substance', in P. Ratcliffe, *'Race', ethnicity and nation: international perspectives on social conflict* (London: UCL Press, 1994), pp. 68–90.

Janjic, D., 'Resurgence of ethnic conflict in Yugoslavia: the demise of communism and the rise of new nationalism', in P. Akhavan, R. Howse, *Yugoslavia, the former and future* (Washington: Brookings Institution, 1995), pp. 29–44.

Jenkins, R., *Social Identity* (London: Routledge, 1996).

Joly, D., *Between Exile and Ethnicity* (Coventry: Centre for Research in Ethnic Relations, University of Warwick, 1996a).

Joly, D., *Haven or Hell? Asylum policy and refugees in Europe* (New York: Macmillan, 1996b).

Nisbet, R. A., *The Sociological Tradition* (London: Heinemann, 1967).

Rabinow, P., *The Foucault reader* (New York: Pantheon, 1984).

Rex, J., D. Joly, C. Wilpert (eds), *Immigrant associations in Europe* (Aldershot: Gower Press, 1987).

Salinas, M., D. Pritchard, A. Kibedi, 'Refugee based organisations: their functions and importance for the refugee in Britain', *Working papers on refugees*, No. 3 (Oxford, London: Refugee Studies Programme and British Refugee Council, 1987).

Shaw, A., *A Pakistani Community in Britain* (Oxford: Blackwell, 1988).

Vertovec, S., C. Peach, 'Introduction: Islam in Europe and the politics of religion and community', in S. Vertovec, C. Peach, *Islam in Europe: the politics of religion and community* (Basingstoke: Macmillan, 1997), pp. 3–47.

Wahlbeck, O., *Kurdish diasporas: a comparative study of Kurdish refugee communities* (Basingstoke: Macmillan, 1999).

Part IV

The Enlargement of the European
Union and the Creation of a Common
Policy on Immigration

11

'Old Europe/New Europe': Ambiguities of Identity

Edward A. Tiryakian

11.1. Introduction

Now, at the beginning of the twenty first century and in light of the momentous events of the preceding half decade, European identity is facing what may be an unprecedented set of regional and international changes that are involved in the transformation of Europe. The 'bundle' of European identity is a very complex one — what else can we expect of an 'old' continent that has such varied ethnic, cultural and historical legacies? Perhaps an 'outsider' can assist European 'insiders' to re-examine their list of components of European identity as Europe — in the midst of Chairman Valéry Giscard d'Estaing's epochal Convention on the Future of Europe (http://european-convention.eu.int) — is reinventing its future.

Let me start with a useful quantitative stocktaking effort undertaken a few years ago by the noted Swedish sociologist Göran Therborn (1995). He began his narrative with the European reconstruction following World War II. The 'old Europe' was abandoned in a period of great economic vitality, which both allowed a rather painless shedding of the empires of 'old Europe' and restrained an outward flow of population for greener economic opportunities. (West) Europe in the glorious quarter century or so after World War II easily adjusted to the post-war structural transformations by moving along the highway of modernity towards political democracy and economic growth.

Therborn notes that Europe experienced and digested a number of important historical turns along the way. Overall, there was a convergence and advancement in beneficial aspects of modernity, like a decline in infant mortality and a rise of GDP/wealth. Western (including Scandinavian) countries have made remarkable strides, but 'catch-up' has also taken place, albeit at lower levels, in Eastern Europe. To be sure, Therborn notes, the trajectory has not been a straight line towards European integration and convergence, but the direction has remained positive across a range of political, social and economic indices (1995, pp. 138, 166, 259). Involved here is a shift in migration patterns, that is from emigration to immigration, as internal labour markets pulled labour into high growth centres rather than pushed surplus labour to other regions. Therborn notes this trend but does not dwell on it. I, however, think it deserves greater attention in discussions of European identity, which he rather glossed over in his chapter on identity (Therborn, 1995, pp. 230–54).

At the end of his mammoth survey, Therborn noted that the economic slowdown of the 1970s and early 1980s was more of a challenge met than an obstacle that derailed the project of bringing Europe together. Out of the economic malaise (ultimately going back to the 1973–74 oil embargo shock) came new European responses: the European Monetary System and the Single European Act (Therborn, 1995, p. 346). So the new defining challenge to European identity, he sensed, would be the fallout from the Soviet collapse of 1989–91, which marked the complete end of the 'post-war' period in Europe, including the dichotomization of Europe into West and East. With this era behind them, the two Europes can, at last, meet if not unite (Therborn, p. 351).

Therborn has a very keen eye for social change, and I do not pretend to have done justice to his analysis. It is not an overly flattering work, for the social democrat in Therborn does not equate Europe's socio-economic performance as a guarantee for modernity, far from that. Writing in 1995, Therborn sees the European Union as having to think through its identity in terms of membership and geography: where does Europe end southward and eastward? Will economic self-limitation to 'sustainable development', if adopted, be compatible with 'collective democracy and … personal and social emancipation' (Therborn, p. 365)? He ends by admonishing that the Enlightenment tradition of autonomy, liberation, and emancipation is far from reducible to economic growth — a theme that is central in Jürgen Habermas's (1989) notion of the colonization of the life-world. The challenge of modernity for Therborn, then, is this: 'To be successful and important, the European Union needs to be a project of social construction, not just a marketplace or a museum' (Therborn, p. 364).

Therborn is much more of a European 'insider' than I am, and certainly he saw a great many major trends with great perspicacity. A parallel presentation of the dynamics of European modernity that stressed the political democratization process was published at about the same time as Therborn's work by British political scientist Richard Rose (1996). Using their complementary analyses as a springboard, I will discuss three challenges to European identity using European integration and the evolving European Union as a focus. It should be understood that I approach 'identity', both personal and collective, as fundamental in the representation of the self, in defining who we are and whom we would like to be. Further, self-identity as reflexive awareness of the subject in a situation is not a constant but rather is expressed and modified in interaction with others.[1]

Given that premise and granting that most of the secular trends noted by Therborn and Rose still hold, what are some salient challenges a decade after their presentations? I will touch on three. The first is the challenge of *expansion*. The second is the challenge of *immigration*. The third is a new American challenge. Discussing these in turn and in relation to one another will bring out some of the intriguing ambiguities of 'Old' and 'New' Europes.

* * *

Antecedent to this discussion, it might be heuristic to relate in functionalist terms the present identity situation of Europe to the European Union, viewing the latter as an emergent dynamic and differentiated action system acting on behalf of 'Europe'.[2] Here I allude to the four-function paradigm of Talcott Parsons (Treviño, 2001), who postulated that every social system (including the EU, regarded as a very large system) needs to have certain institutional mechanisms functioning to maintain operations in its environment. This is especially true if the environment undergoes changes that impact the action system at various points. Parsons, during many years of refining this schema, changed terminology and added complexity, for example in proposing that there are symbolic media of exchange, like money and power, linking the functional areas to each other. But, for purpose of this discussion, only certain basic aspects of this frame of reference need be reviewed.

The four functional areas were designated *Adaptation*, *Goal Attainment*, *Integration*, and *Pattern Maintenance* or *Value Consensus*. These were represented on a 2x2 table, as shown in Figure 11.1.

A

G

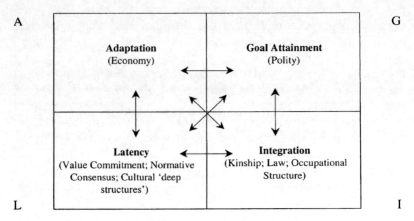

L

I

Figure 11.1 Four-function paradigm of societal (action) systems
Source: Adapted from Parsons, Platt and Smelser (1973) and Treviño (2001, p. xlvii)

As a preliminary methodological note, it should be remembered that the frame of reference is a conceptual one, with flowing boundaries between the differentiated structures. The functional areas are institutionally interdependent and interrelated, indicated by the double arrows connecting the four cells. For the present discussion, the European Union may be viewed as a totality with components contributing to the system as a whole, each of which may furthermore acquire new functions as other parts of the system become modified over time — thus, for example, the European Parliament over time has evolved or may evolve from a deliberative body to one with greater decision-making processes.

Adaptation refers to a social system needing to adapt resources from its environment, generally via the economy. *Goal Attainment* or goal specification emphasizes that a social system requires directionality, goals, purposefulness — a broad area that entails political decisions made at the institutional level by the polity. Both adaptation and goal specification, in the Parsonian perspective, address themselves to outside factors, to boundary relations with the environment (including socially, economically and politically constructed environments and intersocietal relations).

The second set may be thought of (in non-Marxist terms) as constituting the 'infrastructure' of social systems, that is areas attending to endogenous factors. *Integration* refers to a differentiated social system featuring and comprising a multiplicity of roles and institutions that require mechanisms for coordination and integration. Without such mechanisms or institutions (for example the kinship system for pre-industrial societies, and bureaucratic organizations, legal systems and an advanced division of labour for industrial societies), centrifugal tendencies may lead to fragmentation and loss of solidarity. *Pattern Maintenance* or *Value Consensus* (Parsons also called this the 'Latency' area, suggesting that it is a covert or 'deep structure') is the sector where the cultural values of the 'societal community' are generated and regenerated in the public sphere. During both the mundane and exceptional activities of a society, tensions and frictions accumulate; recourse to fundamental values or ideologies through religious or secular rituals serves to reaffirm the baseline of operations. When a society lacks or ignores this fundamental area, which is perhaps the paramount functional area for a collectivity's identity, its system is prone to Emile Durkheim's general condition of *anomie*, to revolution or, as the world saw in 1989–91, to the implosion of a system that had seemed monolithic.

The identity of Europe, which I take to be a collective enterprise of the European Union — a very large 'action system' — entails attending to all four major functional areas. The system as a whole has had remarkable success in economic and political development, so much so that individuals and states outside of the 'club' wish to enter and no member state has sought 'exit'. Integration has come about in several institutional and more striking ways, such as new cross-border regions and free circulation for EU passport holders. A shared value cluster with a focus on Enlightenment and 'post-modern' values, combined with pre-modern religious rituals and holidays,[3] has more or less provided a satisfactory matrix of a recognisable, non-imperial 'European civilization'.

It is at this moment that we need to consider the major challenges that the broad 'environment' poses to this rather well-integrated but vibrant system. It does not matter where we begin because we shall see that the problem areas are interrelated. As a caveat, there is one 'environmental' challenge that I will not discuss despite its importance: the broad economic challenge of international economic integration and related aspects of 'globalization' (Kierzkowski, 2002).

11.2. Expansion

An immediate challenge to European identity is the expansion of Europe from 15 to 25 member states. From an organizational point of view, so sizeable an enlargement is not going to be easy if the organization is to retain its collective identity. In this instance, the expansion to the East entails significant material, political and psychological challenges, since eight of the ten countries acceding the EU are, in a sense, 'old Europe' in those three respects.[4] That is, they were part of the Soviet system, which differed dramatically from the predominant Western system of post-World War II modernity.

Economically, the Baltic States and Central Europe were client states of the Soviet economic system, which had Russia as its core; economic production was subordinated to political considerations favouring heavy industry rather than a diversified economy favouring consumer products. This led, on one hand, to an economy with 'full' employment and job security and, on the other, to scarcity of consumer goods and severe environmental degradation. Although significant progress has been achieved in ten years in providing consumer goods and some diversification of the economy, the economic costs of expansion are enormous, since eastward expansion of the EU means, in the short-term at least, sizeable transfers from the developed West to the 'old' East. If one considers the enormous financial costs for West Germany of incorporating East Germany, which was by many accounts the most advanced East European country at the time of (re)unification, one can understand the strains that the EU's 'Adaptation' functional area will have to overcome.[5]

Expansion to the East brings also challenges for the polity ('G') since 'old Europe' is barely a decade into feeling comfortable in its new political mode of Western political democracy, including the institutionalized concept of 'her majesty's loyal opposition'. The Soviet system did not allow for a 'loyal opposition', though elections were held routinely in the single party state. Some of the 'old Europe' once had pre-war political systems with recognized places for opposition parties, but most Central European democracies were still in a tender stage of development when the lights went out under Hitler, Stalin and their puppet leaders. In the past ten years or so, although political opposition has flourished and public opinion favours the new forms of political democracy (Rose, 1996), declining voter turnouts in many Central European countries indicate that the novelty of multiple-candidate elections is beginning to wear off. The rumblings among voters inside the EU today about a lack of transparency in the political process and that bureaucrats rather than the people are in charge may seem very familiar to East Europeans of a certain age. In the 'new Europe' too the younger generation still must be motivated to participate fully in the political process. Failure to do so will reproduce the sort of apathy and political anomies East Germans experienced after unification, whereby locals sometimes feel like second-class citizens or even 'colonized' in their own territory (Meier, 1994).

In terms of integration, a whole variety of networks and voluntary associations that can provide strong, broad ties between East and West needs to be developed. Whereas the enlargement of NATO to the East had been a matter of great controversy and national debate just a few years ago (Mattox and Rachwald, 2001), the tide has turned in favour of expansion, partly since NATO candidates see this as expediting EU membership and as a potential economic boon when NATO bases are moved eastward, across the Elbe.

Of course, integration entails more than a new, broader military defence network. Some questions about the overall benefits of this mode of integration will be discussed shortly. For now, the discussion will turn to a particular challenge confronting European integration. In many areas of 'old Europe', there are minorities and ethnic groups that have only partially integrated into the wider societies and in certain respects feel like aliens mistreated by the state.[6] After the collapse of communism, nationalist tensions and ethnic mobilization threatened to disrupt the internal peace of some Central and Eastern European countries, nowhere more violently shown than in the civil wars and ethnic cleansing that ravaged what used to be Yugoslavia. Western 'new Europe' has gone a long ways towards accommodating regional ethnic differences — for example, greater autonomy for Scotland and Wales within Great Britain and the constitutional arrangements of 'new Spain' doing the same for the Basque area, Catalonia, and Galicia.

One action that should enhance the integration process is an extension and expansion of exchanges of students and faculty that the EU has undertaken via various secondary and higher education exchange programmes (Erasmus, Comenius, Socrates, Leonardo da Vinci). This may be expensive short-term but it seems to me that having students of the same generation criss-cross Europe's educational map and learning more about 'the other' as classmates, friends and colleagues is an excellent long-term investment.

Expansion, lastly, relates to the Latency or a value dimension. This is perhaps the hardest and most nebulous area. 'Old Europe' *as understood here in terms of Eastern Europe* has borne the historical cultural imprints of four empires: most recently, the Soviet empire and its value orientations of modernity based on a strong, secular welfare state, collective enterprises, and a transnational 'Soviet' identity. Prior to the Soviet period, 'old Europe' had fallen under three empires: the Tsarist Empire, the Austro-Hungarian Empire, and the Ottoman Empire. Although one may say there was a certain common denominator of values, such as respect for 'traditional authority', hierarchical status distinctions, and a certain controlled allowance for ethnic diversity, a core difference was in the religious orientation of the public sphere: Catholic Vienna, Orthodox Moscow and Islamic Constantinople/Istanbul. The cultural integration of 'East Europe', in terms of the countries scheduled for EU incorporation in 2004, does mean that its deep cultural values have to be accommodated by means of new cultural entries and new cultural symbols providing a sense of identity and legitimating other activities in several spheres, including social and political ones (Shore, 2000).

My feeling is that such expansion at the cultural level is manageable, albeit with some difficulty, in terms of the present set of 'new Europe' and 'old Europe' countries. The Baltic states have common religio-cultural ties with the West: Catholicism in Lithuania and Protestantism in Estonia and Latvia.[7] Still, visits to that part of Europe indicate no great religiosity in the younger generation, either of nationals (that is Lithuanians, Latvians and Estonians) or of ethnic minorities (predominantly ethnic Russians, Ukrainians, and so on). I cannot speak directly about the Central European countries but, in an historical context, Hungary, the Czech Republic, Poland, and Slovakia have long had contacts — cultural, scientific, and educational — with Western Europe, so I am rather confident that a value consensus can be achieved. The 'L' area of the EU matrix gels around Christianity and the Enlightenment. In the nineteenth century, these two were antagonistic, clearly shown in the *Kulturkampf* in Germany and in the equally bitter battles over laïcisme and the Ferry laws in Third Republic France. Today the lingering dispute is between Orthodoxy and the Vatican (with the Fall of Constantinople still rankling Orthodox church leaders), but I do not see it as a permanent divide in the value sector of the evolving EU. In key sectors of value consensus, the convergence of 'new Europe' and 'old Europe' is a matter of one or two generations, as is convergence within 'new Europe' (Abramson and Inglehart, 1995; Inglehart et al., 1998).

11.3. Immigration

The very post-war economic and social successes of post-war Western Europe — notably sustained economic growth and sharp improvements in health and living standards — generated short- and long-term labour problems. Not 'old-style' labour problems in the form of strikes and class conflicts so much as a shortage of domestic labour in Western Europe. For the early post-war period, the northern tier could attract service workers from the southern tier (Portugal, Spain, and later Yugoslavia) as temporary workers, but when the southern tier in the 1980s underwent its own socio-economic transformation, that surplus labour pool began to dry up. Since they had been taken in as 'guest workers' on temporary visas, there were few issues relating to the maintenance of guest workers' cultural identity in the host countries.

But the real challenge, of course, is the significant rise in a permanent immigrant population from outside Europe that is ethnically and culturally, if not racially, distinct from the 'indigenous' host society. The areas of emigration have been Asia (South and Southeast), sub-Saharan Africa, North Africa, and the eastern Mediterranean, particularly from Turkey. Except for the latter, the other sending regions were tied to European countries by virtue of colonial empires until half a century ago. Decolonization in the 1950s and 1960s and the lack of significant economic development in the ex-colonies led to many colonial subjects seeking employment opportunities in the former colonial powers. They and their European-born children have become part of the socioscape of contemporary Europe.

This has led to a demographic dilemma that has far-reaching consequences for European identity. Western Europe had understood and represented itself as homogeneous societies in the framework of their respective nation-states. Whereas in the nineteenth and early twentieth centuries, it was a territory of *emigration* due to surplus population that could not be adequately sustained with available economic resources, in the late twentieth century it had (surplus) economic resources that could not be adequately sustained by its own demographic resources, particularly as birth rates pointed downward below replacement value. In the past quarter of a century, Europe rediscovered itself as a territory of *immigration*, with marked ethnic and racial diversity.[8] In terms of skin pigmentation, one might speak of a 'darkening' of 'white' Europe; at another level, in terms of culture, one may speak of a 'new Orientalism', given the proliferation of Islam, Buddhism, and Hinduism in various European centres.

Canada and the United States have had a longer awareness of themselves as countries of immigrants. Although this may be accepted and reflected in their collective identities, there are still sharp disagreements involving the institutionalization of 'multi-culturalism', particularly in the educational system. In Europe, perhaps because of the recent large-scale immigration combined with the general economic downturn of the past 15 years or so, 'multiculturalism' seems to be a more recent recognition of changing demographic conditions and its problematics for social integration. Although Great Britain, France, Germany and Belgium have attracted more attention in this respect, ethnic/racial heterogeneity and its attendant integration issues face all the societies of the European Union and economically advanced regions such as the Scandinavian countries, including Sweden and Finland (Forsander, 2002; Ylänkő, 2002). The question of social integration is that of the complex relation of the national state to nascent migrant community enclaves, including educational policies involving religious observance (Rex, 1995, p. 29; Rex and Singh, forthcoming; Todd, 1994; Kurthern, 1998; *Le Figaro Magazine*, 2003). Although nationalist and more right-wing parties and groups have not succeeded in 'ethnic cleansing' of the 'homeland', they have led to governments' introduction of more restrictive immigration policies.

Down the road looms an even larger, albeit related, challenge for European identity. If Turkey, Albania, and Bosnia are welcomed into the European Union as member states, the integration of three predominantly Islamic countries, with a combined year 2000 population of 73 million and relatively very high birth rates would be a formidable task. Since the total population of Europe at the turn of the century was roughly 730 million, their accession into the EU would entail an Islamic population of 10 per cent.[9] Of course, given the EU's policy of the free internal circulation of EU citizens, this could only mean a confrontation of the 'new' EU identity with a ghost of its past. Gerard Delanty has cogently argued that the origins of modern European identity is an adversarial one tracing back to the sixteenth century joint resistance to Turkish military inroads in the Balkans and Central Europe up until the siege of Vienna (Delanty, 1995, p. 37). This represented the second major wave of Islamic intrusion into Europe, after the penetration of the Iberian peninsula in the seventh century. How will Europe in the twenty first century react to a third Islamic wave, even a non-military one, is far from certain. Its reaction is even more uncertain in the current global anti-terrorism climate, which seems to have strong correlation with an 'Islamic' anti-West jihad phenomenon. This leads to the third, and perhaps the toughest, challenge facing European identity.

11.4. The New American Challenge

I deliberately insert 'new' in this section because the present challenge is the third time in less than a hundred years that the United States has profoundly challenged European identity. The first time was at the end of World War I when President Woodrow Wilson went to Versailles with a moral challenge for 'old' Europe. He sought a 'new' moral order of states based on his 'Fourteen Points' advocating, among others, freedom of self-determination, open covenants openly arrived at and a drastic reduction in national armaments.[10] Despite some acquiescence, such as the symbolic Kellogg-Briand Peace Pact of 1928, neither Europe, nor the United States for that matter, was ready to change, and so the 'old' order persisted.

The second American challenge had a greater impact. Rather than a political or presidential one, it was raised in the 1960s by American firms' new methods of management and organization and more efficient production and distribution. The challenge was to the 'old Europe's' ways of doing business by taking away market share even in protected European territory and provoked an informed cry of alarm in the continental corporate world itself (Servan-Schreiber, 1969).[11] Obviously, globalization (sometimes viewed suspiciously as another form of Americanization) was not halted at the European frontier. However, the challenge is being satisfactorily handled through new and more transparent economic procedures, greater efficiency and accountability to shareholders and so on, even if overall the economy still has a way to go to match American productivity. And European corporatist values found in the welfare state impose constraints that the more brutal American capitalist system does not have, especially in the American neo-liberal climate of the past 20 years. Still, overall, Europe has come a long ways in modernizing its economy.[12]

It is the third challenge that is the most troublesome. This is the challenge of the Bush administration. After its enormous political windfall in 11 September 2001, it has adopted as its central mission a war against terrorism at home and overseas irrespective of material and social costs. War as a foreign policy option seems to have received high priority and, in practice, has taken on the form of a war against parts of the Islamic world. In the brief span of a year since President Bush declared a war against an 'axis of evil', American military intervention has toppled regimes in Afghanistan and Iraq.

During the war against Iraq (really a war against its head of state and his party), the American administration, out of desire for United Nations legitimation, challenged Europe anew, namely, to rally behind the 'new Europe' and reject the authority of 'old Europe'. This is a very different dichotomy from the 'old Europe/new Europe' that I have discussed earlier, and very different from the same dichotomy discussed as recently as 2001 by a long-time Europe watcher, who thought that a 'new Europe' would emerge as America withdrew its traditional post-war military hegemony over Western Europe. The same analyst had speculated that a new transatlantic relationship would have to be found, one in which Europe would depend more on its own indigenous forces, institutions and balances (Calleo, 2001, p. 5).

For the Bush administration, as voiced by its Secretary of Defence Rumsfeld, 'old Europe' is the European countries that are unwilling to acquiesce and support America's military interventions anywhere arising from the September 11 attacks on the United States. Russia, Germany, Belgium and especially France have been denounced as fair-weather allies meriting scorn and economic reprisals. 'New' Europe, embracing all regimes that supported, with various levels of commitment, the war against Iraq, seems to especially refer to Eastern European countries that only yesteryear were 'old Europe'.[13] So, in one of the great ironies of the new century, what had been pillars of democracy in the twentieth century are now being demonized in the United States, while the countries that were on the margins of modernity for most of the twentieth century are now being hailed by America's military strategists as 'new' allies against terrorism. This reshuffling accompanies the relocation of American military bases and personnel, not away from Europe, but within Europe to more 'friendly' climes, for example to Romania and Bulgaria.

The use of strong-arm tactics by the American administration has extremely serious consequences for the United States, for Europe and for the world. This is not the occasion to detail the changes in American society that have been taking place in the spheres of civil liberties, government surveillance of the citizenry and the like. Nor is it the time to decry that the 'military-industrial' complex President

Eisenhower warned against in his farewell address 40 years ago has entrenched its interests into foreign policy so much that new large-scale military enterprises are likely to continue for the rest of this decade.

This chapter does, however, represent an occasion to show that the present American administration has not only undone the long-standing multilateralist orientation of American foreign policy towards Europe (that is treating Europe as a necessary bulwark of democracy and economic partnership), but also that the administration is pursuing an aggressive policy of separating Europe by means of its 'for us or against us' mentality. This policy seeks to make Europe part of its large toolkit for American interests outside of Europe, stripping Europe of its sphere of influence beyond its geographical borders (including the oil regions of the Middle East and Central Asia). At the military level, the American policy is to make use of NATO outside the European theatre while doing its utmost to prevent Europe from developing its own military force independent of American command.

While I am confident about Europe's ability to answer the long-term challenges of American hegemony — East Asia is a region that has maintained its cultural identity while also having significant economic development — I do have concerns that, short-term, American blandishments and strong-arm tactics will have a divisive impact on Europe, especially with some of the 2004 EU entrants being viewed as American satellites by their fellow Europeans. March 2003's acrimony among the present member states generated by an America poised to go to war against Iraq and seeking legitimacy and resources from Europe is a bitter taste of things to follow. The sound democratic and economic growth of Europe — west, east, and south — and the internal construction of a really 'new' Europe should not be diverted into overseas military adventurism whose shots are called on the other side of the Atlantic.

What Europe needs to maintain and renew its identity is a new De Gaulle, a new Delors, a new Adenauer, a new De Gasperi — just as what the United States needs to regain its authentic democratic and multilateral orientation is another Wilson, Roosevelt or Kennedy. At present, the 'new' America is a far cry from the 'old' American democracy that Europeans knew about from Tocqueville and Bryce and recognized up until the end of the twentieth century. It is uncomfortably closer to the brief but harrowing McCarthy period when even the national media were silent for fear of being tainted with anti-Americanism. The United States, just as much as Europe, is going through a critical period of challenge to its cultural identity. The multiculturalism forged in the cold war has been thrown overboard by an American administration that seems only to revel in its hegemony. Yet, perhaps, sanity will return when the 'new' America wakes up to how much it needs 'old' Europe to safeguard common principles of democracy.

Figure 11.2 is a rough summation of the challenges facing Europe that have been discussed in this chapter.

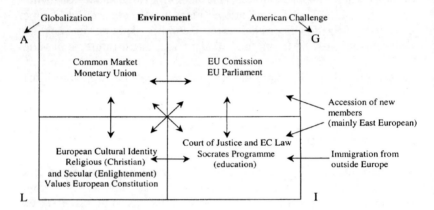

Figure 11.2 Challenges Facing the European Union
Source: Author's elaboration

11.5. Closing Remarks

In summary, I have limited my discussion to some challenges facing European identity, taking the EU 15 as the central reference. In the mid-1990s, Therborn saw the challenge to European modernity posed by questions of identity and geography in light of the collapse of the Soviet system. In a sense, these are still present because the European Union has become a magnet for all countries claiming some European connection, even as far as the Urals. Expansion may be reaching its limit in terms of economic marginal utility, since the financial and cultural costs to the European Union of bringing in new states may exceed the benefits of widening markets. Yet, there are some ideals of European integration unreducible to economics and a certain sentiment of *noblesse oblige* may still be operative, especially among the more economically robust member states.

I have given attention to some challenges to the EU coming from the non-physical environment and, in particular, from the new American challenge, which has derided what it calls the 'old Europe' in favour of 'new Europe'. Implied in this dichotomy is an instrumental approach to Europe by the present administration: the 'new Europe' is the one that provides allegiance to American policy; the 'old' is the one that demands partnership and dialogue on European and global affairs. This represents an important external challenge to European identity. Figure 11.2 also points out to the reader the internal structures and processes that are part of the ongoing dynamic reality of the European Union. The present deliberations on a European Constitution, which seek to work out a cultural baseline of identity and values, are of the utmost significance in formulating Europe as something other than 'a market or a museum'. To this American observer, it appears as a sort of juncture similar but not identical to when the newly-independent American states were deliberating between being a confederation or a federation. What made the path easier in the eighteenth century was that the constituent units had had a very similar trajectory leading to the constitutional convention and that the geo-political environment did not exercise constraints on the evolution of the polity. Still, when all is said and done, I believe that a 'new Europe', one different from Washington's conception of what it should be, will carve out internally and externally an identity appropriate for the modernity of this century.

Notes

1   Giddens (1991) provided a very useful initial sociological discussion of self and identity at the micro level of the individual, and Archer (2000) has greatly expanded this in her recent theoretical volume of agency.
2   It might also be fruitful to see the EU at its present stage of development sharing similarity with the nascent United States at the end of the eighteenth century with problems of identity involving separation of church and state, forms of government and powers of the different branches of government, representation in government of states as a function of size of population, and other contentious issues.
3   Davie (2002) has carefully documented the vestigial aspects of a Christian past in the European collective memory; to non-Christian visitors to Europe, at least, they are far from being trivial.
4   Malta and Cyprus are front-runner accession countries that were not in the Soviet orbit.
5   To be sure, there will also be significant costs for the new member states, such as rising unemployment in some sectors that will not be competitive in the common market. In this article, I am taking the European Union as the

focal point, but a fuller analysis would have to consider challenges to identity from the reciprocal perspective of the periphery, that is, those countries seeking admission.

6   Even in the modern, 'new' West Europe there are still sore spots. To bring in an autobiographical touch, while in August 2002 in Bastia, Corsica for another purpose, I chanced on the annual meeting of cultural autonomists not only from Corsica, but also from the Basque area, Catalonia, Brittany, Sardinia and Sicily, all sharing common experiences of having friends as political prisoners of the respective nation-states. Though perhaps not a major political force, they did prove that ethnocultural sentiments induce some people in these regions to feel that present institutional arrangements are far from those of 'representative democracy'.

7   Of course, the substantial ethnic Russian population in Estonia and Latvia is nominally Russian Orthodox rather than Protestant or Roman Catholic.

8   It was also the case for France, Spain, and Great Britain that the representation of the unified nation-state was shattered by the rise of ethnonationalism in the 1960s and 1970s that, at least in Spain and Great Britain, has led to significant devolution away from the central state.

9   Data calculated from the US Census Bureau, *Statistical Abstract of the United States 2002*, Tables 1306 and 1308. Washington, D.C. US Department of Commerce. Albania and Bosnia have a combined total of about 7,300,000, that is 1/9 of that of Turkey.

10   For the complete list, see 'Fourteen Points' *Encyclopædia Britannica* from Encyclopædia Britannica Online. http://search.eb.com/eb/article.edu=35688 [accessed 12 May 2003].

11   Incidentally, the American business challenge had a parallel in the social sciences. French researchers returned from the United States taken with new quantitative methods for empirical research, including survey analysis. This generated a reaction in the traditional centres of higher learning, one manifestation of which was the creation of a new trans-national professional organization: the Association Internationale des Sociologues de Langue Française, which, in part, has sought to protect the use of French as a scientific language at international meetings.

12   America's economic challenge to Europe has recently taken on a new hue, in the form of European Union resistance to opening up its doors to American genetically modified (GM) crops, following the EU resistance to American hormone-injected poultry.

13   Regime support for the war is not the same thing, of course, as popular support. My impressions based on recent visits to Italy, Great Britain and one Baltic state is that the regime provided support to the American war initiative whereas a substantial majority of the population was opposed.

References

Abramson, P. R., R. Inglehart, *Value Change in Global Perspective* (Ann Arbor, MI: University of Michigan Press, 1995).

Archer, M. S., *Being Human. The Problem of Agency* (Cambridge: Cambridge University Press, 2000).

Calleo, D. P., *Rethinking Europe's Future* (Princeton, NJ: Princeton University Press, 2001).

Cederman, L-E. (ed.), *Constructing Europe's Identity. The External Dimension* (Boulder, CO, London: Lynne Rienner, 2001).

Cordell, K. (ed.), *Ethnicity and Democratisation in the New Europe* (London, New York: Routledge, 1999).

Davie, G., *Europe: the Exceptional Case. Parameters of Faith in the Modern World* (London: Darto, Longman & Todd, 2002).

Delanty, G., *Inventing Europe. Idea, Identity, Reality* (Houndsmills, London: Macmillan, 1995).

Dinan, D., *Ever Closer Union. An Introduction to European Integration*, Second Edition (Boulder, CO, London: Lynne Rienner, 1999).

Forsander, A. (ed.), *Immigration and Economy in the Globalisation Process. The Case of Finland* (Helsinki: Sitra Reports Series, 2002).

Giddens, A., *Modernity and Self-Identity. Self and Society in the Late Modern Age* (Stanford: Stanford University Press, 1991).

Habermas, J., *The Theory of Communicative Action*, Vol. 2: 'Liefeworld and System: A Critique of Functionalist Reason' (Boston: Beacon Press, 1989).

Inglehart, R. A., M. Basáñez, A. M. Moreno, *Human Values and Beliefs: Political, Religious, Sexual, and Economic Norms in 43 Societies* (Ann Arbor, MI: University of Michigan Press, 1998).

Kierzkowski, H. (ed.), *Europe and Globalisation* (New York: Palgrave Macmillan, 2002).

Kurthern, H., *Immigration, Citizenship and the Welfare State in Germany and the United States* (Stamford, CT: JAI Press, 1998).

Le Figaro Magazine,'La laïcité en danger', Special Issue, Cahier No. 3 (24 May, 2003).

Mattox, G. A., A. R. Rachwald (eds), *Enlarging NATO. The National Debates* (Boulder, London: Lynne Rienner, 2001).

Meier, A., 'Take-off or Take-over? The Westernisation of East German Higher Education', paper presented at the RC04 session 11, World Congress of Sociology (Bielefeld, July 1994), unpublished.

Rex, J. 'Ethnic Identity and the Nation State: The Political Sociology of Multicultural Societies', *Social Identities*, Vol. 1, No. 1 (1995), pp. 21–35.

Rex, J., G. Singh (eds), *Governance in Multicultural Societies: Comparative Lessons in Public Policy* (Aldershot: Ashgate, 2004), forthcoming.

Rose, R., *What is Europe? A Dynamic Perspective* (New York: HarperCollins, 1996).

Servan-Schreiber, J-J., *The American Challenge* (New York: Atheneum, 1969 (1967)).

Shore, C., *Building Europe. The Cultural Politics of European Integration* (London, New York: Routledge, 2000).

Therborn, G., *European Modernity and Beyond. The Trajectory of European Societies 1945–2000* (London: Sage, 1995).

Todd, E., *Le destin des immigrés. Assimilation et ségrégation dans les démocraties occidentales* (Paris: Editions du Seuil, 1994).

Treviño, A. J., 'Introduction', in A. J. Treviño (ed.), *Talcott Parsons Today* (London, Boulder, CO: Rowman & Littlefield, 2001), pp. xv–lviii.

US Department of Commerce, Bureau of Census, *Statistical Abstract of the United States 2002* (Washington: Department of Commerce, 2003).

Ylänkö, M., *La Finlande, Pays d'Acceuil. Approche Historique et Anthropologique* (Helsinki: Societas Scientiraum Fennica, 2002).

12

Russia and the Enlargement of the European Union

Vladimir Iontsev, Irina Ivakhniouk

The invitation for Russian experts to contribute to this book/publication/joint project was extended in order to get 'a view from the outside', in this case Russia's view, of the EU. To start with, we would like to say a couple of words about current migration trends in Russia, because since the EU is getting Russia as its next-door neighbour, it should be interested in finding out what is this neighbour like. Naturally, knowing the neighbour living next door is very important for your own well being. If your neighbour is calm, friendly and successful then you can feel secure. But if your neighbour is hostile, secretive, and has a household full of strange, suspicious guests, then there are grounds for concern. For this reason, it would be useful to make a very brief overview of the recent migration trends in Russia.

12.1. Migration in Russia: Current Trends and Perspectives

The EU usually regards Russia as a peripheral zone for the exodus of migrants heading to the west. That is true. This migration flow has already turned Central European countries, such as Poland, the Czech Republic and Hungary into 'new' destination and transit countries. Relatedly, the flow from Russia into more traditional Western European destination countries has increased. However, at the same time Russia is at the centre of a new migration region that covers the territory of the former Soviet Union. In this context, it acts as a sending and — to a much greater extent — as a receiving and transit country.

The last decade was the most vigorous period ever in Russia's migration history. This history is rich; migration flows within the

Russian Empire and the Soviet Union were numerous. Their most common trend was centrifugal: the central government ordered the colonization of the Empire's border regions, primarily Siberia and the Far East as well as the assimilation of fertile lands along the Volga River and in the South of Russia. This accelerated the economic development of the Soviet republics — mainly by means of Russian specialists and technicians sent from the cities of central Russia (during certain historical periods, international migrants were also involved in this process, for example, the settlement of Volga provinces by German colonists in the mid-eighteenth century).

These phenomena greatly stimulated a high migration potential in this region of the world, which resulted in the 'international migration boom' after the collapse of the USSR and the subsequent political and economic crisis. The migrations in and into Russia at the beginning of the 1990s were mainly panicked, extraordinary ones, caused by the post-collapse shock and political and economic uncertainty. Nationalist unrest and civil wars provoked flows of refugees and forced migrants.

European demographers' predictions of mega emigration from the former USSR (the estimates varied from 1.5 to 50 million persons by 2000) probably had some basis. Given economic depression, unemployment, a crisis in food supply and the violation of civil rights according to nationality, people started to emigrate. Despite the tenfold growth of annual emigration from Russia — from 10,000 in 1987 to 104,000 in 1991 — to non-former Soviet Union states (in the context of a total emigration leap from post-Soviet states — from 39,000 to 452,000 correspondingly) (Goskomstat, 2001), the exodus did not reach into the millions. In particular, its failure to hit such proportions was due to many European countries' restrictive migration regulations, which amounted to a sort of 'iron curtain' for many former Soviet citizens and would-be migrants. The restrictions were quite natural or understandable for those countries to defend their social stability under the circumstances.

As a result, the main stream of migration was directed at Russia. Russia's net migration resulting from migration exchange with ex-Soviet states between 1992 and 2001 was +4.7 million (Goskomstat, 2001, p. 128). Population movements were bilateral; however, the ratio of those who arrived in Russia from former Soviet Union states to those who left was 4:1. The centrifugal tendency of migration movements in this region changed to a clearly centripetal one — directed primarily at the heavily populated provinces of Central

Russia (this tendency was also prevailing in internal migration — from Russia's Far East and Far North).

At the same time, emigration from Russia and other CIS[1] states to foreign countries also increased. It was primarily ethnic by nature and directed to those few countries that offered an open migration policy towards people of specific ethnic groups. First of all, to Germany which received in 1992–2000 about 550,000 emigrants from Russia, or 60 per cent of all *émigrés* from Russia (approximately 900,000 persons). The second country of destination was Israel, which received around 180,000 persons, or 20 per cent of Russia's emigrants. The USA with its large Jewish diaspora that accepted Russia's Jews is also worth mentioning. In total, these three countries — Germany, Israel and the USA — received 92 per cent of Russia's emigration as of 2000 (Iontsev et al., 2001, p. 317).

As a whole, registered emigration from Russia to outside the ex-USSR was relatively stable during the 1990s, at around 100,000 persons per year and gradually declined at the very beginning of the twenty first century to 60,000 persons a year (Goskomstat, 2002). However, its structure and direction during the last 3–4 years demonstrated significant changes caused by essential shifts in the overall migration picture in and around Russia.

The stage of panicked, reactive and largely forced migration is over (having peaked in 1990–93). As well, the ethnic factor is considerably decreasing in both internal and external migration flows (in 1993–95, almost half of emigrants from Russia were ethnically German and around 12 per cent were Jews, whereas in 2000 the proportion of Germans fell to a third. At the same time, emigration of ethnic Russians increased 1.5 times in comparison with 1993. In 2000, 40 per cent of emigrants were Russians, significantly surpassing Germans and almost quintuple the number of Jews) (Vishnevsky, 2002, p. 116). Very notably, the motivations behind migration shifted; economic factors (both push and pull ones) played a greater role.

These changes in migration causes and motives are restructuring migratory flows to and from Russia, with regard to both ex-USSR states and other countries of the world. The prevalence of economic motivations in migration suggests well-analyzed, considered individual decisions about when, why and where to move (in contrast to forced migration). In recent years, Russia has looked economically more attractive than the majority of its neighbouring countries. Therefore, the citizens of the CIS countries come to Russia mainly in quest of jobs and higher salaries (common language, culture, mutually-recognized diplomas and qualifications, and so on, have significance here). At the same time, Russians — those who are unsatisfied with their economic situation or have some other reasons to emigrate — choose nearby European countries that are successfully going through their economic transition (Czech Republic, Poland, Hungary, and so on) and developed European countries, which have been attractive for migrants for decades because of their stable economic development, traditional respect for civil rights, social benefits (including for foreigners) and growing need for labour due to the aging of the indigenous population.

Here, we mention several ways of how Russian citizens carry out their westward migration. Firstly, (regarding emigration) for the constantly growing number of prosperous Russians (who nonetheless wish to change the country of their permanent residence), immigration to the country of destination as business migrants — investors, entrepreneurs, or property owners — is becoming prevalent (despite few reliable statistics, we can still assume — from information from immigration agencies — that no less than half of the above-mentioned increasing emigration of ethnic Russians took this form during recent years).

Secondly, temporary migration by Russian citizens to Europe (education, business, labour, tourism) is in fact 'pregnant' with emigration: graduates of European universities sometimes choose to stay and work in their countries of education, labour migrants enjoying successful employment start applying for permanent residence permits, 'tourists' often turn out to be illegal labour migrants, and so on.

Thirdly, experience acquired from short-term trips to the European countries (circular migration of petty traders, intermediary business, temporary labour-migration, and so on) is conducive to the formation of migrants' networks in certain European countries (Poland, Romania, Germany, Italy, Greece, and so on). Things favouring such networks include reliable contacts with partners and employers in these countries, which allow migrants to find long-term work there (usually illegally), as well as to inform their relatives, friends and other compatriots about the opportunities and conditions for staying, living and working or running a business there. Often, migrants' networks are interrelated with criminal networks, primarily due to semi-legal residence and employment. This is true not only for Russian citizens, but also for citizens of the other European CIS states — Belarus, Ukraine and Moldova.

Overall, migration flow from Russia towards the West consists of various categories: business migrants, temporary labour migrants, circular ('shuttle') migrants, irregular migrants, and so on, all of whom are motivated primarily by economic factors.

This point is closely related to the change of the internal European migration zone and makes the issue of regulation of the migration between the CIS countries and new member-states of the EU very topical. In Russia (as well as in Ukraine, for example) there exists a certain segment whose well-being strongly depends on their trips abroad. According to some estimates, the incomes of around two million households in Russia are derived from international migration (Vorobyeva, 2001, p. 21). However, we suppose that the real number is much higher if we take into consideration all the categories of economic migrants (seasonal migrants, contract workers, day labourers, petty traders, and irregular migrants). Many of them are oriented to the new EU states of Central Europe. The problem is that EU expansion by making the border restrictions more strict, may leave many of these people either without a source of income or forced to become irregular persons within the EU.

In order to avoid this, it is important to undertake official, governmental efforts to provide migration opportunities under the new conditions, that is when a new, common immigration policy comes into force. This looks especially topical since cheap foreign labour from neighbouring countries has become a structural element in some industries in the central European countries. We do not have reliable statistical data, but we can suppose that, for example, the garment industry in some regions of Poland has increased its competitiveness thanks to female migrants from Ukraine and Russia.

12.2. Migration Regulation in Russia

Nowadays, Russian migration policy is becoming an issue of academic and political debate, as well as in the media. Russia is in need of a policy corresponding to the real migration situation in the country and around it. For several years, migration policy was focused exclusively on forced migration. Now, the situation has changed. Labour migration — and its irregular component — is becoming a matter of particular importance. This shift needs new approaches and strategies. Furthermore, global migration is changing and should be taken into consideration.

During the last decade, the management of migration in Russia was one of the most uncertain and unstable elements of federal government policy. In 1992, the Federal Migration Service (FMS) was founded. Its activities were mainly directed at forced migrants, in accordance with migration situation of the time. However, other forms of international migration dropped from sight. When, in 2000, the FMS was abolished, the responsibility for the management of migration was transferred to the Ministry of Federation, National and Migration Policy. Even the title of the Ministry demonstrates that migration policy was regarded primarily as an internal matter. International migration was again forgotten. One year later, in September 2001, the Ministry was restructured, and since February 2002 the management of migration together with migration policy has come under the Ministry of Home Affairs. This time, actions against irregular migration became the core principle in the field of migration. Terrorist attacks in the USA stimulated the worldwide campaign against terrorism, which, in the Russian context, became synonymous with efforts against migration to Russia in general.

Besides 'institutional musical chairs', other obstacles hindering effective migration policy include imperfections in regulatory legislation on migration and the lack of important, up-dated laws to guarantee social and legal rights for migrants (both for those who come to Russia and those who leave Russia temporarily or permanently). The laws on citizenship, refugees and forced migrants and social guarantees for international migrants were formulated during a very short period of time following Russia's emergence as a sovereign state, when there was an urgent need for national legislation. Laws were hastily written under conditions of panicked and/or forced migration flows. However, during the last decade the situation has been radically changing, and the laws have grown outdated. In recent years, a new packet of laws was under development. On 1 November 1 2002 the new Law on the Legal Status of Foreign Citizens in the Russian Federation came into force. New laws on citizenship, labour migrants and others are on agenda. At the same time, there is an obvious lack of bilateral, inter-governmental agreements on international migration, in particular concerning social security for labour migrants from one country working in the territory of another country.[2]

The undeveloped and inadequate state of national legislation on migration improperly narrows the scope of legitimate migration and consequently broadens the scope of irregular migration. However, migration legislation is not drafted in a vacuum. It is a manifestation of official migration policy. The debates on a reasonable concept for a migration policy have been going on in Russia for over ten years; however, so far there has been no common attitude towards migration either in society or among policy-makers. Many groups are now calling for a scrutinization of migration policy, especially in the field of immigration and transit migration. If this entails improved border controls, restrictions on irregular migration and illegal employment, the scrutiny could be regarded as advantageous. However, if it results in restrictions on labour migration and permanent immigration to Russia, it can damage national interests (mostly, in economic and demographic dimensions).

The more or less accepted opinion is that the spontaneous character of migration processes in the territories of Russia and other CIS states should be legally regulated. The opinion is the same for both temporary and permanent types of migration. Once a legitimate legal foundation has been made to cover migration, international co-operation and agreements in this sphere should become possible.

In our opinion, migration regulation should be a sphere of active cooperation among the interested countries: countries of destination, countries of origin and countries of transit. The effectiveness of this cooperation highly depends on whether the mutual interests will be fully and properly understood and addressed. Crucial issues related to migration — such as the Kaliningrad muss — highlight the correctness of this idea.

12.3. Russia as the East-West Transit 'Corridor'

While forecasting migration flows between Russia and the EU countries, it is important to take into account the geopolitical location of Russia: it is not merely an eastern neighbour of the EU — it is a waystation on numerous overt and covert migration routes from Asian and African countries to Europe.

The attractiveness of Russia as a transit 'staging post' for (mainly illegal) migrants is determined by the relatively 'transparent' borders within the post-Soviet territory. Furthermore, some CIS states have signed agreements on visa-free entry with third countries[3] and the Russian legislation regulating foreigners' entry, residence and employment on the territory of Russia is poor. Other important factors are Russia's geographic location, which stands between Asia and Europe, and the disorganization of the domestic labour market, with a significant informal sector, where irregular migrants most often derive their income. According to Ministry of Internal

Affairs statistics, at the present time there are around 300,000 transit migrants from Afghanistan, China, Angola, Pakistan, India, Sri-Lanka, Turkey and Ethiopia 'stuck' in Russia. (IOM, 2002a, p. 4). Furthermore, there is a significant flow of migrants who illegally penetrate Russian borders trying to reach EU countries.

The presence of illegal/irregular transit migrants in Russia is incompatible with the national interests of the country. Many of these migrants are involved in crime and the places of their concentration become sources of 'exotic' infectious diseases, drug addiction and prostitution.

It is admittedly unfortunate that, until now, Russian official structures did not manage to properly control the arrival and staying of transit migrants in the country. After entering with a transit or tourist visa (or crossing the border illegally) they often get lost in the vast spaces of Russia. At the same time, their departure towards the intended countries of destination is quite strictly controlled at Russian frontiers. By prohibiting the illegal exit of those migrants who have violated the terms of their visas, or had used forged documents and so on, the Russian frontier services are in effect turning Russia into a 'settling tank' for illegal migrants.

Migrant smuggling (and trafficking in migrants) is a serious, well-organized business in many countries. According to a number of estimates, the overall annual profit from the smuggling of migrants in the world is 5–7 billion dollars. Nowadays it became widespread in Russia as well, being stimulated by its extremely high profitability. Along the borders of Russia, especially on the Russian-Chinese, Russian-Kazakh and Russian-Ukrainian borders, there exist numerous well-organized channels for migrant smuggling (90 per cent of illegal migration to Russia comes from Kazakhstan, where there are almost 7600 km of practically open border). A hasty agreement on visa-free entry for citizens of the PRC to Russia at the beginning of the 1990s opened a 'floodgate' of Chinese migration, which — as a consequence of huge differences in demographic potential on both sides of Russian-Chinese border — has brought many labour migrants to Russia as well as people whose ultimate goal is to reach Western Europe via Russian territory.

Over the past five years, the number of those detained at Russian borders has increased almost tenfold. This figure includes citizens of 30 countries with which Russia shares no common border. In 1999–2000, the Russian Federal Frontier Service, together with law-enforcement agencies, detained more than 2000 irregular migrants and exposed about 400 criminal groups specializing in moving irregular migrants (IOM, 2001, p. 3). This activity of the Russian law-enforcement agencies is primarily aimed at protecting Russia's interests and its national security while simultaneously safeguarding the interests of those transit migrants' target countries. It would be logical to assume that common interests need common efforts (in the framework of information exchange, international agreements counteracting illegal migration, and so on). If European countries are interested in preventing illegal migration 'from afar' — as they should — then they should initiate international programs and agreements in this domain, joint scientific projects in international migration in all its forms and in-depth studies on the most topical issues (for example, the prospects of cross-border cooperation in preventing illegal migration; the impact of Russian temporary/ irregular labour migrants on the EU accession-countries' industries; the migration situation and its regulation in the Kaliningrad Province a foreign enclave within the enlarged EU).

12.4. Kaliningrad Province as an Enclave in the Enlarged EU

The eastward enlargement of the EU raises a series of problems for policymakers on both sides. Some of these problems required making concerted decisions urgently, before Poland, Czech Republic, Hungary, Lithuania and other accession states joined the EU. One pressing issue concerned Kaliningrad Province, which is non-contiguous with the main territory of the Russian Federation. With the inclusion of Lithuania and Poland into the UE, Kaliningrad Province becomes an enclave surrounded by the EU on three sides and the Baltic Sea on the other. Thus, the question has been raised about how to regulate the movement of people and goods between this enclave and the rest of Russia.

A likely thorn in the side of the European Union may be irregular migration from (and through) Kaliningrad Province towards West. For these reasons, a small province of fewer than one million people has become the stumbling block for Russian and EU decision-makers. The problem is exacerbated by trends in the province's demographic and economic development. Population dynamics, age structure and labour market demands have made this 'island' heavily dependent on migrants in the past, in the present and likely for the future.

The demographic history of the province is closely linked to migration, to be more precise, to official recruitment campaigns, and migration inflow continues to this day. The migration ratio in

242 Migration in the New Europe: East-West Revisited

Kaliningrad Province (over nine migrants per 1000 economically-active persons) is the highest in Russia (IOM, 2002b, p. 12). Net migration — both internal (from other territories of Russia) and international (from neighbouring Poland, Lithuania and some CIS states) has become an important compensatory factor for the natural population decrease and for the replenishment of the local labour supply. The provincial economy is based on transportation and construction industries, which are integrated with similar industries in neighbouring countries. Besides, it strongly depends on supplies from 'continental' Russia. The transformation of EU boundaries can increase the Province's isolation from both directions.

On the other hand, the investment inflow to Kaliningrad over the past couple of years is stimulating an economic revival and a correspondingly inflow of migrants from other, less successful regions of Russia, as well from other countries. According to the economic forecast of the Russian government, within a few years Kaliningrad Province will become one of the most developed regions in Russia. If this happens, the province will become even more attractive for migrants. This situation will definitely raise the question: to what extent and under what conditions can a society based on democratic values provide freedom of movement for those who choose to live and to work in Kaliningrad Province.

The November 2002 EU — Russia summit in Brussels agreed on a special 'Facilitated Transit Document' (FTD) regime for Russian citizens travelling through Lithuanian territory. Under this agreement, two types of FTD will be issued. For multi-entry transit by rail citizens of Kaliningrad Province or any other regions of Russia are to apply to a Lithuanian consulate; after necessary checking procedures an application will be satisfied or rejected. The same regime applies to persons travelling by automobile transport. As for single trips by rail, the FTD will be issued to transit passengers on the basis of a Russian passport (after 31 December 2004 — of international passports only) when buying a railway ticket. The FTD is to be the statistical and immigration control method covering the passage of people through the EU territory. The FTD regime looks like the most reasonable solution under existing and foreseen circumstances.

However, a year after the Brussels summit, transit practicalities are still a 'hot item' under discussion. While Lithuania agrees to follow EU decisions on this item, in fact it intends to link transit regulations to its own political interests. Thus, regulation of vexed questions concerning 'disputed territories' at the Lithuanian-Russian border[4] was closely tied to conditions of Kaliningrad transit for Russian citizens. Therefore, in the short time before EU enlargement, Kaliningrad Province remained a politically sensitive and technically difficult to resolve issue in Russia — EU relationships.

Russian President Vladimir Putin's call for a visa-free regime between Schengen countries and Russia seems to be too optimistic for the present. However, over a long-term perspective issue this call can be promising, since to enter the Schengen zone, a country must undertakes certain responsibilities, including securing its borders with third countries. For Russia, this would mean strengthening its eastern border control, restricting transit migrants, developing a general migration database and combating irregular migration in all its forms, migrant-smuggling in particular. Who will benefit from these positive changes in Russia's management of migration? Certainly Russia itself and undoubtedly its neighbouring western countries — the expanded European Union — as well. It would be best to remember that the present shift in European migration trends seemed unrealistic not so long ago but now we are witnessing the most profound and positive change in the enlarged European migration space.

12.5. Conclusion

Arriving at coordinated decisions is a long and arduous process, which increasingly highlights the problems and intricacies under discussion. As the situation unfolds, new agenda items keep emerging. Currently, as Europe becomes increasingly integrated and national interests are converging, cooperation in migration policy with 'outside countries' is becoming a point of vital interest for all involved parties.

Ethnic migrations from Russia (of Russian citizens, including Slavic and non-Slavic populations) and through Russia's territory (of transit migrants, primarily from Asia) can have a serious influence on ethnic processes in the countries of Central and Western Europe. Analysis of these migrations is especially topical in the context of the enlarged European migration space.

Practical cooperation between the EU and Russia, an important link in the migration chain between Asia and Europe (which will probably bring the largest 'ethnic' migration inflow to the European Union), looks both possible and promising.

Irregular migration from Russia and through Russia is a painful item in EU-Russia cooperation in the migration sphere. It is important to understand that irregular migrants are primarily motivated by economic/employment/labour reasons. Therefore, their number is closely related to the labour absorption capacity in receiving countries. 'Grey' labour market sectors are most attractive for irregular migrants. Domestic labour market regulation and control could be the most effective method to limit irregular migration.

The post-September 11 attacks tendency for unfavourable attitudes on migration (see, for example, Kritz, 2002) is leading tothe mis-association of migrants, particularly irregular ones, with terrorists. This misconception — when expressed in anti-migration actions — can have the opposite result to the desired one. The experience of the last four decades of migration policy in different countries of the world shows that restrictive migration regulations were always followed by increases in irregular migration (in the 1960s in the USA, in the 1970s and in the 1990s in Europe). Another lesson from this history is the impossibility of eliminating irregular migration without enormous compromises to citizens' rights and freedoms. The alternative way is to develop legitimate, regular forms of international migration, primarily labour migration. This should be the essence of practical cooperation between the EU and Russia in view of the enlargement of the European internal migration sphere.

Notes

1 Countries of the former Soviet Union excluding Baltic States.
2 Russia has agreements on employment and social security for the citizens of one country working in the territory of another country with some former Soviet states — Armenia (1994), Belarus, Ukraine, Moldova (1993), Kyrghyzstan (1996), and agreements on social and legal guaranties for permanent migrants who have moved from one country to another — with Azerbaijan (1997), Armenia (1997), Georgia (1994), Kazakhstan (1995), Kyrghyzstan (1995), Tadjikistan (1992), Turkmenistan (1993) and Ukraine (2001). As to non-former Soviet Union states, there are several agreements on co-operation in the field of social security with the countries of the former socialist block, signed in the 1950s and 1960s: with Czechoslovakia signed on 1 December 1959 (now valid for the Czech Republic and Slovakia); with Bulgaria signed on 11 December 1959; with Romania signed on 24 December 1960; with Hungary signed on 20 December 1962 and with Mongolia signed on 6 April 1981. Nowadays, they are obviously outdated. The agreement on social security between Russia and Spain, signed 11 April 1994, is the only example of modern bilateral regulation of social guaranties for international migrants in the Russian legislation.

3   For example, agreements on visa-free entry between China and Kyrghyzstan and between Kyrghyzstan and Kazakhstan and between Kazakhstan and Russia provides a rather comfortable and cheap land route for transit migrants from China to Russia or for onward travel to the West (Sadovskaya, 2002, p. 51).

4   'The Agreement on a State Border with Lithuania' was ratified by the Russian Gosudarstvennaya Duma (Parliament) on 21 May 2003.

References

Chesnais, J-C. 'L'Emigration Sovietique: Passe, Present et Avenir', in *Migrations internationales: le tournaut* (Paris: OCDE, 1993), pp. 117–26.

Goskomstat, *Chislennost' i migratsia naseleniya v Rosijskoy Federatsii v 2001 godu* (Moscow: Goskomstat, 2002).

Goskomstat, *Russia's Statistical Yearbook* (Moscow: Goskomstat, 2001).

IOM, 'Irregular Migration at the Eastern and Western Boundaries of Russia: Primorsky Territory and Kaliningrad Province', *IOM Open Forum, Information Series*, No. 4 (Moscow: IOM, 2002b).

IOM, 'Irregular Migration in Russia: Opening the Debate', *IOM Open Forum, Information Series*, No. 1 (Moscow: IOM, 2001).

IOM, 'Management of Migration in the CIS Countries: Legislation and Cross-Border Cooperation', *IOM Open Forum, Information Series*, Special issue, No. 3 (Moscow: IOM, 2002a).

Iontsev, V., I. Ivakhniouk, 'Russia in the World Migration Flows: Trends of the Last Decade (1992–2001)', in 'The World in the Mirror of International Migration', *International Migration of Population: Russia and the Contemporary World*, Vol. 10 (Moscow: MAX Press, 2002), pp. 34–78.

Iontsev, V. A., *Mezhdunarodnaya migratsiya naseleniya: Teoriya i istoriya izucheniya* (Moscow: Dialog-MGU, 1999).

Iontsev, V. A., N. M. Lebedeva, M. V. Nazarov, A. V. Okorokov, *Emigratsiya i repatriatsiya v Rossii* (Moscow: Trusteeship for Russian repatriates' needs, 2001).

Ivakhniouk, I. V., '"Perekhodniye" formy mezhdunarodnoy migratsii v Rossii', in *Lomonosovskiye Chteniya — 2000* (Moscow: TEIS-MGU, 2001), pp. 214–28.

Kritz, M., 'Time for a National Discussion on Immigration', *International Migration Review*, Vol. 36, No. 1 (2002), pp. 33–6.

Okólski, M., 'Migration Pressures on Europe', in D. Van De Kaa, H. Leridon, G. Gesano, M. Okólski (eds), 'European Populations: Unity in Diversity', *European Studies of Population*, Vol. 6 (Dortdrecht, Boston, London: Kluwer Academic Press, 1999), pp. 141–94.

Sadovskaya, E., 'Predotvrascheniye nezakonnoy migratsii v Kazakhstane', in 'Nelegal'naya immigratsiya', *Mezhdunarodnaya migratsiya naseleniya: Rossiya i sovremenniy mir*, Vol. 9 (Moscow: MAX-Press, 2002), pp. 50–65.

Vishnevsky, A. G. (ed.), 'Naseleniye Rossii v 2001 godu', *Annual Demographic Report* (Moscow, University Publishing House, 2002).

Vorobyeva, O. (ed.), 'Trudovaya migratsiya v Rossii', *Migration of Population Series*, Vol. 2 (Moscow, 2001).

13

Forging a Common Immigration Policy for the Enlarging European Union: for Diversity of Harmonization

Agata Górny, Paolo Ruspini

13.1. Introduction

13.1.1. Setting a context

In 1957, the Treaty of Rome set up the European Economic Community and introduced the free movement of persons as one of the four freedoms to be established, along with freedom of movement of services, capital and goods. The commitments to establish a common market and the free movement of persons have been counterbalanced by some member states' reluctance to transfer their immigration and asylum responsibilities to the European level (Favell and Geddes, 2000). It can be argued that member states did not fully give up their prerogatives of intergovernmental cooperation underlying collaboration in those two policy areas in the 1980s and 1990s. While the conflict between the prerogatives of national sovereignty and that of the developing supranational European entity has remained harsh, the ongoing process of integrating into a single entity has drawn immigration and asylum into a web of evolving supranational interdependencies (Favell and Geddes, 2000).

Even though work on principles of a common European approach to migration date back to the early 1990s,[1] the need for a common EU immigration policy has been fully recognized by all the member states only since the Tampere meeting of the European Council in October 1999. Due to difficulties and delays on the part of member states, European policy-makers are still discussing the shape of a EU immigration policy. At present, achieving manageability of migration in Europe has become a priority, at least in the official European discourse (compare, for example, Niessen, 2000; Papademetriou, 2003). A key component of management of European migration is cooperation among all the countries involved in a given migration system, in particular, between sending and receiving countries. This includes cooperation in defining the goals and needs of migration policy and a broad perspective that transcends the national interests of the countries involved (Crawley, 2003).

It is notable that, apart from a general agreement on the need for a common EU immigration policy, the query 'to what degree should/could this policy be harmonized?' still leaves unanswered questions. General directives built upon a concept (and legal instrument), first introduced by Title VI of the Maastricht Treaty, of joint actions to be employed when 'the objectives of the Union can be attained better by joint action than by the member states individually' lacks precision in a variety of respects. European integration has opened the doors to many activities that are no longer subject to the control of the intergovernmental actors that once were responsible for them (Favell and Geddes, 2000). In order to determine the common denominators for a EU immigration policy and an appropriate degree of its harmonization, one must first identify those aspects that relate to problems of continent-wide significance. The harmonization is to be based on the fundamental principles of the European polity promoted by international organizations like the Council of Europe — democracy, rule of law and human rights. At the same time, some satisfactory level of sovereignty has to be secured so as to enable national governments to deal with country-specific aspects of both immigration and emigration, such as labour migration. A balance between the increasing prerogatives of the European polity and securing some degree of sovereignty for EU member states is to be pursued through discussions and negotiations involving actors from all the present and prospective member states.

On 1 May 2004, two processes tend to converge: the EU enlargement on one hand and the setting up of common standards for EU immigration policy on the other. As the ten new member countries accede to the EU, the migratory diversity within and to the Union will further diversify. Consequently, the complex task of creating a common EU immigration policy will become even more complicated. One might even question whether a far-reaching harmonization is possible in the light of considerable differences between migratory experiences of the EU and accession countries. Nevertheless, due to the fact that the enlarged European Union is to constitute a unified migration space with internal freedom of movement, effective management of migration on both the European and national levels requires a broad, European perspective.

13.1.2. Approach taken

The previous chapters of this book have presented country- and region-specific developments in migratory and policy processes. The chapters have pointed out and focused on similarities but, nevertheless, have also illustrated several of the considerable differences observed among European countries. This chapter will now expand its scope to propose fields of action in which a European-level approach can bring particularly effective outcomes. In this way, selected aspects of forming a common EU immigration policy are to be addressed and, in particular, areas of possible harmonization of national migration policies demonstrated.

Developing a common EU immigration policy, as understood in this chapter, entails setting up a framework for an appropriate harmonization of respective national policies in the European Union. We focus on prospects for the management of European migration, as attaining its manageability is the *condicio sine qua non* to harmonize national policies on migration and to forge a common EU immigration policy. We argue that achieving manageability of European migration requires identification of migration fields where cooperation among European countries can reward all present and future member states.

Peter F. Drucker's classic work on management theory (1988) lists what he sees as the preconditions for successful management. '[Management] requires simple, clear and unifying objectives ... The goals that embody it have to be clear, public and often reaffirmed' (Drucker, 1988, p. 76). These postulates apply also to management of European migration. The search for common denominators for the EU immigration policy should consist not only of identification of similarities in migratory processes but, most of all, of identification of similarities in interests across Europe. Migration is such a sensitive issue that even the most comprehensive and enlightened policy solutions proposed by the European Commission often encounter resistance on the country-level because they clash with long-established governmental interests in the area as well as with powerful electoral lobbies. Thus, this chapter focuses on proposing selected fields of management of European migration wherein a broad European level of governance can result in positive outcomes for the Union overall, including its current and future members. It should be noted that we will take into account not only the economic side of the problem, but also aspects like satisfying social stability and securing human rights within the enlarged European Union.

Most material presented in this chapter derives from the discussion on prospects for European migration policy carried out during the conference 'In Search for a New Europe: Contrasting Migratory Experiences' held on 22–24 March 2002.[2] It gathered policy makers and experts in migration representing chief international organizations, academia and selected NGOs from both member and accession countries (participating organizations and their representatives are listed in Appendix). The outcomes of this debate have been enriched with our own reflections and information about some of the most recent developments in the field. One value of this contribution lies in the analysis of the current stage of discussion about the formation of European migration policy. Some fundamental aspects of this debate are of a universal nature whereas others will change conceptually and/or in importance in the future. All the aspects, however, do represent important points of reference for further developments in the migration policy of the enlarged European Union.

It should be noted that, while presenting our analyses, we assume that EU immigration policy harmonization is inevitable in the light of progressing European integration. Moreover, this chapter presents views of migration experts who, as a group, can be considered having a broad European outlook on policy processes underway in European migration. Consequently, the opinions and recommendations presented come mainly from advocates of EU immigration policy harmonization, whereas their opponents can mainly be found among policy-makers defending the national interests of their respective countries. Therefore, this contribution emphasizes the advantages of setting up a common European approach to migration addressing, at the same time, selected disadvantages of its inappropriate harmonization.

The chapter starts with the presentation of the principal goals of the European Commission in migration and the main actions that it has already undertaken. Subsequently, the analysis focuses on the demonstration of preconditions for designing a common EU immigration policy and its three areas requiring appropriate European management, as advocated by the migration experts. The proposed management areas include: asylum vs. migration, European labour market and the Union's eastward enlargement. Their demonstration is followed by appropriate policy recommendations. The chapter closes with reflections about possible levels of harmonization of EU immigration policy.

13.2. European Commission

13.2.1. Short historical outlook

In 1986, the Single European Act gave birth to a unified market comprising an area without internal frontiers with guaranteed free movement of persons. As a result, immigration and asylum became matters of common concern. However, cooperation under the umbrella of the European Union in the field of Justice and Home Affairs (JHA) is a relatively new development and its significant advancement has only been underway since the late 1990s. The meeting of the European Council in Tampere established an Area of Freedom, Security and Justice, called for in the 1997 Treaty of Amsterdam, which came into force on 1 May 1999 and elaborated the political guidelines for the following years, including in the field of migration. These proceedings, together with plans for semi-annually updated 'scoreboard' to assess implementations of Council conclusions and the later approval of the Charter of Fundamental Rights of European Union at the Nice Council in December 2000, were quantum leaps in developing European cooperation in the field of JHA and, hence, of managing migration in Europe.

At the moment, all decisions on immigration and asylum are subject to intergovernmental agreements between EU member states and third countries and to unanimous votes among the EU member states — as established in the 1992 Maastricht Treaty. The entry into force of the following Treaty of Amsterdam established a period of five years for these decisions to become the official European Community legislation, subject to co-decision and qualified majority. Immigration and asylum have been therefore 'communitarized' in the sense that they have been gradually placed under the authority of the European Union.[3] Furthermore, making them subject to qualified majority voting would make respective proceedings faster.[4]

The main intervention areas for European Commission include: 1. a comprehensive approach to the management of migratory flows; 2. fair treatment of third country nationals; 3. partnership with countries of origin; and 4. development of a common European asylum system (CEC, 2000a). The selection of intervention areas demonstrates the recognition by the European Commission that, given declining population and labour shortages in some sectors of a number of EU countries, 'the existing "zero" immigration policies, which have dominated thinking over the past 30 years, are no longer appropriate' (CEC, 2000a, p. 6).[5]

13.2.2. Guiding principles of migration policy formation

The currently agreed-upon overall objective is to achieve manage-ability of migration in Europe. It applies to management of migration on both EU and national levels. In other words, it is to set up a long-term common migration policy for the European Union. Obviously, these objectives cover a variety of issues and related social, economic and political phenomena. The European Commission semi-annual 'scoreboard' objectives include areas like: establishing a coherent European Union policy on asylum, migration, readmission and return; combating trafficking in human beings, improving European statistics on migratory phenomena; and a wide collection of aspects related to internal and external borders and visa policy (CEC, 2003c). In general, forming a common immigration policy for the European Union requires an appropriate framework to achieve the ambitious goals settled on for the upcoming period. As noted above, there are four main areas for the European Commission's intervention. Their selection corresponds with some basic principles formulated by the Commission for the development of the European migration policy.[6]

Necessity of comprehensiveness. Migration intersects with a variety of social, economic and political phenomena. Thus, migration policy cannot be tackled separately from problems relating to labour markets, border control and controlling illegal work, trade and movement. This involves the crucial importance of comprehensiveness during the formation of a common migration policy for the European Union.

Working out an adequate *framework for fair treatment of legally-resident third country nationals.* This designates an effort to secure possibly comparable rights and obligations for third country nationals resident in the member states. The integration of migrants and related social, economic and political inclusion/exclusion problems is and will be an important issue since the European Union hosts an enormous number of foreigners. A framework for this is to be based on the Charter of Fundamental Rights, implying a series of rights that seem to provide for a future, uniform 'European legal status for migrants' (Mafrolla and Nascimbene, 2002, p. 57). Its driving principles are to be built upon an anti-discrimination and anti-racism approach. It is, at the same time, assumed that the involvement of various actors of civil society (among others, NGOs and migrants' associations) from European countries operating on different levels — local, regional and national — is necessary to set up the appropriate framework for migrants' integration.

Necessity of partnership and dialogue. Notions of partnership and dialogue are to play a pivotal role in what the European Commission does concerning migration policy. It hopes to establish a dialogue between countries of destination, origin and transit that goes beyond issues of readmission and return. The aim is to identify possible advantages (for example, opportunities for economic development) of, increasingly circular, migration for not only receiving but also sending areas. Particularly, the emphasis is put on a dialogue with third countries, which is to be developed in relevant contexts such as trade and development. The dialogue is also expected to deal with the impact of emigration on the countries of origin and the orderly management of migratory flows (consular cooperation, appropriate policies for recruiting labour migrants in countries of origin, which could eventually lead to the establishment of 'one-stop shops' in these countries as well as control of illegal migration) (Pratt, 2001, pp. 5–6). Partnership and dialogue can be of particular importance in the light of European Union enlargement; promising scenarios exist for discussion between accession countries and the enlarged Union's eastern neighbours.

Emphasis on asylum policy. An asylum policy for the European Union has to be developed distinctly from the broad issue of migration, particularly from labour migration, and must be done in accordance with the Geneva Convention of 1951 and other related international conventions. Securing asylum-seekers' rights in the European Union should be a principle consistent with the human rights approach underlying Union policy. Development of an appropriate asylum policy is related to the introduction of effective measures for economic migration. It is hoped that providing a satisfactory legal alternative will reduce illegal flows (for example, trafficking in people) and pressure on asylum systems (Pratt, 2001).

13.2.3. Works of the Commission — achievements and plans for the future

The above-presented four basic EU principles match all the elements that the Heads of State and Government called for to identify the guiding principles for the elaboration of a European migration policy at the European Council Tampere meeting. As far as the Commission's practical works are concerned, they form two phases. The first of which, establishing a framework for the admission and stay of third country nationals and related pieces of legislation covering a variety of migratory aspects, started in 1999. The second phase is at a relatively early stage and concerns development of discussion, dialogue and exchange of information concerning an appropriate migration policy for the European Union and its member states. These efforts are being made to set up a basis for a common EU immigration policy and are of undeniable importance for further developments.[7]

First phase: Setting up a legal framework for admission and conditions of stay of third country nationals. The framework is to be based on prerogatives included in the Treaty of Amsterdam and covers a wide range of issues related to asylum. On the migration side, legislation and proposals of legislation introduced as an outcome of the overall works of this phase include:

- a Council Directive on the right to family reunification (CEU, 2003),[8]
- a Council Directive concerning the status of third-country nationals who are long-term residents (CEU, 2004),
- a proposal for a Council Directive on the conditions of entry and residence of third-country nationals for the purpose of paid employment and self-employment economic activities (CEC, 2001b),[9]
- a proposal for a Council Directive on the entry and residence conditions for third country nationals for the purposes of study, vocational training or voluntary activity (CEC, 2002).[10]

The presented legislative acts and proposals are to establish minimum standards for migration policy in Europe and to constitute its base. It should be noted that vigorous discussions that ensue from various legal proposals of the Commission slow down the implementation procedure and the designing of a legal framework for the European migration policy. It applies particularly to legislation on labour migration, since in the field of asylum policy, the controversies seem to be smaller. In addition, due to the relative novelty of the migration issue in the works of the Commission, the decision-making process still lacks appropriately adjusted procedures. This issue will grow in importance after the enlargement when the number of countries involved in the decision-making process will jump from 15 to 25.

Second phase: Establishing discussion, dialogue and information exchange on policy formation. Communication is to be a pivotal element in the formative process of a common EU immigration policy. The rich diversity of migratory experiences and political interests of all the member states means that it is difficult to achieve an agreement on joint policy solutions in the migration field. Thus, the Commission aims, first of all, at setting minimum policy standards and at providing a relatively broad range of options for adapting solutions appropriate for a variety of country scenarios. This implies that, even after implementing basic pieces of European legislation, there will be many differences in how migration policies are put into practice across the European Union. Such a perspective has resulted in the Commission's proposal to employ the so-called open method of coordination in the field of European migration policy (CEC, 2001a). This would be based on an exchange of information about how legislation is put in place, about the effectiveness of chosen policy solutions and about the impacts that their implementation has on different European countries.

One key element of the open method of coordination is the Council's adoption of multi-year guidelines for the Union accompanied by specific timetables for achieving the goals set for the short, medium and long term. These guidelines will then be translated into national policy solutions by the setting of specific targets, which take into account national and regional differences (CEC, 2001a). For each set of guidelines, member states should prepare national action plans, which will be reviewed and updated on an annual basis. The action plans will provide the basis for an overall evaluation of the implementation of the common policy and the results obtained. They will also provide inputs into the way in which the guidelines should be developed to reflect changing needs (CEC, 2001a). One purpose of the Commission is to build a bottom-up approach and bring into debate not only experts and policy-makers operating on European and national levels, but also civil society, local authorities, social partners and others actors in the field. Thus, for the first time, the open method of coordination leaves room for the active involvement of migrants' associations and non-governmental organizations, at both national and European levels, as part of the group of target actors for the success of the policies and the achievement of the goals set out in its guidelines (CEC, 2001a). It is a valuable recognition to the work of migrants not only in assisting their fellow migrants in adjusting to the hardships of integrating into the host country but also in actively promoting their own rights and thus helping in forging local and national policies sensitive to their needs.

Implementing the open method of coordination is quite a complex task requiring the creation of an appropriate framework for migration debate. Plans include the creation of a European Migration Observatory, which is to be a network of institutions working closely on migratory phenomena and stimulating exchanges of information and research activities (CEC, 2001b, p. 16).[11] The Commission stresses the need to improve the quality and comparability of statistics on migration in Europe by adopting an *ad hoc* action plan (CEC, 2003b) and to carry out comparative research programs on migration and asylum, which will help inform debate on migration policy for the European Union. All moves of the Commission aiming at establishing information exchange and dialogue between various actors are to identify a sensible direction for the development of the European immigration policy in both medium- and long-term perspectives.

13.3. Managing Migration in the Enlarged Europe — Necessary Preconditions and Pivotal Fields of Action

13.3.1. Preconditions for managing migration in Europe

Management of European migration is a far more complex task than management of any, even the most sophisticated, organization. Nevertheless, selected basic principles of management theory appear to be fully relevant to the problem discussed. In particular, we want to present three preconditions for the effective management, which we have translated into the language of migration management:

- management should secure the ability to establish a self-learning migratory European system (policy developments vs. social dynamics of migration),[12]
- management requires communication, that is information exchange within the European Union,[13]
- management requires appropriate indicators of migratory processes underway[14].

We argue that the above postulates set a context that should be applied to the management of European migration. They directly suggest two pivotal requirements for the effective development of a common EU immigration policy: improvement of data system on migration in Europe and a need for intensive and well coordinated cooperation between the various actors dealing with the issue.

Migration processes and undocumented flows are difficult to grasp using official data and quantitative indicators. Obtaining a coherent migratory picture for Europe overall seems even less realistic. Nevertheless, monitoring of European migration and improvement of the existing data sources is a widely recognized necessity. Achieving comparability of various national data sets is a priority for the European level of migration management. Information objectivity is also needed. Various bodies collect data in different manners depending on their statutory objectives. For example, data concerning racial violence and crimes coming from police and NGOs' records differ. In order to acquire an objective picture of the issues concerned, an appropriate balance between different sources of data has to be elaborated. Reliability of data can be achieved only by careful testing of data sources. Attention to this aspect can contribute to the improvement of data sets on migration available in European countries.[15] Last but not least, even though accession countries do already take part in various international initiatives aimed at developing a reliable statistical system on migration (for example, Eurostat and OECD Sopemi network), it appears that wider inclusion of these countries in EU research should be pursued as soon as possible.[16]

In the realm of improving knowledge about migration, efficient exchange of information within the Union has to be ensured. In order to achieve a self-learning capacity in the European migration system, however, cooperation between various actors operating in the field should go beyond the exchange of information. In fact, the open method of coordination for migration policy formation, promoted by the European Commission, implies and requires the active involvement of a variety of European actors: scientists, policy-makers, international organizations, NGOs and migrant associations. We further argue that civil society can play in this cooperation a particular role that should not be neglected. Experience of NGOs and various migrant associations that assist immigrants in their every-day problems can be particularly useful for elaborating a framework for integrating immigrants. As well, NGOs can be an important source of information not only about migrants but also for migrants. Active lobbying by NGOs can, thus, effectively contribute to the creation of integration policies (Niessen, 2000). Societal involvement in the process of policy formation should be particularly encouraged in accession countries. In some of them, conditions were unfavourable for the development of the non-governmental sector during their Communist era and so the tradition of involving it in policy formation is relatively new. Therefore, there is a need to stimulate cooperation between NGOs and policy makers in these countries. This will have a positive impact not only on migration policy developments, but also on the process of policy formation as a whole.

The postulates presented above are nothing new. It is worth noting, however, that proposals of academics and practitioners in the field of European migration are consistent with the work by the European Commission to promote dialogue and information exchange within the Union. It seems that there is a willingness to cooperate among European migration experts. The challenge for the European-level governing bodies is to set up a coordinating procedure for this cooperation and set standards high enough to achieve a satisfactory outcome.

13.3.2. Managing migration and asylum in Europe

Managing migration in Europe, it has been agreed, is a major objective for a common EU immigration policy. One can argue that the related managing of asylum may be inserted in this broad framework.[17] Whether it is a satisfactory solution is worthy of discussion. Obviously, migration and asylum are two interrelated phenomena. The first level of intersection is that asylum seekers have to take up migration in their search for safe countries of residence. The second aspect is that some asylum seekers are simply economic migrants who use the asylum procedure to get access to the labour markets of more prosperous countries. These 'persons not in need of international protection' seek not safety but a better life and job prospects using asylum procedures to satisfy their economic needs. This phenomenon is conditioned by limitations in access to the EU labour market and goes against principles and purposes of the asylum system, designed to protect those who face real threats to their lives and freedom. Thus, even though labour migration and asylum both concern human mobility, they should be separated in terms of policy.[18] This involves not only distinct policy systems, but also the formulation of adequate measures to distinguish and separate these two phenomena. In other words, to create appropriate asylum policy, the problem raised by 'persons not in need of international protection' should be effectively eliminated.

It should be emphasized that, although we argue that managing asylum should be tackled distinctly if not separately from managing (labour) migration, the refugee issue is overwhelmingly important in the European Union, which receives many asylum seekers at present. Thus, the Union needs a universal implementation of asylum procedures to divide more evenly the responsibility for managing asylum among all the Community's countries. It should relieve the countries now bearing the greatest part of this responsibility, such as the United Kingdom, Germany and France (compare UNHCR, 2002). Effective implementation of universal procedures requires reinforcing the credibility of the asylum institution in Europe, which has been challenged by some lack of efficiency in recent decades.[19] This involves the reestablishment of fair, efficient and fast procedures of refugee status identification, which would diminish the possibility of their misuse.

One example of procedural problems in the asylum field is as follows:

> Some 88,000 refugees enter the UK annually. There are real practical problems in administrating such numbers. The waiting list for processing is two years even though numbers have recently been reduced from 70,000 to 40,000. Applicants can expect their appeal to take four years before a decision is made. Each appeal costs around 3000 [GBP]. In the end, only 14% are ever deported (Stubbs, 2002, p. 1).

Achieving efficiency in asylum procedures requires cooperation between countries of refugees' origin and destination, particularly in returning unsuccessful asylum seekers. Another related problem is the credibility of public information about refugee issues in the hosting countries. Namely, education on differences between asylum seekers and economic migrants and on the positive impacts that refugees may have on the host societies needs to be developed. The latter is to include not only economic consequences, but also refugees' contribution to the social and cultural reality of the countries involved. On the other hand, to act positively in the destination areas, refugees need to have appropriate access to the labour market and integration programmes. This will enable them to become self-supporting members of the hosting societies.

The complexity of the asylum issue in the European Union requires a multi-faceted approach. Thus, it is worth presenting here a multi-track proposal addressing, in a broad perspective, the most urgent and delicate issues of asylum in Europe. These have been elaborated by Sukhvinder Kaur Stubbs from her many years' experience in the refugee field and on expertise developed within the Barrow Cadbury Trust (UK). Stubbs speaks in particular about the trafficking of women and children.

> Without realistic, progressive and comprehensive policies, this sort of abuse and exploitation will flourish. The UK and other member states should accept that they need migrants now, much as they have throughout the centuries relied on the positive contributions made by immigrants. Well-managed migration policies should be instigated which take into account the rise in economic refugees and the continued existence of political asylum seekers.

A clampdown on trafficking is an essential component of such policies but alongside this, legitimate routes to employment need to be created for migrants. Meanwhile, levels of protection afforded to political refugees should be raised and the universal implementation of asylum legislation secured. Policies need to demonstrate a stronger stance in challenging the media perceptions and negative stereotyping. This combination of approaches enables migrants and refugees to play their role in society (Stubbs, 2002, p. 2).

The above, proposal is an approach advocating universalism of asylum legislation in Europe. Moreover, it attracts attention to an increasing phenomenon, human trafficking, which not infrequently causes severe personal harm and tragedies. Due to a lack of transparency in asylum procedures, this problem is also connected with managing asylum in the European Union at the moment.

To sum up, effective dealing with asylum issue in the European Union requires a multi-level and multi-aspect approach involving cooperation between countries of asylum seekers' origin and destination. The three chief elements of managing asylum should include:

- satisfactorily separating asylum from economic migration,
- strengthening the effectiveness of asylum procedures,
- promoting integration of refugees into the destination countries.

13.3.3. Managing migration and labour market in Europe

Management of labour mobility within and to the European Union is an important issue constantly under discussion. Low fertility rates in European countries and the ageing of their societies have already caused labour force shortages on the old continent, which will persist into the future. At present, it applies to certain sectors of the labour market but the problem is likely to grow in importance. At the same time, the prospective enlargement and opening up of the European labour market for citizens of new member states will most likely not solve this problem. The precision of estimates of future demographic patterns in CEE countries is currently quite low due to ongoing social and economic transitions in these countries. It seems, however, likely that accession countries will follow the demographic patterns of present member states, characterized by low fertility rates and ageing populations (de Beer and van Wissen, 1999; Fassmann and Münz, 2002). Thus, it is argued more and more often that the European Union will need a foreign labour force, that is migrants, to fill gaps and shortages in its native labour force (see, for instance, Orzechowska, 2002). Labour immigration should be perceived, however, only as a partial solution to the problem and not as a remedy that would stop the ageing of the European societies (Orzechowska, 2002; UN, 2001).[20] Nevertheless, in the light of European demographic trends, the development of an appropriate policy covering labour migration to the European Union is highly important and requires a broad, European perspective. This should take into account not only short- and medium-term prospects but also long-term consequences. Controlled immigration may help to alleviate labour shortages as part of an overall strategy of structural policies in the field of employment and human resource development.

It is vital that the European policy on labour mobility is comprehensive. On the one hand, the extent and rapidity of the population's aging is likely too great to be offset solely by an influx of foreign workers. On the other hand, however, long-run consequences of a policy encouraging foreigners to work in the Union should be taken into consideration. Experience has shown, for example, in Germany and France in the 1970s, that labour migrants tend to become permanent migrants who want to bring or establish their families in the destination countries (see, for example, Castles, 1985). This involves further growth of migrant communities and cultural diversity in the receiving countries and hence an increasing need for appropriate integration measures. Furthermore, in times of recession and unemployment, many of the invited foreign workers contribute to a group of jobless people needing and/or expecting social benefits and governmental help.[21]

In general, satisfying the needs of the European labour market should go beyond appropriate employment programmes for foreign workers. It can be argued that some deeper reforms of European labour market regulations should be made. First of all, better distribution of skills across the Union should be achieved. In fact, labour force mobility within the Community is low at the moment, as it is estimated that only 5 per cent of the European labour force is internationally mobile (Orzechowska, 2002). Among other things, this phenomenon is conditioned by the high regulation of the European labour market. A variety of measures, such as generous unemployment benefits programmes in some European countries and other employment regulations, restrain the mobility of workers within the Union. It appears that some deregulation of the European labour market can stimulate the mobility of European citizens and enable a more effective circulation of labour, thereby contributing to a better distribution of skills across Europe (compare, for example, Peixoto, 2001).[22] It should be also born in mind that labour immigration to the Union consists of, to a large extent, short-term, very short-term and seasonal mobility and includes a variety of modern types of work such as part-time jobs, telecommuting and others (Gesano, 1999). These novel forms of work do not fit in with traditional labour regulations. Thus, they often exist outside the official labour market to say the least. This component of labour frequently represents a particular type of the shadow economy that is contributing, as other forms of illegal work, to the *de facto* deregulation of the European labour market and is likely to grow in the near future. It seems that formation of more flexible labour market institutions and regulations can both help tackle the skills shortages in the European Union and take advantage of some sorts of foreigners' currently-illegal labour activities while not necessary increasing immigration pressure on the European Union.[23]

Advocating that illegal mobility and employment can have a positive impact on the European labour market is not surprising considering the breadth of migratory activities falling into this category. Such activities range from short-term and seasonal labour trips taken up by foreigners in response to European demand for unskilled workers to organized crime and trafficking in human beings. Whereas increased criminality associated with illegal mobility of labour should be effectively fought, other 'less abusive' forms of illegal activities should be validated, where appropriate, in proportion to their positive and negative impacts on the sending and receiving areas. In this respect, the characteristics of the destination labour markets matter, since in countries with a well-developed shadow economy the supply of illegal foreign work can be particularly easy accommodated. This is the case for most southern European countries (Martin and Miller, 2000) as well as for CEE accession countries (referring to Poland see, for example, Grabowski, 2000). Thwarting illegal work in such countries is rather unlikely as long as there are favourable conditions for it in the form of a welcoming shadow market. It seems that an approach proposing a 'better combination of regularization campaigns and fewer legal restrictions on the would-be immigrants' (Garnier, 2000, p. 90) should be evaluated on the European level. Unfortunately, the discussion on illegal migration and work is prevalently on control measures in the European Union (see, for instance, CEC, 2001c). It can be argued that the notion of management should not be limited to legal types of labour migration but rather applied also to illegal mobility and work, with careful attention to the appropriate classification of their various forms (Mattila, 2000).

Managing the European labour market and related labour migration in the Union is highly complex and controversial when compared, for example, with the asylum issue, for which a consensus is easier to achieve.[24] Finding consensus between a broad, pan-European perspective and individual countries' interests in safeguarding their labour markets is still a challenge for European governing bodies. Obvious requirements for achieving such consensus include taking into account aspects like: demographical trends in Europe, the structure of the European labour market and long-term consequences of the employment programmes for foreigners. We would argue that the following can also positively impact management of labour market and labour mobility in the European Union:

▪ some deregulation of the European labour market that, if properly applied, can enable more efficient distribution of skills across Europe,

▪ taking into account the present diversity and novel nature of various forms of mobility (including 'less abusive' forms of illegal employment) while designing respective policy solutions.

13.3.4. *Managing migration and European Union enlargement*

The enlargement of the European Union and the 'communitarization' of the EU countries immigration policy both scheduled for May 2004 are two simultaneous and interrelated processes that need to be further coordinated. This presents an additional challenge for the creation of a common EU immigration policy in Europe and involves two general aspects: the migration policy of present member states towards accession countries and harmonization/ formation of migration policies in the future member countries. For the second aspect, the difficulties in securing satisfactory control on the external borders of the enlarged Europe have been attracting particular attention for some time (for instance, CEU 2001, p. 5) urging the establishment of a European Agency for their cooperative management (CEC, 2003f).

Setting up a political framework for post-enlargement migration from accession countries to the EU member states has been a challenge for politicians taking part in negotiations on accession. EU member states' fear that emigration from accession countries may number into the millions, challenging social cohesion and European labour market stability, thwarted acceptance of the full freedom of movement between 'old' and 'new' members of the Union upon enlargement (see, for example, Okólski, 2001; Jileva, 2002).[25] Various analyses indicate that these expectations are unfounded (see, for example, Kaczmarczyk in this volume); however, this has not eliminated the fear of a flood of Central Europeans seeking work in present member states. Consequently, an optional transitional period preceding full freedom of movement has been negotiated. This period is to last at most seven years and apply to all accession countries except Malta and Cyprus. However, its *de facto* duration is subject to individual decisions of 'old' member states. Some of them have already announced that they would not introduce transitional periods at all.[26] In practice, there will be a variety of transitional periods negotiated with each accession country.[27] Even though 'current member states must give preference to candidate country nationals over non-EU labour' (CEC, 2003f, p. 7), as long as transitional agreements are in force, they will challenge the free movement of people in the European Union and thus hinder real harmonization of the European immigration policy. Experts in the field advocate either shortening the transition periods (Niessen, 2001) or finding alternative solutions, since the alarmist scenarios that drove demand for transitional periods do not seem to be supported by convincing evidence (Krenzler and Wolczuk, 2001). In this regard, it has been mentioned that 'a safety clause is a more sophisticated instrument as it allows the monitoring of the actual level of labour migration and adjustment of policy measures accordingly' (Krenzler and Wolczuk, 2001, p. 16).

Nevertheless, the most likely scenario for the near future is that a EU member state's immigration policy towards inflow from accession countries will vary dependently on its labour market situation and geopolitical locale. In addition, Austria and Germany have the right to flanking national measures to protect some 'sensitive' sectors of their labour markets (EC, 2003). During the transitional periods, bilateral agreements between 'old' and 'new' member countries concerning workers' employment should be a migration management tool. This will enable the European labour market to benefit from the enlargement by achieving satisfactory skill and labour force distributions throughout the European Union. On the other hand, this can prevent the brain drain in new member states that, some experts predict, may arise after opening the European Union market to Central European workers (de Sousa Ferreira, 2002). At the same time, appropriate recognition of skills and diplomas within the European Union will grow in importance upon the Union's eastward enlargement. This applies to both the transitional periods and the future, as the variety of education systems will expand with the increase in the number of Union members.[28] The improvement in this field should eliminate losses of productivity as highly-educated people take up work in other member states (compare, Peixoto, 2001; de Sousa Ferreira, 2002).

As mentioned above, another important aspect of managing eastward enlargement of the European Union and the drafting of a common immigration policy is further development of candidate countries' respective policies, which have been already considerably adjusted to the European standards in the accession process.[29] In fact, pre-accession preparations have had a profound impact on the present shape of immigration policy in CEE countries (see Kępińska and Stola in this volume). Due to these countries' recent transformation from emigration to immigration-emigration areas, their migration policies have been formed virtually from scratch since the beginning of the 1990s. The policy-making has intersected with the accession process. On the one hand, this has had a positive impact on advancing the policy formation process in the CEE region. However, circumstances have led to a reactive nature of their new migration policies as a response to nascent migratory trends and the requirements of the European Union. It is evident that the accession countries need to develop coherent premises for their future migration policies because solutions implemented in the European Union cannot be fully copied in CEE.[30] For example, the complicated ethnic composition of this region, as a heritage of shifting state borders in past centuries, requires specific policy solutions for both minorities and migration. The Hungarian Parliament's introduction of a Special Status Law on 19 June 2001, under which ethnic Hungarians living in neighbouring countries (Slovakia and Romania) will enjoy a right to medical, employment and educational services in Hungary, has already incited much controversy. The law, intended to avert mass immigration of ethnic Hungarians once Hungary joins the European Union and to accommodate the needs of the Hungarian labour market, would create a privileged group — according to the European representatives in Budapest (van Krieken, 2002). Similar attempts have been made by Slovakia and work on a similar legislative solution is underway in Poland. The scope of rights that the above accession countries are eager to give to their co-ethnics living abroad is exceptionally broad compared to European Union standards and becomes particularly problematic when applied to people living outside the Schengen area. Here, an agreement satisfying both the European Union's prerogatives and the specific needs of accession countries has to be found. Nevertheless, the expertise of the EU member states with long-lasting experience with immigration can serve as an important point of reference. Frameworks for dealing with some aspects of migration (for example, integration of second-generation migrants) can be elaborated well ahead of time for the relatively new immigrant populations of CEE countries.[31]

Finally, an important aspect of the EU enlargement is the introduction of a new border regime in Europe. There is high pressure in and from the European Union to strengthen border controls on its future frontiers. This is accompanied by high financial allocations directed not only to accession countries but also to the future neighbouring countries of the European Union (for example, Russia and Ukraine).[32] Apart from strengthening border controls, accession countries have to introduce stricter visa regimes with countries that will remain outside the Union. It is usually agreed that these restrictions will restrain migration to accession countries, since an overwhelming majority of immigrants to accession countries originate from the non-Baltic republics of the former Soviet Union (compare, for example, Paszewski, 2000). It can also slow down economic and political cooperation in the CEE region divided by the Schengen border, which has been vibrantly developing since the late 1980s. Restrictions on the movement of people can especially afflict border regions of future Schengen members and countries staying outside, where transborder relations and mobility play a particular economic role (compare Mync and Szul, 1999). For their inhabitants, short-term, shuttle mobility has become a strategy to earn a living despite the ongoing period of economic crisis, high unemployment and other deleterious effects of the post-Communist transition. In fact, as far as mobility to accession countries is concerned some transitional periods are also possible. As long as a visa to a given accession country will not be tantamount to a Schengen visa, some intermediary measures can be in force. This appears to be a solution that would ease the negative effects of the restrictions put on movements. Nevertheless, we argue that there is a need to initiate a broad 'neighbourhood policy' between the European Union and its future neighbours. Such a policy would foster the development of a new 'friendly neighbourhood' area, wherein measures facilitating the movement of people and trade between the European Union and its neighbours would be gradually implemented. This would benefit particularly neighbour and accession countries by preserving the economic, social and political links existing in the CEE region. Less directly, it would benefit also the overall European Union by securing factors of economic development (in accession countries) resulting from international cooperation in the CEE region. Last but not least, an active 'neighbourhood policy' of the Union would prevent the formation of another 'iron curtain', this time moved further east.[33]

To sum up, the formation of a common EU immigration policy and the eastward enlargement of the Union require careful coordination. In fact, as long as transitional periods are in force, the free movement of labour, one of the cornerstones of the European Union treaties, will not apply to all members of the enlarged Europe. This will affect 'comprehensiveness' and 'inclusiveness' in the process of making a real common EU immigration policy. Nevertheless, the harmonization of policy developments in present and future member countries should proceed. The countries joining the European Union still differ from present member states, in particular, in their economic characteristics stemming from their Communist past and in the nature of their ethnic issues and problems. This requires elaboration of an appropriate framework for migration policy in the overall acceding region — a task to be pursued on both the European and national levels. The active involvement of the CEE governments in this process seems a precondition for a satisfactory outcome. As well, cooperation and exchange of information between experts from EU member states and accession countries should be effectively stimulated. One important outcome of such a cooperative policy formation would be a real, comprehensive effort in establishing a 'neighbourhood policy' for the enlarged European Union.

13.4. Concluding Remarks — for Diversity of Harmonization

Work on the formation of a common EU immigration policy dates back to the late 1990s. Developments in this field are slow and controversy-riven among European policy-makers. Integration of CEE countries with the European polity compounds challenges relating to managing the European migration space. Notwithstanding the efforts towards harmonization, policy developments in this area remain a combination of intergovernmental and European Union policy decisions (Jordan, Stråth and Triandafyllidou, 2003, p. 208). National governments' determination to retain sovereign control over immigration seems confirmed by the results of the European Council in Laeken in December 2001.[34] In this context, it is interesting to note that the Council, while assessing the progresses of the Tampere conclusions, admitted that: 'the scoreboard produced by the Commission reveals a wealth of achievements in the various areas of police cooperation and judicial cooperation in civil and criminal matters and, to a lesser extent, asylum and immigration' (CEU, 2001, p. 1). At the same time, however, the Council stressed the need for ensuring greater convergence in member states' legislation on asylum and immigration, as the necessary adoption of national laws sometimes complicates the adoption of Community legislative acts (CEU, 2001, p. 3). More recently, in the last update of the scoreboard of December 2002, the Commission argued that the subsequent June 2002 European Council in Seville 'had given a fresh impetus towards the implementation of the Tampere programme by declaring its determination to speed up every aspect' (CEC, 2003c, p. 4). At the same time, the Commission 'had also noted that the backlogs identified on the occasion of the scoreboard for the Laeken European Council had not gone away' (CEC, 2003c, p. 4). This picture seems only partially changed by the steps forward of the June 2003 European Council in Thessaloniki which successfully recorded the agreement on the directives on family reunification and long-term resident status (European Council, 2003, p. 8).[35] It can be argued that progress in this area of common policy formation is often negated or reversed in the practice or implementation of joint policy, which explains why the policy process has been called 'pendulum like' (Sciortino and Pastore, 2002). Thus, the question that remains is whether there are realistic prospects for developing an efficient, working European approach towards migration. The floor is divided between enthusiasts of common European solutions and advocates of state sovereignty in the field of migration.

The unquestionable reality is, however, a progressing European integration and the fact that cooperation in the field of JHA is advocated by most European migration experts (academics and practitioners). Moreover, experts' views are consistent with the principles adopted by the European Commission in the migration area. They emphasize the needs for coordination in migration management in Europe, for comprehensiveness and inclusiveness within the policy-making process and for dialogue between various actors in the field.

Therefore, we argue that progressive integration of the common European migration space requires pan-European solutions. The policy formation should involve mutual learning from similarities in migratory phenomena observed in various European countries and tackling existing differences by leaving enough space for national governance. European-level management of migration should take place in fields where European countries share not only common problems but also interests and values. In such areas, European migration policy harmonization is likely to proceed particularly efficiently.

The collection of management areas that this chapter has asserted require a European approach is certainly not exhaustive. We did not touch, for example, the issue of the highly pivotal policy framework for immigrants' integration into their host countries and, more broadly, into the EU (European Council, 2003, p. 9). We argue, however, that the three management fields, as proposed in this chapter, should be prioritized in the formation of a common EU immigration policy. Yet, it is important to remember that the extent of possible harmonization of the European migration policy differs among these various fields. Management of asylum vs. migration appears to be least controversial, as it is based on a shared European value of securing individuals' human rights. In contrast, managing the European labour market and related labour migration is highly conflict-ridden due to the sensitiveness of protecting national labour markets. Thus, in the sphere of labour migration, much autonomy should be secured for national governments whereas at the pan-European level effort should be directed towards some deep structural reforms of the overall European labour market. Finally, managing the eastward geopolitical enlargement and migration still poses a variety of unresolved problems that require certain novel solutions on a Europe-wide basis. This process is, by definition, highly monitored and governed by the pertinent European bodies, but further developments in migration policy should involve consultation and the systematic participation of both the accession countries and the governments of the EU's 'new' neighbouring states. Policy formation in this regard should be aimed at developing a specific framework, in particular an appropriate 'neighbourhood' policy of the enlarged Union, that would also satisfy the interests of the 'neighbours' and the accession countries and, hence, the interests of the Union as a whole.

Notes

1   The intergovernmental cooperation, formalized by the 1992 Maastricht Treaty, produced a series of non-binding policy recommendations (on issues such as migration for employment, border control, visa, asylum and irregular

migration), binding international agreements (such as the Schengen Agreements and the Dublin Convention) and instruments for information exchange (see Niessen, 2001).

2　Reflections presented in this chapter are greatly derived from the contributions of participants of the round table discussion on 'Forging a common immigration policy: new and old migratory trends in the light of the European Union enlargement', held during the conference. The overall discussion has been transcribed verbatim ('Forging a New Immigration Policy', 2002). In addition, some participants prepared written contributions that have been also used in this chapter (see description of materials from the conference in the reference list).

3　The Treaty of Amsterdam moved the focus from intergovernmental co-operation to protect a common interest to supranational governance (Jordan, Stråth and Triandafyllidou, 2003, p. 209).

4　The adoption of the qualified majority for voting of the European Council in the JHA area, hence in common immigration and asylum decisions was inserted in the Constitution for Europe recently drafted by the European Convention (European Convention, 2003a). However, the lack of agreement on the voting system within the European Council impeded the adoption of the EU's first constitution.

5　One may argue that the EU member states have never fully prevented labour immigration since they have, in fact, implemented a variety of entry programmes for foreign labour (Sciortino and Pastore, 2002, p. 8).

6　As proposed by S. Pratt ('Forging a new immigration policy', 2002, pp. 1–3).

7　Following S. Pratt ('Forging a new immigration policy', 2002, pp. 1–5).

8　Member states shall comply with it by 3 October 2005.

9　This proposal establishes, among other things, the principle that third-country nationals may only accede to the EU labour market if a post cannot be filled by EU-nationals (principle of 'Community preference') or by privileged third-country nationals. The principle is a reflection of the rules already in force in most member states, which require, for the admission of third countries workers, a thorough assessment of the domestic labour market situation (Pratt, 2001, p. 8).

10　The European Commission has scheduled an action plan and another proposal for a directive on conditions for entry and stay of researchers, aimed at increasing the supply of researchers from third-countries in Europe (CEC, 2003c, p. 6).

11　This action was launched by establishing national contact points in December 2002 (CEC, 2003c, p. 32).

12　Originally: 'It is also management's job to enable the enterprise and each of its members to grow and develop as needs and opportunities change. This means that every enterprise is a learning and teaching institution' (Drucker, 1988, p. 76).

13　Originally: '[Management] must be built on communication and on individual responsibility' (Drucker, 1988, p. 76).

14　Originally: 'We need a diversity of measures for an enterprise. Performance has to be built into the enterprise and management, it has to be measured — or at least judged — and it has to be continuously improved.' (Drucker, 1988, p. 76).

15   Based on a contribution of B. Löwander ('Forging a new immigration policy', 2002, pp. 10–1).

16   Ibid. See also CEC (2003b, p. 12) where the need to fully involve the accession countries in data cooperation and exchange has been also reaffirmed by the European Commission.

17   Based on a contribution of D. Dessalegne ('Forging a new immigration policy', 2002, pp. 6–7).

18   Ibid. Also, according to the European Commission, immigration and asylum need specific approaches while being 'closely related'. (Pratt 2001, p. 3). This instance is reflected in two separate Communications on the two phenomena (see CEC, 2000a and 2000b).

19   Based on a contribution of D. Dessalegne ('Forging a new immigration policy', 2002, pp. 6–7).

20   The European Commission shares this view stressing also that, in the long term, it is not an effective way to offset demographic changes, since migrants once settled tend to adopt the fertility patterns of the host country (CEC, 2000a, p. 25).

21   Based on a contribution of A. Leas ('Forging a new immigration policy', 2002, pp. 8–10).

22   Based on a contribution of D. Stola ('Forging a new immigration policy', 2002, pp. 13–4).

23   Ibid.

24   Based on a contribution of S. Pratt ('Forging a new immigration policy', 2002, pp. 1–5).

25   This argumentation was supported by taking up a regional perspective — most migration models while looking at national averages cannot account for regional developments. As a result of considerable wage differentials between neighbouring regional labour markets of some Eastern and Western parts of the future EU, labour will flow from the low-wage region to the high-wage region generating in the short term higher unemployment and perhaps decreasing wages (Fassmann and Münz, 2002).

26   As of April 2003, Denmark, Ireland, Netherlands, the United Kingdom, Sweden, as well as the associated Iceland and Norway, declared that they would open their labour markets to Polish citizens immediately upon Poland's accession to the European Union in May 2004. Later, Denmark and Netherlands decided to tighten up their rules, for example, by making work permits conditional on finding a job or having a contract (Castle, 2003).

27   After five years, the *acquis* will automatically apply unless a particular member state requests the extension (for a maximum of two years) of the national provisions because of disturbances to its domestic labour market (Pratt, 2001, p. 11).

28   The European Union's standards of recognition of skills and diplomas will start to be effective for the candidate countries immediately upon their accession (EC, 2003).

29   The Accession Partnerships urged the candidate countries to aim for institutional isomorphism — becoming like the EU in their approach to the variety of JHA policies — rather than for a straightforward transfer of specific policies. However, the language used in the accession documents is fairly vague, full of general claims that only later have been supplemented with country-specific instructions how to implement these policies (Grabbe,

2002, p. 94).
30   Based on a contribution of D. Stola ('Forging a new immigration policy',
      2002, pp. 13–4).
31   Ibid.
32   Improvements of the technical border infrastructure and reinforcement of the
      border controls are financed by the European Union through the TACIS
      programme. Funds are mainly directed to support transformation towards
      market economies and democratic societies in the newly independent, post-
      Soviet states and Mongolia and through the Phare programme in the
      accession countries (Grabbe, 2002, p. 95).
33   In fact, the Communication issued by the European Commission on 'Wider
      Europe — Neighbourhood: A New Framework for Relations with our
      Eastern and Southern Neighbours' seems to fully adopt this policy
      orientation. The document set out a vision for EU links with those countries
      that 'do not currently have a perspective of membership but who will soon
      find themselves sharing a border with the Union', namely Russia, the western
      former Soviet states and the Southern Mediterranean. Further advancement of
      this policy could lead to free movements of persons, goods, services and
      capital (CEC, 2003a, pp. 3–4). The Commission further implemented this
      policy advocating the creation of a new Neighbourhood Instrument 'which
      build on the experience of promoting cross-border cooperation within the
      PHARE, Tacis and INTERREG programmes' (CEC, 2003e).
34   Stalker (2002, p. 168) argues that the Council 'while calling for closer
      cooperation to protect external frontiers, rejected a proposal to create
      a common European border patrolled by EU border guards'.
35   The Council called also for an 'Annual Report on Migration and Integration
      in Europe' as included in a Commission's communication to closely monitor
      and evaluate EU immigration policy (CEC, 2003d, p. 28).

References

Beer De J., L. Van Wissen, 'Europe: one continent, different worlds. Population
    scenarios for the twenty first century', *European Studies of Population*, Vol. 7
    (Dordrecht, Boston, London: Kluwer Academic Publishers, 1999).
Castle, S., 'Workers from "New Europe" left out in cold', *The Independent (UK)*
    (6 December, 2003), available at http://news.independent.co.uk/europe/
    story.jsp?story=470576.
Castles, S., 'The guests who stayed — the debate on "foreign policy" in the German
    Federal Republic', *International Migration Review*, Vol. 19, No. 3 (1985),
    pp. 517–34.
CEC, 'Biannual Update of the Scoreboard to Review Progress on the Creation of an
    Area of "Freedom, Security and Justice" in the European Union (First Half of
    2003)', Communication from the Commission to the Council and the European
    Parliament, COM 291, Final (Brussels, 22 May 2003c).
CEC, 'On a Common Policy on Illegal Immigration', Communication from the
    Commission to the Council and the European Parliament, COM 672, Final
    (Brussels, 15 November 2001c).
CEC, 'On a Community Immigration Policy', Communication from the Com-
    mission to the Council and the European Parliament, COM 757, Final (Brussels,
    22 November 2000a).

CEC, 'On an Open Method of Coordination for the Community Immigration Policy', Communication from the Commission to the Council and the European Parliament, COM 387, Final (Brussels, 11 July 2001a).

CEC, 'On Immigration, Integration and Employment', Communication from the Commission to the Council, the European Parliament, the European Economic and Social Committee of the Regions, COM 336, Final (Brussels, 3 June 2003d).

CEC, 'Paving the way for a New Neighbourhood Instrument', Communication from the Commission, COM 393, Final (Brussels, 1 July 2003e).

CEC, 'Proposal for a Council Regulation establishing a European Agency for the Management of Operational Co-operation at the External Borders', COM 687, Final/2 (Brussels, 20 November 2003f).

CEC, 'Proposal for a Council Directive on the conditions of entry and residence of third-country nationals for the purpose of paid employment and self-employed economic activities', COM 386, Final (Brussels, 11 July 2001b).

CEC, 'Proposal for a Council Directive on the conditions of entry and residence of third-country nationals for the purposes of studies, vocational training or voluntary service', COM 548, Final (Brussels, 7 October 2002).

CEC, 'To present an action plan for the collection and analysis of community statistics in the field of migration', Communication from the Commission to the Council and the European Parliament, COM 179, Final (Brussels, 15 April 2003b).

CEC, 'Towards a common asylum procedure for a uniform status, valid throughout the Union, for persons granted asylum?', Communication from the European Commission to the Council and the European Parliament, COM 755, Final (Brussels, 22 November 2000b).

CEC, 'Wider Europe — Neighbourhood: A New Framework for Relations with our Eastern and Southern Neighbours', Communication from the Commission to the Council and the European Parliament, COM 104, Final (Brussels, 11 March 2003a).

CEU, 'Council Directive 2003/86/EC of 22 September 2003 on the right to family reunification', Official Journal of the European Union, L 251, (Brussels, 3 October 2003), pp. 12–8.

CEU, 'Council Directive 2003/109/EC of 25 November 2003 concerning the status of third-country nationals who are long-term residents', Official Journal of the European Union, L 16, (Brussels, 23 January 2004), pp. 44–53.

CEU, 'Evaluation of the conclusions of the Tampere European Council', Note from Presidency to General Affairs Council/European Council (Brussels, 6 December 2001).

Crawley, H., 'How Europe Selects Immigrants Today' in Athens Migration Policy Initiative and Migration Policy Institute, *Policy Briefs & Recommendations: The Greek Presidency Conference on Managing Migration for the Benefit of Europe*, Policy Brief 7 (Athens, 15–16 May 2003), available at www.migrationpolicy.org/AMPI.

Drucker, P. F., 'Management and the World's Work', *Harvard Business Review*, Vol. 88, No. 5 (1988), pp. 65–76.

EC, 'Report on the results of the negotiations on the accession to of Cyprus, Malta, Hungary, Poland, the Slovak Republic, Latvia, Estonia, Lithuania, the Czech Republic and Slovenia to the European Union' (Brussels: EC, 2003), available at http://europa.eu.int/comm/enlargement/negotiations.

European Convention, 'Draft revised text of Parts Two, Three and Four', Cover note from Presidium to Convention, CONV 802/03, Vol. 2 (Brussels, 12 June 2003b), available at http://european-convention.eu.int.

European Convention, 'Text of Part I and Part II of the Constitution', Cover note from Presidium to Convention, CONV 797/1/03, Vol. 1 (Brussels, 12 June 2003a), available at http://european-convention.eu.int.

European Council, 'Presidency Conclusions — Thessaloniki' (Thessaloniki, 19–20 June, 2003), unpublished.

Fassmann, H., R. Münz, 'EU Enlargement and Future East-West Migration', in F. Laczko, I. Stacher, A. Klekowski von Koppenfels (eds), *New Challenges for Migration Policy in Central and Eastern Europe* (The Hague: T.M.C. Asser Press and International Organisation for Migration, 2002), pp. 59–86.

Favell, G., A. Geddes, 'Immigration and European Integration: New Opportunities for Transnational Mobilization?', in R. Koopmans, P. Statham (eds), *Challenging Immigration and Ethnic Relations Politics* (Oxford: Oxford University Press, 2000), pp. 407–28.

Garnier, P., 'Illegal migration for employment in the light of ILO policy and standards', in K. Hakola (ed.), *Articles on migration management on the eastern border of the EU* (Jyvaskyla: Jyvaskyla University, 2000), pp. 79–91.

Geddes, A., *The Politics of Migration and Immigration in Europe* (London: SAGE Publications, 2003).

Gesano, G., 'Who is working in Europe?', in D. Van de Kaa, H. Leridon, G. Gesano, M. Okólski (eds), 'European populations. Unity in diversity', *European Studies of Population*, Vol. 6 (Dordrecht, Boston, London: Kluwer Academic Publishers, 1999), pp. 77–139.

Grabbe, H., 'Stabilizing the East While Keeping Out the Easterners: Internal and External Security Logics in Conflict', in S. Lavenex, E. M. Uçarer (eds), *Migration and the Externalities of European Integration* (Lanham, Maryland: Lexington Books, 2002), pp. 91–104.

Grabowski, M., 'Informal Labour and Foreigners — the Polish Case', in K. Hakola (ed.), *Articles on migration management on the eastern border of the EU* (Jyvaskyla: Jyvaskyla University, 2000), pp. 99–111.

Jileva, E., 'Visa and free movement of labour: the uneven imposition of the EU acquis on the accession states', *Journal of Ethnic and Migration Studies*, Vol. 28, No. 4 (2002), pp. 683–700.

Jordan, B., B. Stråth, A. Triandafyllidou, 'Contextualizing immigration policy implementation in Europe', *Journal of Ethnic and Migration Studies*, Vol. 29, No. 2 (2003), pp. 195–224.

Krenzler, H.G., K. Wolczuk, 'EU Justice and Home Affairs in the Context of Enlargement', *Policy Papers*, RSC No. 4 (Florence: European University Institute, 2001).

Krieken van, P., 'Candidate Countries, Enlargement and Migration: Living up to the Acquis', in F. Laczko, I. Stacher, A. Klekowski von Koppenfels (eds), *New Challenges for Migration Policy in Central and Eastern Europe* (The Hague: T.M.C. Asser Press and International Organisation for Migration, 2002), pp. 175–214.

Mafrolla, E. M., B. Nascimbene, 'Gli orientamenti comunitari', in Fondazione ISMU, *Settimo Rapporto sulle migrazioni 2001* (Milan: Franco Angeli, 2002), pp. 45–59.

Martin, P., M. Miller, 'Employer sanctions: French, German and US experience', *International Migration Papers*, Vol. 36 (Geneva: International Labour Office, 2000).

Mattila, H., 'Preventing, combating, regularizing irregular migration — the various experiences of Western Europe', in K. Hakola (ed.), *Articles on migration management on the eastern border of the EU* (Jyvaskyla: Jyvaskyla University, 2000), pp. 32–43.

Mync, A., R. Szul, *Rola granicy i współpracy transgranicznej w rozwoju regionalnym i lokalnym* (Warsaw: The Publishing House for Regional and Local Development, Warsaw University, 1999).

Niessen, J., 'The shaping of EU policies on free movement, internal mobility and immigration', in J. Niessen (ed.), *Policy recommendations for EU migration policies (a joint document of 10 European and American migration experts)* (Brussels, Berlin: King Baudouin Foundation and German Marshall Fund of the United States, 2001).

Niessen, J., *Diversity and cohesion: new challenges for the integration of immigrants and minorities* (Strasbourg: Council of Europe Publishing, 2000).

Okólski, M., 'O rzeczową argumentację w kwestii swobodnego przepływu pracowników', in A. Stepniak (ed.), *Swobodny przepływ pracowników w kontekście wejścia Polski do Unii Europejskiej* (Warsaw: Office of the Committee for European Integration, 2001), pp. 19–40.

Orzechowska, E., 'Migracja zastępcza — sposób przeciwdziałania starzeniu się i ubytkowi zasobów pracy w Unii Europejskiej', *Studia Demograficzne*, Vol. 142, No. 2 (2002), pp. 73–92.

Papademetriou, D. G., 'Reflections on Managing Rapid & Deep Change in the Newest Age of Migration', paper presented at the conference 'Managing Migration for the Benefit of Europe' (Athens, 15–16 May 2003), available at http://www.migrationpolicy.org/AMPI.

Paszewski, T (ed.), 'Polska granica wschodnią granicą Unii Europejskiej', *Raporty i Analizy*, Vol. 7 (Warsaw: Centre for International Relations, 2000).

Peixoto, J., 'Migration and Policies in the European Union', *International Migration*, Vol. 29, No. 1 (2001), pp. 31–61.

Pratt, S., 'The European Dimension: Development of a Community Competence', Discussion Paper presented at IPRP Seminar Series on the Future of UK Migration (London, 24 September 2001), unpublished.

Ruspini, P., 'L'area dell'Unione europea', in Fondazione I.S.MU., *Ottavo Rapporto sulle migrazioni 2002* (Milan: Franco Angeli, 2003), pp. 269–77.

Ruspini, P. 'Migratory Flows and Policies in the New European Space', in S. Giusti, L. Tajoli (eds), *Convergence in the Enlarged European Union* (Milan: Egea-ISPI, 2003), pp. 221–41.

Sciortino, G., F. Pastore, 'Immigration and European immigration policy: myths and realities', paper presented at the conference 'Extending the area of Freedom, Justice and Security through Enlargement: Challenges for the European Union' (Trier, 4–6 July 2002), unpublished.

Stalker, P., 'Migration Trends and Migration Policy in Europe', *International Migration*, Vol. 40, No. 5 (2002), pp. 151–77.

Tóth, J., 'Connections of Kin-minorities to the Kin-state in the Extended Schengen Zone', *European Journal of Migration and Law*, Vol. 5, No. 2 (2003), pp. 201–27.

UNHCR, 'Asylum applications lodged in Europe, North America, Australia, New Zealand and Japan: January-December 2002' (2003), available at http://www.unhcr.ch/cgi-bin/texis/vtx/home/opendoc.pdf.

UN, *Replacement Migration. Is it a solution to declining and ageing populations?* (New York: UN, 2001).

Widgren, J., 'Immigration and EU Enlargement', keynote speech at the European Seminar 'Immigration: Labour Market and Integration' held by the Ministry of Labour and Social Policies within the framework of the semester of Italian Presidency of the European Union (Villa Erba, Como, 21 November 2003), unpublished.

Materials from the conference 'In search for a new Europe: contrasting migratory experiences' held on 22–24 March at the University of Warwick, United Kingdom

'Forging a common immigration policy', verbatim transcript of the discussion during the round table on 'Forging a new immigration policy: new and old migratory trends in the light of the European Union enlargement' (Coventry, 2002), unpublished.

Stubbs, S. K., 'Forging a common EU policy', paper prepared for the round table on 'Forging a new immigration policy: new and old migratory trends in the light of the European Union enlargement' (Coventry, 2002), unpublished.

De Sousa Ferreira, E., 'The EU enlargement to the east and the effects on migration policies', paper prepared for the round table on 'Forging a new immigration policy: new and old migratory trends in the light of the European Union enlargement' (Coventry, 2002), unpublished.

Walczak, P., 'Council of Europe: towards migration policy respectful of migrants' human rights and dignity', paper prepared for the round table on 'Forging a new immigration policy: new and old migratory trends in the light of the European Union enlargement' (Coventry, 2002), unpublished.

Appendix

Participants to the Round Table — 'Forging a Common Immigration Policy: New and Old Migratory Trends in the Light of the European Union Enlargement' — held during the Conference 'In Search for a New Europe: Contrasting Migratory Experiences', 22–24 March 2002, University of Warwick, Coventry, United Kingdom

Address speech:

Sandra Pratt, Unit Immigration and Asylum, Justice and Home Affairs Directorate-General, European Commission, Brussels, Belgium — "The Common EU Immigration Policy and the Current State of Play"

Discussants:

Damtew Dessalegne, United Nations High Commissioner for Refugees, Geneva, Switzerland

Eduardo de Sousa Ferreira, CEDEP, Research Centre for International Economics, Universidade Autónoma de Lisboa, Lisbon, Portugal   .

Allan Leas, European Council on Refugees and Exiles, London, United Kingdom

Birgitta Löwander, European Union Monitoring Centre on Racism and Xenophobia, Vienna, Austria

Sylvia de Palacios, UK New Citizen, London, United Kingdom

Dariusz Stola, Warsaw University and Polish Academy of Sciences, Warsaw, Poland

Sukhvinder Stubbs, Director of the Barrow Cadbury Trust, Birmingham, United Kingdom; previously Chair of the European Network Against Racism

Piotr Walczak, Council of Europe, Strasbourg, France

Ernest Zienkiewicz, Helsinki Foundation for Human Rights, Warsaw, Poland

Index